WELCOME

Thanks for purchasing these training notes for the **AWS Certified SysOps Administrator Associate** exam from Digital Cloud Training. The information in these Cheat Sheets relates to the latest SOA-C02 version of the exam.

The SOA-C02 exam covers a broad set of AWS services. The aim of putting this exam-specific information together is to provide a centralized, detailed list of the facts you need to know before you sit the exam. This will shortcut your study time and maximize your chances of passing the AWS Certified SysOps exam the first time.

I trust that you get great value from this popular resource that has been well received by our pool of over 750,000 students. Through diligent study of these learning materials, you will be in the perfect position to ace your AWS Certified SysOps Administrator Associate exam with confidence.

Wishing you the best for every step in your cloud journey!

Neal Davis

Neal Davis
Founder of Digital Cloud Training

WHAT DO OTHER STUDENTS SAY?

Check out the excellent reviews from our many students who passed their AWS exam with an average passing score of over 850:

* * * * *

Helped me pass the exam! Excellent book!

* * * * *

The author did an excellent job in explaining each subject in a comprehensive and methodical approach that is very easy to understand. This book covers all subjects for the AWS SysOps exam.

* * * * *

After successfully passing my SysOps exam, I'm now using this book as a valuable reference on the job.

* * * * *

TABLE OF CONTENTS

GETTING STARTED

ABOUT THESE TRAINING NOTES

Please note that this document does not read like a book or instructional text. We provide a raw, point-to-point list of facts backed by tables and diagrams to help with understanding.

For easy navigation, the information on each AWS service in this document is organized into the same categories as they are in the AWS Management Console.

The scope of coverage of services, and what information is included for each service, is based on feedback from our pool of over 750,000 students who have taken the exam, as well as our own experience.

YOUR PATHWAY TO SUCCESS

⊘ Enroll in Instructor-led Video Course
   Familiarize yourself with the AWS platform

⊘ Take our AWS Practice Exams
   Identify your strengths and weaknesses and assess your exam readiness

⊘ Study Training Notes
   Focus your study on the knowledge areas where you need to most

⊘ Get AWS Certified
   This pathway will let you pass your AWS exam first time with confidence

HOW CAN YOU BEST PREPARE?

So, you're excited to get started with the AWS Certified SysOps Administrator Associate certification and wondering what resources are out there to help you. Let's start with the free options. Visit https://digitalcloud.training/free-aws-certification-training/ for links to free resources including cheat sheets, practice questions, blog articles and video tutorials.

For the full training experience though, your best bet are the following training courses:

ON-DEMAND VIDEO COURSE

To get you started with your exam prep, we'd suggest first enrolling in the online instructor-led AWS Certified SysOps Administrator Associate Video Course from Digital Cloud Training to familiarize yourself with the AWS platform before returning to the Training Notes to get a more detailed understanding of the AWS services.

To learn more, visit https://digitalcloud.training/aws-certified-sysops-administrator-associate/

PRACTICE EXAM COURSE

To assess your progress on your AWS journey, we recommend taking the AWS Certified SysOps Administrator Associate Practice Exams on the Digital Cloud Training website. The **online exam simulator** will help you identify your strengths and weaknesses. These practice tests are designed to reflect the difficulty of the AWS exam and are the closest to the real exam experience available.

To learn more, visit https://digitalcloud.training/aws-certified-sysops-administrator-associate/

Our online Practice Exams are delivered in 4 different variations:

- **Exam Mode**

    In exam simulation mode, you complete one full-length practice exam and answer all 65 questions within the allotted time. You are then presented with a pass / fail score report showing your overall score and performance in each knowledge area to identify your strengths and weaknesses.

- **Training Mode**

    When taking the practice exam in training mode, you will be shown the answers and explanations for every question after clicking "check". Upon completion of the exam, the score report will show your overall score and performance in each knowledge area.

- **Knowledge Reviews**

    Now that you have identified your strengths and weaknesses, you get to dive deep into specific areas with our knowledge reviews. You are presented with a series of questions focused on a specific topic. There is no time limit, and you can view the answer to each question as you go through them.

- **Final Exam Simulator**

    The exam simulator randomly selects 65 questions from our pool of questions – mimicking the real AWS exam environment. The practice exam has the same format, style, time limit and passing score as the real AWS exam

STEP 3: TRAINING NOTES

As a final step, use these training notes to focus your study on the knowledge areas where you need to most. Get a detailed understanding of the AWS services and deep dive into the SOA-C02 exam objectives with detailed facts, tables and diagrams that will shortcut your time to success.

LIMITED TIME BONUS OFFER

To assess your AWS exam readiness, we have included one full-length practice exam from Digital Cloud Training. These 65 exam-difficulty practice questions are timed and scored and simulate the real AWS exam experience. To gain access to your free practice test on our interactive exam simulator online, simply navigate to the CONCLUSION at the back of this book where you'll find detailed instructions.

REQUEST YOUR FREE PDF VERSION OF THIS BOOK

Based on the feedback we've received from our Amazon clients, we understand that studying complex diagrams in black and white or accessing reference links from a kindle device may NOT offer the best learning experience.

That's why we've decided to provide you with a PDF version of this book at **no additional charge**. Simply navigate to the CONCLUSION of this book for instructions on how to access your free PDF version.

CONTACT, SUPPORT & FEEDBACK

We want you to get great value from these training resources. If for any reason you are not 100% satisfied, please contact us at support@digitalcloud.training. We promise to address all questions and concerns, typically within 24hrs. We really want you to have a 5-star learning experience!

The AWS platform is evolving quickly, and the exam tracks these changes with a typical lag of around 6 months. We are therefore reliant on student feedback to keep track of what is appearing in the exam. If there are any topics in your exam that weren't covered in our training resources, please provide us with feedback using this form https://digitalcloud.training/student-feedback/. We appreciate any feedback that will help us further improve our AWS training resources.

REVIEWS REALLY MATTER

If you enjoy reading reviews, please consider paying it forward. Reviews guide students and help us continuously improve our courses. We celebrate every honest review and truly appreciate it. We'd be thrilled if you could leave a rating at amazon.com/ryp or your local amazon store (e.g. amazon.co.uk/ryp).

JOIN THE AWS COMMUNITY

Our private Facebook group is a great place to ask questions and share knowledge and exam tips with the AWS community. Join the AWS Certification QA group on Facebook and share your exam feedback with the AWS community: https://www.facebook.com/groups/awscertificationqa

CONNECT WITH NEAL ON SOCIAL MEDIA

To learn more about the different ways of connecting with Neal, visit: https://digitalcloud.training/neal-davis

 digitalcloud.training/neal-davis

 youtube.com/c/digitalcloudtraining

 facebook.com/digitalcloudtraining

 Twitter @nealkdavis

linkedin.com/in/nealkdavis

 Instagram @digitalcloudtraining

HOW HARD IS THE AWS CERTIFIED SYSOPS ADMINISTRATOR ASSOCIATE?

The AWS Certified SysOps Administrator Associate certification has a reputation for being the hardest of the associate level certifications in Amazon Web Services' certification programs. But how difficult is it really?

The AWS SysOps Administrator exam focusses on exam scenarios that cover deployment and operational aspects of AWS services. This means it can be a bit challenging for those who don't have on-the-job experience. There is also a lot more coverage of monitoring, auditing and managing resources, as well as troubleshooting issues.

If you work with AWS services regularly then that will make the exam significantly easier.

IS IT WORTH GETTING?

Some people skip the SysOps Associate as they don't work in a systems operations role, so they assume it is not that useful. However, one may argue that it is a valuable certification to gain for a couple of reasons:

1. Firstly, it's considered to be harder and fewer people have it on their resumes, so it does provide a bit of differentiation.

2. Secondly, if you're already doing the other associate level certifications, due to the amount of overlap you'll already be most of the way there – so it's definitely worth a bit of extra effort.

ARE THERE ANY PRE-REQUISITES?

There are no pre-requisites for taking the exam. However, we recommend taking at least one of the other associate level certifications first or having equivalent industry experience. This will provide you with a broader understanding of AWS services and more hands-on experience (assuming you follow along with the labs).

WHAT TOPICS ARE COVERED?

There are six domains in the AWS Certified SysOps Administrator Associate S0A-C02 exam guide:

Domain 1: Monitoring, Logging, and Remediation

- Implement metrics, alarms, and filters by using AWS monitoring and logging service
- Remediate issues based on monitoring and availability metrics

Domain 2: Reliability and Business Continuity

- Implement scalability and elasticity
- Implement high availability and resilient environments
- Implement backup and restore strategies

Domain 3: Deployment, Provisioning, and Automation

- Provision and maintain cloud resources
- Automate manual or repeatable processes

Domain 4: Security and Compliance

- Implement and manage security and compliance policies
- Implement data and infrastructure protection strategies

Domain 5: Networking and Content Delivery

- Implement networking features and connectivity
- Configure domains, DNS services, and content delivery
- Troubleshoot network connectivity issues

Domain 6: Cost and Performance Optimization

- Implement cost optimization strategies
- Implement performance optimization strategies

HOW MUCH OVERLAP IS THERE WITH OTHER ASSOCIATE LEVEL CERTIFICATIONS?

There is a lot of overlap between all associate level certifications. The core set of services are very similar to the AWS Solutions Architect Associate and AWS Developer Associate. However, there are some differences in the objectives of the AWS Certified SysOps Administrator being more geared towards deployment, management and operational activities.

In addition to different objectives, there are some services covered in more detail, including:

- AWS Systems Manager (lots of coverage of inventory, patching, software management, etc.)
- AWS CloudFormation (at least compared to the AWS Solutions Architect Associate)
- Amazon ElastiCache (more focus on deployment types)
- AWS Config (for compliance)
- Amazon CloudWatch (lots of coverage of performance monitoring, events, logs, etc.)
- AWS IAM (more geared towards understanding IAM policies)
- AWS Organizations (know your SCPs!)
- AWS Cost management tools (fairly light coverage but more than the other associates: Cost Explorer, Cost and Usage Report, AWS Budgets)

WHAT ARE THE EXAM QUESTIONS LIKE?

Here are some resources you can use to check out the format of the exam questions:

1. You can find **20 FREE AWS Certified SysOps Administrator questions** here: https://digitalcloud.training/aws-sysops-administrator-associate-free-practice-exam-questions/
2. At the end of this document, you'll find some example exam scenarios with solutions

The exam scenarios are extracted from many common scenarios that students have seen come up on the exam so they are a really useful resource to gain an understanding of the types of questions you will see on the exam. This can also really help you in knowing what you need to learn to prepare yourself.

HOW LONG WILL IT TAKE TO PREPARE FOR THE EXAM?

We recommend taking at least one of the other associate level certifications first. If you do that then you'll already be 60-80% of the way there. Generally speaking, you need to put aside an additional 2-3 weeks to prepare for the SOA-C02 exam.

Download your **FREE Study Plan** to successfully prepare for your AWS SysOps Administrator Associate in 21 days here: https://digitalcloud.training/aws-certification-study-plan-sysops-administrator-associate/

The AWS Certified SysOps Administrator Associate is a great certification to get on your CV so we hope you're excited to get started with your exam preparation!

HOW TO GET THE HANDS-ON EXAM PREPARATION

With the SOA-C02, AWS introduced exam labs that require you to complete a practical task using the AWS Management Console. To best prepare you for these practical exercises, sign up for Challenge Labs. These hands-on exercises run in a secure sandbox environment and offer extensive hands-on practice opportunities. Gain practical, real-world cloud skills with Challenge Labs from Digital Cloud Training: https://digitalcloud.training/hands-on-challenge-labs/

COMPUTE

AMAZON EC2

AMAZON EC2 FEATURES

Amazon Elastic Compute Cloud (Amazon EC2) is a web service that provides resizable compute capacity in the cloud.

With Amazon EC2 you launch virtual server instances on the AWS cloud.

Each virtual server is known as an "instance".

You use preconfigured templates for your instances known as Amazon Machine Images (AMIs).

Each AMI includes the information needed to launch your EC2 instance (including the operating system and any included software packages).

Amazon EC2 currently supports a variety of operating systems including:

- Amazon Linux.
- Ubuntu.
- Windows Server.
- MacOS.
- Red Hat Enterprise Linux.
- SUSE Linux Enterprise Server.
- Fedora.
- Debian.
- CentOS.
- Gentoo Linux.
- Oracle Linux.
- FreeBSD.

EC2 compute units (ECUs) provide the relative measure of the integer processing power of an Amazon EC2 instance.

With EC2 you have full control at the operating system layer (root/admin access).

Key pairs are used to securely connect to EC2 instances:

- A key pair consists of a **public key** that AWS stores, and a **private key file** that you store.
- For Windows AMIs, the private key file is required to obtain the password used to log into your instance.
- For Linux AMIs, the private key file allows you to securely SSH (secure shell) into your instance.

Metadata and User Data:

- User data is data that is supplied by the user at instance launch in the form of a script.
- Instance metadata is data about your instance that you can use to configure or manage the running instance.
- User data is limited to 16KB.
- User data and metadata are not encrypted.

- Instance metadata is available at http://169.254.169.254/latest/meta-data/ (the trailing "/" is required).
- Instance user data is available at: http://169.254.169.254/latest/user-data.
- The IP address 169.254.169.254 is a link-local address and is valid only from the instance.
- On Linux you can use the curl command to view metadata and user data, e.g. "curl http://169.254.169.254/latest/meta-data/".
- The Instance Metadata Query tool allows you to query the instance metadata without having to type out the full URI or category names.

EC2 INSTANCE TYPES

Amazon EC2 provides a wide selection of instance types optimized to fit different use cases.

Instance types comprise varying combinations of CPU, memory, storage, and networking capacity and give you the flexibility to choose the appropriate mix of resources for your applications.

Each instance type includes one or more instance sizes, allowing you to scale your resources to the requirements of your target workload.

Category	Families	Purpose/Design
General Purpose	Mac, T4g, T3, T3a, T2, M6g, M6i, M5, M5a, M5n, M5zn, M5, A1	General Purpose Instances provide a balance on compute, memory, and networking resources, and can be used for a variety of diverse workloads.
Compute Optimized	C6g, C6gn, C6i, C5, C5a, C5n, C4	Compute optimized are ideal for compute bound applications that benefit from high performance processors.
Memory Optimized	R6g, R5, R5a, R5b, R5n, R4, X2gd, X1e, X1, High Memory, z1d	Memory optimized instances are designed to deliver fast performance for workloads that process large data sets in memory.
Accelerated Computing	P4, P3, P2, DL1, Inf1, G5, G4dn, G4ad, G3, F1, VT1	Accelerated Computing instances use hardware accelerators, or co-processors to perform functions such as floating-point number calculations, graphics processing, or data pattern matching.
Storage Optimized	I3, I3en, D2, D4, D3en, H1	This instance family provides Non-Volatile Memory Express (NVMe) SSD-Backed instance storage optimized for low latency, very high random I/O performance, high sequential read throughput and high IOPS at a low cost.

LAUNCHING EC2 INSTANCES

Choose an Amazon Machine Image (AMI).

Choose whether to auto-assign a public IP – default is to use the subnet setting.

Can add an instance to a placement group (more about this below).

Instances can be assigned to IAM roles which configures them with credentials to access AWS resources.

Termination protection can be enabled and prevents you from terminating an instance.

Basic monitoring is enabled by default (5-minute periods), detailed monitoring can be enabled (1-minute periods, chargeable).

Can define shared or dedicated tenancy.

T2 unlimited allows applications to burst past CPU performance baselines as required (chargeable).

Can add a script to run on startup (user data).

Can join to a directory (Windows instances only).

There is an option to enable an Elastic GPU (Windows instances only).

Storage options include adding additional volumes and choosing the volume type.

Use Amazon Elastic File System (EFS) for mounting a shared filesystem to multiple EC2 instances.

Non-root volumes can be encrypted.

Root volumes can be encrypted at launch.

There is an option to create tags (or can be done later).

You can select an existing security group or create a new one.

You must create or use an existing key pair – this is required if you want to access your instances via SSH. However, you can also attach the 'AmazonEC2RoleforSSM' IAM role to your EC2 instance to allow connection to your instance via Systems Manager (Session Manager).

AMAZON MACHINE IMAGES

An Amazon Machine Image (AMI) provides the information required to launch an instance.

An AMI includes the following:

- A template for the root volume for the instance (for example, an operating system, an application server, and applications).
- Launch permissions that control which AWS accounts can use the AMI to launch instances.
- A block device mapping that specifies the volumes to attach to the instance when it's launched.

AMIs are regional. You can only launch an AMI from the region in which it is stored. However, you can copy AMIs to other regions using the console, command line, or the API.

Volumes attached to the instance are either EBS or Instance store:

- Amazon Elastic Block Store (EBS) provides persistent storage. EBS snapshots, which reside on Amazon S3, are used to create the volume.
- Instance store volumes are ephemeral (non-persistent). That means data is lost if the instance is shut down. A template stored on Amazon S3 is used to create the volume.

BILLING AND PROVISIONING

There are several options for how you consume and pay for Amazon EC2 instances.

On demand

- Pay for hours used with no commitment.
- Low cost and flexibility with no upfront cost.
- Ideal for auto scaling groups and unpredictable workloads.
- Good for dev/test.

Spot

- Amazon EC2 Spot Instances let you take advantage of unused EC2 capacity in the AWS cloud.
- Spot Instances are available at up to a 90% discount compared to On-Demand prices.
- You can use Spot Instances for various stateless, fault-tolerant, or flexible applications such as big data, containerized workloads, CI/CD, web servers, high-performance computing (HPC), and other test & development workloads.
- You can request Spot Instances by using the Spot management console, CLI, API or the same interface that is used for launching On-Demand instances by indicating the option to use Spot.
- You can also select a Launch Template or a pre-configured or custom Amazon Machine Image (AMI), configure security and network access to your Spot instance, choose from multiple instance types and locations, use static IP endpoints, and attach persistent block storage to your Spot instances.
- **New pricing model:** The Spot price is determined by long term trends in supply and demand for EC2 spare capacity.
  - You don't have to bid for Spot Instances in the new pricing model, and you just pay the Spot price that's in effect for the current hour for the instances that you launch.
  - Spot Instances receive a two-minute interruption notice when these instances are about to be reclaimed by EC2, because EC2 needs the capacity back.
  - Instances are not interrupted because of higher competing bids.
- To reduce the impact of interruptions and optimize Spot Instances, diversify, and run your application across multiple capacity pools.
- Each instance family, each instance size, in each Availability Zone, in every Region is a separate Spot pool.
- You can use the RequestSpotFleet API operation to launch thousands of Spot Instances and diversify resources automatically.
- To further reduce the impact of interruptions, you can also set up Spot Instances and Spot Fleets to respond to an interruption notice by stopping or hibernating rather than terminating instances when capacity is no longer available.

Reserved

- Purchase (or agree to purchase) usage of EC2 instances in advance for significant discounts over On-Demand pricing.
- Provides a capacity reservation when used in a specific AZ.
- AWS Billing automatically applies discounted rates when you launch an instance that matches your purchased RI.
- Capacity is reserved for a term of 1 or 3 years.
- EC2 has three RI types: Standard, Convertible, and Scheduled.
- Standard = commitment of 1 or 3 years, charged whether it's on or off.
- Scheduled = reserved for specific periods of time, accrue charges hourly, billed in monthly increments over the term (1 year).
- Scheduled RIs match your capacity reservation to a predictable recurring schedule.
- For the differences between standard and convertible RIs, see the table below.
- RIs are used for steady state workloads and predictable usage.
- Ideal for applications that need reserved capacity.
- Upfront payments can reduce the hourly rate.
- Can switch AZ within the same region.
- Can change the instance size within the same instance type.
- Instance type modifications are supported for Linux only.
- Cannot change the instance size of Windows RIs.
- Billed whether running or not.
- Can sell reservations on the AWS marketplace.
- Can be used in Auto Scaling Groups.
- Can be used in Placement Groups.
- Can be shared across multiple accounts within Consolidated Billing.
- If you don't need your RI's, you can try to sell them on the Reserved Instance Marketplace.

	Standard	Convertible
Terms	1 year, 3 year	1 year, 3 year
Average discount off On-Demand price	40% - 60%	31% - 54%
Change AZ, instance size, networking type	Yes via ModifyReservedInstance API or console	Yes via ExchangeReservedInstance API or console
Change instance family, OS, tenancy, payment options	No	Yes
Benefit from price reductions	No	Yes

RI Attributes:

- Instance type – designates CPU, memory, networking capability.

- Platform – Linux, SUSE Linux, RHEL, Microsoft Windows, Microsoft SQL Server.
- Tenancy – Default (shared) tenancy, or Dedicated tenancy.
- Availability Zone (optional) – if AZ is selected, RI is reserved, and discount applies to that AZ (Zonal RI). If no AZ is specified, no reservation is created but the discount is applied to any instance in the family in any AZ in the region (Regional RI).

Comparing Amazon EC2 Pricing Models

The following table provides a brief comparison of On-demand, Reserved and Spot pricing models:

On-Demand	Reserved	Spot
No upfront fee	Options: No upfront, partial upfront or all upfront	No upfront fee
Charged by hour or second	Charged by hour or second	Charged by hour or second
No commitment	1-year or 3-year commitment	No commitment
Ideal for short term needs or unpredictable workloads	Ideal for steady-state workloads and predictable usage	Ideal for cost-sensitive, compute intensive use cases that can withstand interruption

You are limited to running up to a total of 20 On-Demand instances across the instance family, purchasing 20 Reserved Instances, and requesting Spot Instances per your dynamic spot limit per region (by default).

Dedicated hosts

- Physical servers dedicated just for your use.
- You then have control over which instances are deployed on that host.
- Available as On-Demand or with Dedicated Host Reservation.
- Useful if you have server-bound software licenses that use metrics like per-core, per-socket, or per-VM.
- Each dedicated host can only run one EC2 instance size and type.
- Good for regulatory compliance or licensing requirements.
- Predictable performance.
- Complete isolation.
- Most expensive option.
- Billing is per host.

Dedicated instances

- Virtualized instances on hardware just for you.
- Also uses physically dedicated EC2 servers.
- Does not provide the additional visibility and controls of dedicated hosts (e.g. how instances are

placed on a server).
- Billing is per instance.
- May share hardware with other non-dedicated instances in the same account.
- Available as On-Demand, Reserved Instances, and Spot Instances.
- Cost additional $2 per hour per region.

The following table describes some of the differences between dedicates instances and dedicated hosts:

Characteristic	Dedicated Instances	Dedicated Hosts
Enables the use of dedicated physical servers	X	X
Per instance billing (subject to a $2 per region fee)	X	
Per host billing		X
Visibility of sockets, cores, host ID		X
Affinity between a host and instance		X
Targeted instance placement		X
Automatic instance placement	X	X
Add capacity using an allocation request		X

Partial instance-hours consumed are billed based on instance usage.

Instances are billed when they're in a running state – need to stop or terminate to avoid paying.

Charging by the hour or second (by the second with Linux instances only).

Data between instances in different regions is charged (in and out).

Regional Data Transfer rates apply if at least one of the following is true, but are only charged once for a given instance even if both are true:

- The other instance is in a different Availability Zone, regardless of which type of address is used.
- Public or Elastic IP addresses are used, regardless of which Availability Zone the other instance is in.

NETWORKING

Networking Limits (per region or as specified):

Name	Default Limit
EC2-Classic Elastic IPs	5
EC2-VPC Elastic IPs	5
VPCs	5

Subnets per VPC	200
Security groups per VPC	500
Rules per VPC security group	50
VPC security groups per elastic network interface	5
Network interfaces	350
Network ACLs per VPC	200
Rules per network ACL	20
Route tables per VPC	200
Entries per route table	50
Active VPC peering connections	50
Outstanding VPC peering connection requests	25
Expiry time for an unaccepted VPC peering connection	168

IP ADDRESSES

There are three types of IP address that can be assigned to an Amazon EC2 instance:

- Public – public address that is assigned automatically to instances in public subnets and reassigned if instance is stopped/started.
- Private – private address assigned automatically to all instances.
- Elastic IP – public address that is static.

Public IPv4 addresses are lost when the instance is stopped but private addresses (IPv4 and IPv6) are retained.

Public IPv4 addresses are retained if you restart the instance.

Elastic IPs are retained when the instance is stopped.

Elastic IP addresses are static public IP addresses that can be remapped (moved) between instances.

All accounts are limited to 5 elastic IPs per region by default; however this is a soft limit which can be raised by a service limit increase to AWS Support.

AWS charges for elastic IP's when they're not being used.

An Elastic IP address is for use in a specific region only.

You can assign custom tags to your Elastic IP addresses to categorize them.

By default, EC2 instances come with a private IP assigned to the primary network interface (eth0).

Public IP addresses are assigned for instances in public subnets (VPC).

DNS records for elastic IP's can be configured by filling out a form.

Secondary IP addresses can be useful for hosting multiple websites on a server or redirecting traffic to a standby EC2 instance for HA.

You can choose whether secondary IP addresses can be reassigned.

You can associate a single private IPv4 address with a single Elastic IP address and vice versa.

When reassigned the IPv4 to Elastic IP association is maintained.

When a secondary private address is unassigned from an interface, the associated Elastic IP address is disassociated.

You can assign or remove IP addresses from EC2 instances while they are running or stopped.

When you stop and start and EC2 instance, it will generally be moved to different underlying hardware.

Exam tip: You can stop and start an EC2 instance to move it to a different physical host if EC2 status checks are failing or there is planned maintenance on the current physical host.

You can modify the following attributes of an instance only when it is stopped:

- Instance type.
- User data.
- Kernel.
- RAM disk.

All IP addresses (IPv4 and IPv6) remain attached to the network interface when detached or reassigned to another instance.

You can attach a network interface to an instance in a different subnet if it's within the same AZ.

You can bring part or all your publicly routable IPv4 or IPv6 address range from your on-premises network to AWS. This is called BYOIP.

You continue to own the address range, but AWS advertises it on the internet by default. After you bring the address range to AWS, it appears in your AWS account as an address pool.

BYOIP is not available in all Regions and for all resources.

The following table compares the different types of IP address available in Amazon EC2:

Name	Description
Public IP address	Lost when the instance is stopped Used in Public Subnets No charge Associated with a private IP address on the instance Cannot be moved between instances
Private IP address	Retained when the instance is stopped Used in Public and Private Subnets
Elastic IP address	Static Public IP address You are charged if not used Associated with a private IP address on the instance

	Can be moved between instances and Elastic Network Adapters

PLACEMENT GROUPS

Placement groups are a logical grouping of instances in one of the following configurations.

Cluster – clusters instances into a low-latency group in a single AZ:

- A cluster placement group is a logical grouping of instances within a single Availability Zone.
- Cluster placement groups are recommended for applications that benefit from low network latency, high network throughput, or both, and if most of the network traffic is between the instances in the group.

Spread – spreads instances across underlying hardware (can span AZs):

- A spread placement group is a group of instances that are each placed on distinct underlying hardware.
- Spread placement groups are recommended for applications that have a small number of critical instances that should be kept separate from each other.

Partition — divides each group into logical segments called partitions:

- Amazon EC2 ensures that each partition within a placement group has its own set of racks.
- Each rack has its own network and power source. No two partitions within a placement group share the same racks, allowing you to isolate the impact of hardware failure within your application.
- Partition placement groups can be used to deploy large distributed and replicated workloads, such as HDFS, HBase, and Cassandra, across distinct racks.

The table below describes some key differences between clustered and spread placement groups:

	Clustered	Spread	Partition
What	Instances are placed into a low-latency group within a single AZ	Instances are spread across underlying hardware	Instances are grouped into logical segments called partitions which use distinct hardware
When	Need low network latency and/or high network throughput	Reduce the risk of simultaneous instance failure if underlying hardware fails	Need control and visibility into instance placement
Pros	Get the most out of enhanced networking Instances	Can span multiple AZs	Reduces likelihood of correlated failures for large workloads.
Cons	Finite capacity: recommend launching all you might need up front	Maximum of 7 instances running per group, per AZ	Partition placement groups are not supported for Dedicated Hosts

Launching instances in a spread placement group reduces the risk of simultaneous failures that might occur when instances share the same underlying hardware.

Recommended for applications that benefit from low latency and high bandwidth.

Recommended to use an instance type that supports enhanced networking.

Instances within a placement group can communicate with each other using private or public IP addresses.

Best performance is achieved when using private IP addresses.

Using public IP addresses the performance is limited to 5Gbps or less.

Low-latency 10 Gbps or 25 Gbps network.

Recommended to keep instance types homogenous within a placement group.

Can use reserved instances at an instance level but cannot reserve capacity for the placement group.

The name you specify for a placement group must be unique within your AWS account for the Region.

You can't merge placement groups.

An instance can be launched in one placement group at a time; it cannot span multiple placement groups.

On-Demand Capacity Reservation and zonal Reserved Instances provide a capacity reservation for EC2 instances in a specific Availability Zone.

The capacity reservation can be used by instances in a placement group. However, it is not possible to explicitly reserve capacity for a placement group.

Instances with a tenancy of host cannot be launched in placement groups.

IAM ROLES

IAM roles are more secure than storing access keys and secret access keys on EC2 instances

IAM roles can be used to allow EC2 to interact with several different services like S3, DynamoDB etc.

IAM roles are easier to manage and more secure than access keys.

You can attach an IAM role to an instance at launch time or at any time after by using the AWS CLI, SDK, or the EC2 console.

IAM roles can be attached, modified, or replaced at any time.

Only one IAM role can be attached to an EC2 instance at a time.

IAM roles are universal and can be used in any region.

BASTION/JUMP HOSTS

You can configure EC2 instances as bastion hosts (aka jump boxes) to access your VPC instances for management.

Can use the SSH or RDP protocols to connect to your bastion host.

Need to configure a security group with the relevant permissions.

Can use auto-assigned public IPs or Elastic IPs.

Can use security groups to restrict the IP addresses/CIDRs that can access the bastion host.

Use auto-scaling groups for HA (set to 1 instance to just replace if it fails).

Best practice is to deploy Linux bastion hosts in two AZs, use auto-scaling and Elastic IP addresses.

You can also use AWS Systems Manager Session Manager instead of using bastion hosts

MONITORING EC2

EC2 status checks are performed every minute, and each returns a pass or a fail status.

If all checks pass, the overall status of the instance is **OK.**

If one or more checks fail, the overall status is **impaired.**

System status checks detect (StatusCheckFailed_System) problems with your instance that require **AWS** involvement to repair.

The following are examples of problems that can cause system status checks to fail:

- Loss of network connectivity.
- Loss of system power.
- Software issues on the physical host.
- Hardware issues on the physical host that impact network reachability.

Instance status checks (StatusCheckFailed_Instance) detect problems that require **your** involvement to repair.

The following are examples of problems that can cause instance status checks to fail:

- Failed system status checks..
- Incorrect networking or startup configuration.
- Exhausted memory.
- Corrupted file system.
- Incompatible kernel.

Status checks are built into Amazon EC2, so they cannot be disabled or deleted.

You can, however, create or delete alarms that are triggered based on the result of the status checks.

You can create Amazon CloudWatch alarms that monitor Amazon EC2 instances and automatically perform an action if the status check fails.

Actions can include:

- Recover the instance (only supported on specific instance types and can be used only with StatusCheckFailed_System).
- Stop the instance (only applicable to EBS-backed volumes).
- Terminate the instance (cannot terminate if termination protection is enabled).
- Reboot the instance.

It is a best practice to use EC2 to reboot an instance rather than restarting through the OS.

CloudWatch Monitoring frequency:

- Standard monitoring = 5 mins.
- Detailed monitoring = 1 min (chargeable).

Unified CloudWatch Agent

The unified CloudWatch agent enables you to do the following:

- Collect more system-level metrics from Amazon EC2 instances across operating systems. The metrics can include in-guest metrics, in addition to the metrics for EC2 instances. The additional metrics that can be collected are listed in Metrics Collected by the CloudWatch Agent.
- Collect system-level metrics from on-premises servers. These can include servers in a hybrid environment as well as servers not managed by AWS.
- Retrieve custom metrics from your applications or services using the StatsD and collectd protocols. StatsD is supported on both Linux servers and servers running Windows Server. collectd is supported only on Linux servers.
- Collect logs from Amazon EC2 instances and on-premises servers, running either Linux or Windows Server.

You can download and install the CloudWatch agent manually using the command line, or you can integrate it with SSM.

LOGGING AND AUDITING

Amazon EC2 and Amazon EBS are integrated with AWS CloudTrail, a service that provides a record of actions taken by a user, role, or an AWS service in Amazon EC2 and Amazon EBS.

CloudTrail captures all API calls for Amazon EC2 and Amazon EBS as events, including calls from the console and from code calls to the APIs.

If you create a trail, you can enable continuous delivery of CloudTrail events to an Amazon S3 bucket, including events for Amazon EC2 and Amazon EBS.

A trail enables you to store records indefinitely.

If you don't configure a trail, you can still view the most recent events in the CloudTrail console by viewing Event history (past 90 days only).

Using the information collected by CloudTrail, you can determine the request that was made to Amazon EC2 and Amazon EBS, the IP address from which the request was made, who made the request, when it was made, and additional details.

TAGS

You can assign metadata to your AWS resources in the form of *tags*.

A tag is a label that you assign to an AWS resource.

Tags are just arbitrary name/value pairs that you can assign to virtually all AWS assets to serve as metadata.

Tags can help you manage, identify, organize, search for, and filter resources.

Each tag consists of a key and an optional value, both of which you define.

Tagging strategies can be used for cost allocation, security, automation, and many other uses. For example, you can use a tag in an IAM policy to implement access control.

Enforcing standardized tagging can be done via AWS Config rules or custom scripts. For example, EC2 instances not properly tagged are stopped or terminated daily.

Most resources can have up to 50 tags.

RESOURCE GROUPS

Resource groups are mappings of AWS assets defined by tags.

Create custom consoles to consolidate metrics, alarms and config details around given tags.

AMAZON EBS

AMAZON EBS FEATURES

EBS is the Amazon Elastic Block Store.

EBS volumes are network attached storage that can be attached to EC2 instances.

EBS volume data persists independently of the life of the instance.

EBS volumes do not need to be attached to an instance.

You can attach multiple EBS volumes to an instance.

You can attach an EBS volume to multiple instances with specific constraints.

For most use cases where you need a shared volume across EC2 instances use Amazon EFS.

EBS volume data is replicated across multiple servers in an AZ.

EBS volumes must be in the same AZ as the instances they are attached to.

EBS is designed for an annual failure rate of 0.1%-0.2% & an SLA of 99.95%.

Termination protection is turned off by default and must be manually enabled (keeps the volume/data when the instance is terminated).

Root EBS volumes are deleted on termination by default.

Extra non-boot volumes are not deleted on termination by default.

The behavior can be changed by altering the "DeleteOnTermination" attribute.

You can now create AMIs with encrypted root/boot volumes as well as data volumes (you can also use separate CMKs per volume).

Volume sizes and types can be upgraded without downtime (except for magnetic standard).

Elastic Volumes allow you to increase volume size, adjust performance, or change the volume type while the volume is in use.

To migrate volumes between AZ's create a snapshot then create a volume in another AZ from the snapshot (possible to change size and type).

Auto-enable IO setting prevents the stopping of IO to a disk when AWS detects inconsistencies.

The root device is created under /dev/sda1 or /dev/xvda.

Magnetic EBS is for workloads that need throughput rather than IOPS.

Throughput optimized EBS volumes cannot be a boot volume.

Each instance that you launch has an associated root device volume, either an Amazon EBS volume or an instance store volume.

You can use block device mapping to specify additional EBS volumes or instance store volumes to attach to an instance when it's launched.

You can also attach additional EBS volumes to a running instance.

You cannot decrease an EBS volume size.

When changing volumes the new volume must be at least the size of the current volume's snapshot.

Images can be made public but not if they're encrypted.

AMIs can be shared with other accounts.

You can have up to 5,000 EBS volumes by default.

You can have up to 10,000 snapshots by default.

INSTANCE STORE

An instance store provides *temporary* (non-persistent) block-level storage for your instance.

This is different to EBS which provides persistent storage but is also a block storage service that can be a root or additional volume.

Instance store storage is located on disks that are physically attached to the host computer.

Instance store is ideal for temporary storage of information that changes frequently, such as buffers, caches, scratch data, and other temporary content, or for data that is replicated across a fleet of instances, such as a load-balanced pool of web servers.

You can specify instance store volumes for an instance only when you launch it.

You can't detach an instance store volume from one instance and attach it to a different instance.

The instance type determines the size of the instance store available, and the type of hardware used for the instance store volumes.

Instance store volumes are included as part of the instance's usage cost.

Some instance types use NVMe or SATA-based solid-state drives (SSD) to deliver high random I/O performance.

This is a good option when you need storage with very low latency, but you don't need the data to persist when the instance terminates, or you can take advantage of fault-tolerant architectures.

EXAM TIP: Instance stores offer very high performance and low latency. If you can afford to lose an instance, i.e. you are replicating your data, these can be a good solution for high performance/low latency requirements. Look out for questions that mention distributed or replicated databases that need high I/O. Also, remember that the cost of instance stores is included in the instance charges so it can also be more cost-effective than EBS Provisioned IOPS.

EBS VS INSTANCE STORE

EBS-backed means the root volume is an EBS volume and storage is persistent.

Instance store-backed means the root volume is an instance store volume and storage is not persistent.

On an EBS-backed instance, the default action is for the root EBS volume to be deleted upon termination.

Instance store volumes are sometimes called Ephemeral storage (non-persistent).

Instance store backed instances cannot be stopped. If the underlying host fails the data will be lost.

Instance store volume root devices are created from AMI templates stored on S3.

EBS backed instances can be stopped. You will not lose the data on this instance if it is stopped (persistent).

EBS volumes can be detached and reattached to other EC2 instances.

EBS volume root devices are launched from AMI's that are backed by EBS snapshots.

Instance store volumes cannot be detached/reattached.

When rebooting the instances for both types data will not be lost.

By default, both root volumes will be deleted on termination unless you configured otherwise.

EBS VOLUME TYPES

SSD, General Purpose – gp2/gp3:

- Volume size from 1 GiB to 16 TiB.
- Up to 16,000 IOPS per volume.
- Performance:
  - 3 IOPS/GiB for gp2.
  - Up to 500 IOPS/GiB for gp3.
- Can be a boot volume.
- EBS multi-attach not supported.
- Use cases:
  - Low-latency interactive apps.
  - Development and test environments.

SSD, Provisioned IOPS – io1/io2:

- More than 16,000 IOPS.
- Up to 64,000 IOPS per volume (Nitro instances).
- Up to 32,000 IOPS per volume for other instance types.
- Performance:
  - Up to 50 IOPS/GiB for io1.
  - Up to 500 IOPS/Gib for io2.
- Can be a boot volume.
- EBS multi-attach is supported.
- Use cases:
  - Workloads that require sustained IOPS performance or more than 16,000 IOPS.
  - I/O-intensive database workloads.

HDD, Throughput Optimized – (st1):

- Frequently accessed, throughput intensive workloads with large datasets and large I/O sizes, such as MapReduce, Kafka, log processing, data warehouse, and ETL workloads.
- Throughput measured in MiB/s and includes the ability to burst up to 250 MiB/s per TB, with a baseline throughput of 40 MB/s per TB and a maximum throughput of 500 MiB/s per volume.

- Cannot be a boot volume.
- EBS multi-attach not supported.

HDD, Cold – (sc1):

- Lowest cost storage – cannot be a boot volume.
- Less frequently accessed workloads with large, cold datasets.
- These volumes can burst up to 80 MiB/s per TiB, with a baseline throughput of 12 MiB/s.
- Cannot be a boot volume.
- EBS multi-attach not supported.

EBS optimized instances:

- Dedicated capacity for Amazon EBS I/O.
- EBS-optimized instances are designed for use with all EBS volume types.
- Max bandwidth: 400 Mbps – 12000 Mbps.
- IOPS: 3000 – 65000.
- GP-SSD within 10% of baseline and burst performance 99.9% of the time.
- PIOPS within 10% of baseline and burst performance 99.9% of the time.
- Additional hourly fee.
- Available for select instance types.
- Some instance types have EBS-optimized enabled by default.

The following EBS volumes appear most often on the AWS exams:

Volume Type	EBS Provisioned IOPS SSD (io1/io2)	EBS General Purpose SSD (gp2/gp3)	Throughput Optimized HDD (st1)	Cold HDD (sc1)
Short Description	Highest performance SSD volume designed for latency-sensitive transactional workloads	General Purpose SSD volume that balances price performance for a wide variety of transactional workloads	Low-cost HDD volume, designed for frequently accessed. Throughput intensive workloads	Lowest cost HDD volume designed for less frequently accessed workloads
Use Cases	I/O-intensive NoSQL and relational databases	Boot volumes, low-latency interactive apps, dev & test	Big-data, data warehouses, log processing	Colder data requiring fewer scans per day
Volume Size	4 GiB - 16 TiB	1 GiB - 16 TiB	125 GB – 16 TiB	125 GB – 16 TiB
Max IOPS** /	64,000	16,000	500	250

Volume				
Max Throughput *** Volume	1,000 MiB/s	250 MiB/s (gp2) 1000 MiB/s (gp3)	500 MiB/s	250 MiB/s
Can be boot volume?	Yes	Yes	No	No
EBS Multi-attach	Supported	Not Supported	Not Supported	Not Supported

AMAZON EBS SNAPSHOTS

Snapshots capture a point-in-time state of an instance.

Cost-effective and easy backup strategy.

Share data sets with other users or accounts.

Can be used to migrate a system to a new AZ or region.

Can be used to convert an unencrypted volume to an encrypted volume.

Snapshots are stored on Amazon S3.

Does not provide granular backup (not a replacement for backup software).

If you make periodic snapshots of a volume, the snapshots are incremental, which means that only the blocks on the device that have changed after your last snapshot are saved in the new snapshot.

Even though snapshots are saved incrementally, the snapshot deletion process is designed so that you need to retain only the most recent snapshot to restore the volume.

Snapshots can only be accessed through the EC2 APIs.

EBS volumes are AZ specific, but snapshots are region specific.

Volumes can be created from EBS snapshots that are the same size or larger.

Snapshots can be taken of non-root EBS volumes while running.

To take a consistent snapshot, writes must be stopped (paused) until the snapshot is complete. if this is not possible the volume needs to be detached; or if it's an EBS root volume the instance must be stopped.

To lower storage costs on S3 a full snapshot and subsequent incremental updates can be created.

You are charged for data traffic to S3 and storage costs on S3.

You are billed only for the changed blocks.

Deleting a snapshot removes only the data not needed by any other snapshot.

You can resize volumes through restoring snapshots with different sizes (configured when taking the snapshot).

Snapshots can be copied between regions (and be encrypted). Images are then created from the

© 2023 Digital Cloud Training

snapshot in the other region which creates an AMI that can be used to boot an instance.

You can create volumes from snapshots and choose the availability zone within the region.

ENCRYPTION

You can encrypt both the boot and data volumes of an EC2 instance. When you create an encrypted EBS volume and attach it to a supported instance type, the following types of data are encrypted:

- Data at rest inside the volume.
- All data moving between the volume and the instance.
- All snapshots created from the volume.
- All volumes created from those snapshots.

Encryption is supported by all EBS volume types.

Expect the same IOPS performance on encrypted volumes as on unencrypted volumes.

All instance families support encryption.

Amazon EBS encryption is available on the instance types listed below:

- General purpose: A1, M3, M4, M5, M5a, M5ad, M5d, T2, T3, and T3a.
- Compute optimized: C3, C4, C5, C5d, and C5n.
- Memory optimized: cr1.8xlarge, R3, R4, R5, R5a, R5ad, R5d, u-6tb1.metal, u-9tb1.metal, u-12tb1.metal, X1, X1e, and z1d.
- Storage optimized: D2, h1.2xlarge, h1.4xlarge, I2, and I3.
- Accelerated computing: F1, G2, G3, G4, P2, and P3.

EBS encrypts your volume with a data key using the industry-standard AES-256 algorithm.

Your data key is stored on-disk with your encrypted data, but not before EBS encrypts it with your CMK. Your data key never appears on disk in plaintext. .

The same data key is shared by snapshots of the volume and any subsequent volumes created from those snapshots.

Snapshots of encrypted volumes are encrypted automatically.

EBS volumes restored from encrypted snapshots are encrypted automatically.

EBS volumes created from encrypted snapshots are also encrypted.

You can share snapshots, but if they're encrypted it must be with a custom CMK key.

You can check the encryption status of your EBS volumes with AWS Config.

There is no direct way to change the encryption state of a volume.

Either create an encrypted volume and copy data to it or take a snapshot, encrypt it, and create a new encrypted volume from the snapshot.

To encrypt a volume or snapshot you need an encryption key, these are customer managed keys (CMK), and they are managed by the AWS Key Management Service (KMS).

A default CMK key is generated for the first encrypted volumes.

Subsequent encrypted volumes will use their own unique key (AES 256 bit).

The CMK used to encrypt a volume is used by any snapshots and volumes created from snapshots.

You cannot share encrypted volumes created using a default CMK key.

You cannot change the CMK key that is used to encrypt a volume.

You must create a copy of the snapshot and change encryption keys as part of the copy.

This is required to be able to share the encrypted volume.

By default only the account owner can create volumes from snapshots.

You can share unencrypted snapshots with the AWS community by making them public.

You can also share unencrypted snapshots with other AWS accounts by making them private and selecting the accounts to share them with.

You cannot make encrypted snapshots public.

You can share encrypted snapshots with other AWS accounts using a non-default CMK key and configuring cross-account permissions to give the account access to the key, mark as private and configure the account to share with.

The receiving account must copy the snapshot before they can then create volumes from the snapshot.

It is recommended that the receiving account re-encrypt the shared and encrypted snapshot using their own CMK key.

The following information applies to snapshots:

- Snapshots are created asynchronously and are incremental.
- You can copy unencrypted snapshots (optionally encrypt).
- You can copy an encrypted snapshot (optionally re-encrypt with a different key).
- Snapshot copies receive a new unique ID.
- You can copy within or between regions.
- You cannot move snapshots, only copy them.
- You cannot take a copy of a snapshot when it is in a "pending" state, it must be "complete".
- S3 Server Side Encryption (SSE) protects data in transit while copying.
- User defined tags are not copied.
- You can have up to 5 snapshot copy requests running in a single destination per account.
- You can copy Import/Export service, AWS Marketplace, and AWS Storage Gateway snapshots.
- If you try to copy an encrypted snapshot without having access to the encryption keys it will fail silently (cross-account permissions are required).

Copying snapshots may be required for:

- Creating services in other regions.
- DR – the ability to restore from snapshot in another region.
- Migration to another region.
- Applying encryption.
- Data retention.

To take application-consistent snapshots of RAID arrays:

- Stop the application from writing to disk.
- Flush all caches to the disk.
- Freeze the filesystem.

© 2023 Digital Cloud Training

- Unmount the RAID array.
- Shut down the associated EC2 instance.

AMIS

An Amazon Machine Image (AMI) is a special type of virtual appliance that is used to create a virtual machine within the Amazon Elastic Compute Cloud ("EC2").

An AMI includes the following:

- A template for the root volume for the instance (for example, an operating system, an application server, and applications).
- Launch permissions that control which AWS accounts can use the AMI to launch instances.
- A block device mapping that specifies the volumes to attach to the instance when it's launched.

AMIs are either instance store-backed or EBS-backed.

Instance store-backed:

- Launch an EC2 instance from an AWS instance store-backed AMI.
- Update the root volume as required.
- Create the AMI which will upload to a user specified S3 bucket (user bucket).
- Register the AMI with EC2 (creates another EC2 controlled S3 image).
- To make changes update the source then deregister and reregister.
- Upon launch the image is copied to the EC2 host.
- Deregister an image when the AMI is not needed anymore (does not affect existing instances created from the AMI).
- Instance store-backed volumes can only be created at launch time.

EBS-backed:

- Must stop the instance to create a consistent image and then create the AMI.
- AWS registers the AMIs automatically.
- During creation AWS creates snapshots of all attached volumes – there is no need to specify a bucket, but you will be charged for storage on S3.
- You cannot delete the snapshot of the root volume if the AMI is registered (deregister and delete).
- You can now create AMIs with encrypted root/boot volumes as well as data volumes (can also use separate CMKs per volume).

Copying AMIs:

- You can copy an Amazon Machine Image (AMI) within or across an AWS region using the AWS Management Console, the AWS Command Line Interface or SDKs, or the Amazon EC2 API, all of which support the CopyImage action.
- You can copy both Amazon EBS-backed AMIs and instance store-backed AMIs.
- You can copy encrypted AMIs and AMIs with encrypted snapshots.

DEPLOYMENT AND PROVISIONING

Termination protection is turned off by default and must be manually enabled (keeps the volume/data when the instance is terminated).

Root EBS volumes are deleted on termination by default.

Extra non-boot volumes are not deleted on termination by default.

The behavior can be changed by altering the "DeleteOnTermination" attribute.

Volume sizes and types can be upgraded without downtime (except for magnetic standard).

Elastic Volumes allow you to increase volume size, adjust performance, or change the volume type while the volume is in use.

To migrate volumes between AZ's create a snapshot then create a volume in another AZ from the snapshot (possible to change size and type).

EBS COPYING, SHARING AND ENCRYPTION METHODS

The following diagram aims to articulate the various possible options for copying EBS volumes, sharing AMIs and snapshots and applying encryption:

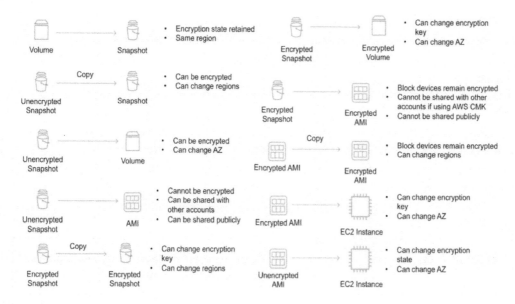

RAID

RAID can be used to increase IOPS.

RAID 0 = 0 striping – data is written across multiple disks and increases performance but no redundancy.

RAID 1 = 1 mirroring – creates 2 copies of the data but does not increase performance, only redundancy.

RAID 10 = 10 combination of RAID 1 and 2 resulting in increased performance and redundancy (at the cost of additional disks).

You can configure multiple striped gp2 or standard volumes (typically RAID 0).

You can configure multiple striped PIOPS volumes (typically RAID 0).

RAID is configured through the guest OS.

EBS optimized EC2 instances are another way of increasing performance.

Ensure the EC2 instance can handle the bandwidth required for the increased performance.

Use EBS optimized instances or instances with a 10 Gbps network interface.

Not recommended to use RAID for root/boot volumes.

MONITORING AND REPORTING

Amazon Elastic Block Store (Amazon EBS) sends data points to CloudWatch for several metrics.

A few specific metrics to understand for the exam:

- DiskReadBytes / DiskWriteBytes:
  - o Relates to Instance Store volumes NOT to EBS.
  - o Included in the AWS/EC2 namespace.
- VolumeReadBytes / VolumeWriteBytes:
  - o Relates to the EBS volume.
  - o Included in the AWS/EBS namespace.

There are two types of Amazon CloudWatch monitoring available for Amazon EBS volumes:

- Basic – Data is available automatically in 5-minute periods at no charge. This includes data for the root device volumes for EBS-backed instances.
- Detailed – Provisioned IOPS SSD (io1) volumes automatically send one-minute metrics to CloudWatch.

Amazon EBS General Purpose SSD (gp2), Throughput Optimized HDD (st1) , Cold HDD (sc1), and Magnetic (standard) volumes automatically send five-minute metrics to CloudWatch.

Provisioned IOPS SSD (io1) volumes automatically send one-minute metrics to CloudWatch. Data is only reported to CloudWatch when the volume is attached to an instance.

Volume status checks enable you to better understand, track, and manage potential inconsistencies in the data on an Amazon EBS volume.

Volume Status	I/O Enabled Status	I/O performance status (only available for Provisioned IOPS volumes)
ok	Enabled (I/O Enabled or I/O Auto-Enabled)	Normal (Volume performance is expected)
warning	Enabled (I/O Enabled or I/O Auto-Enabled) Disabled (Volume is offline and pending recovery or is waiting for the user to enable I/O).	Degraded (Volume performance is below expectations) Severely Degraded (Volume performance is well below expectations)
impaired	Enabled (I/O Enabled or I/O Auto-	Stalled (Volume performance is severely

	Enabled)	impacted)
	Disabled (Volume is offline and pending recovery, or is waiting for the user to enable I/O)	Not Available (Unable to determine I/O performance because I/O is disabled)
insufficient-data	Enabled (I/O Enabled or I/O Auto-Enabled)	Insufficient Data
	Insufficient Data	

LOGGING AND AUDITING

Amazon EC2 and Amazon EBS are integrated with AWS CloudTrail, a service that provides a record of actions taken by a user, role, or an AWS service in Amazon EC2 and Amazon EBS.

CloudTrail captures all API calls for Amazon EC2 and Amazon EBS as events, including calls from the console and from code calls to the APIs.

AMAZON DATA LIFECYCLE MANAGER (DLM)

Automates the creation, retention, and deletion of EBS snapshots and EBS-backed AMIs.

- Protect valuable data by enforcing a regular backup schedule.
- Create standardized AMIs that can be refreshed at regular intervals.
- Retain backups as required by auditors or internal compliance.
- Reduce storage costs by deleting outdated backups.
- Create disaster recovery backup policies that back up data to isolated accounts.

EBS LIMITS (PER REGION)

Name	Default Limit
Provisioned IOPS	300,000
Provisioned IOPS (SSD) volume storage (TiB)	300
General Purpose (SSD) volume storage (TiB)	300
Magnetic volume storage (TiB)	300
Max Cold HDD (sc1) Storage in (TiB)	300

Max Throughput Optimized HDD (st1) Storage (TiB)	300

AWS ELB

AWS ELB FEATURES

Elastic Load Balancing automatically distributes incoming application traffic across multiple targets, such as Amazon EC2 instances, containers, and IP addresses.

Network traffic can be distributed across a single or multiple Availability Zones (AZs) within an AWS Region.

There are four types of Elastic Load Balancer (ELB) on AWS:

- **Classic Load Balancer (CLB)** – this is the oldest of the three and provides basic load balancing at both layer 4 and layer 7.
- **Application Load Balancer (ALB)** – layer 7 load balancer that routes connections based on the content of the request.
- **Network Load Balancer (NLB)** – layer 4 load balancer that routes connections based on IP protocol data.
- **Gateway Load Balancer (GLB)** – layer 3/4 load balancer used in front of virtual appliances such as firewalls and IDS/IPS systems.

Note: *The CLB is not covered in detail on this page as it is on old generation load balancer and is no longer featured on most AWS exams.*

The following table provides a comparison of some of the key features relevant to AWS exams:

Feature	Application Load Balancer	Network Load Balancer	Classic Load Balancer	Gateway Load Balancer
OSI Layer	Layer 7	Layer 4	Layer 4/7	Layer 3 Gateway + Layer 4 Load Balancing
Target Type	IP, Instance, Lambda	IP, Instance, ALB	N/A	IP, Instance
Protocols	HTTP, HTTPS	TCP	TCP, SSL, HTTP, HTTPS	IP
WebSockets	✓	✓		✓
IP addresses as a target	✓	✓		

HTTP header-based routing	✓			
HTTP/2/gRPC	✓			
Configurable idle connection timeout	✓		✓	
Cross-zone load balancing	✓	✓	✓	✓
SSL Offloading	✓	✓	✓	
Server Name Indication (SNI)	✓	✓	✓	
Sticky sessions	✓	✓	✓	✓
Static / Elastic IP Address		✓		
Custom Security policies			✓	

Elastic Load Balancing provides fault tolerance for applications by automatically balancing traffic across targets –

Targets cam be Amazon EC2 instances, containers, IP addresses, and Lambda functions.

ELB distributes traffic across Availability Zones while ensuring only healthy targets receive traffic.

Only 1 subnet per AZ can be enabled for each ELB.

Amazon Route 53 can be used for region load balancing with ELB instances configured in each region.

ELBs can be **Internet** facing or **internal-only.**

Internet facing ELB:

- ELB nodes have public IPs.
- Routes traffic to the private IP addresses of the EC2 instances.
- Need one public subnet in each AZ where the ELB is defined.
- ELB DNS name format: <name>-<id-number>.<region>.elb.amazonaws.com.

Internal only ELB:

- ELB nodes have private IPs.

- Routes traffic to the private IP addresses of the EC2 instances.
- ELB DNS name format: **internal**-<name>-<id-number>.<region>.elb.amazonaws.com.

Internal-only load balancers do not need an Internet gateway.

EC2 instances and containers can be registered against an ELB.

ELB nodes use IP addresses within your subnets, ensure at least a /27 subnet and make sure there are at least 8 IP addresses available for the ELB to scale.

An ELB forwards traffic to eth0 (primary IP address).

An ELB listener is the process that checks for connection requests:

- CLB listeners support the TCP and HTTP/HTTPS protocols.
- ALB listeners support the HTTP and HTTPS protocols.
- NLB listeners support the TCP, UDP and TLS protocols.
- GLB listeners support the IP protocol.

Deleting an ELB does not affect the instances registered against it (they won't be deleted; they just won't receive any more requests).

For ALB at least 2 subnets must be specified.

For NLB only one subnet must be specified (recommended to add at least 2).

ELB uses a DNS record TTL of 60 seconds to ensure new ELB node IP addresses are used to service clients.

By default the ELB has an idle connection timeout of 60 seconds, set the idle timeout for applications to at least 60 seconds.

Perfect Forward Secrecy (PFS) provides additional safeguards against the eavesdropping of encrypted data, using a unique random session key.

Server Order Preference lets you configure the load balancer to enforce cipher ordering, providing more control over the level of security used by clients to connect with your load balancer.

ELB does not support client certificate authentication (API Gateway does support this).

ELB SECURITY GROUPS

Security groups control the ports and protocols that can reach the front-end listener.

In non-default VPCs you can choose which security group to assign.

You must assign a security group for the ports and protocols on the front-end listener.

You need to also allow the ports and protocols for the health check ports and back-end listeners.

Security group configuration for ELB:

Inbound to ELB (allow).

- Internet-facing ELB:
  - Source: 0.0.0.0/0.
  - Protocol: TCP.
  - Port: ELB listener ports.

- Internal-only ELB:
  - ○ Source: VPC CIDR.
  - ○ Protocol: TCP.
  - ○ Port: ELB Listener ports.

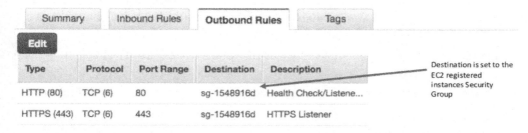

Outbound (allow, either type of ELB):

- Destination: EC2 registered instances security group.
- Protocol: TCP.
- Port: Health Check/Listener.

sg-6b578e13 | Internet-Facing ELB

	Summary	Inbound Rules	Outbound Rules	Tags	

Edit

Type	Protocol	Port Range	Destination	Description
HTTP (80)	TCP (6)	80	sg-1548916d	Health Check/Listene...
HTTPS (443)	TCP (6)	443	sg-1548916d	HTTPS Listener

Destination is set to the EC2 registered instances Security Group

Security group configuration for registered instances:

Inbound to registered instances (Allow, either type of ELB).

© 2023 Digital Cloud Training

- Source: ELB Security Group.
- Protocol: TCP.
- Port: Health Check/Listener.

Outbound (Allow, for both types of ELB).

- Destination: ELB Security Group.
- Protocol: TCP.
- Port: Ephemeral.

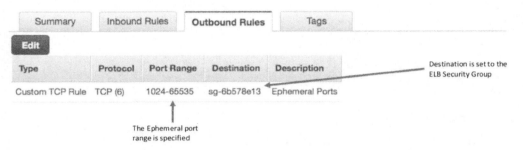

It is also important to ensure NACL settings are set correctly.

DISTRIBUTED DENIAL OF SERVICE (DDOS) PROTECTION:

ELB automatically distributes incoming application traffic across multiple targets, such as EC2 instances, containers, and IP addresses, and multiple Availability Zones, which minimizes the risk of overloading a single resource.

ELB only supports valid TCP requests so DDoS attacks such as UDP and SYN floods are not able to reach EC2 instances.

ELB also offers a single point of management and can serve as a line of defense between the internet and your backend, private EC2 instances.

You can also attach AWS Web Application Firewall (WAF) Web ACLs to Application Load Balancers to protect against web exploits.

ELB MONITORING

Monitoring takes place using:

- CloudWatch – every 1 minute.
  - ELB service only sends information when requests are active.
  - Can be used to trigger SNS notifications.
- Access Logs.
  - Disabled by default.
  - Includes information about the clients (not included in CloudWatch metrics).
  - Can identify requester, IP, request type etc.
  - Can be optionally stored and retained in S3.
- CloudTrail.
  - Can be used to capture API calls to the ELB.
  - Can be stored in an S3 bucket.

TARGET GROUPS

Target groups are a logical grouping of targets and are used with ALB, NLB, and GLB.

Targets are the endpoints and can be EC2 instances, ECS containers, IP addresses, Lambda functions, and other load balancers.

Target groups can exist independently from the ELB.

A single target can be in multiple target groups.

Only one protocol and one port can be defined per target group.

You cannot use public IP addresses as targets.

You cannot use instance IDs and IP address targets within the same target group.

A target group can only be associated with one load balancer.

The following diagram illustrates the basic components. Notice that each listener contains a default rule, and one listener contains another rule that routes requests to a different target group. One target is registered with two target groups.

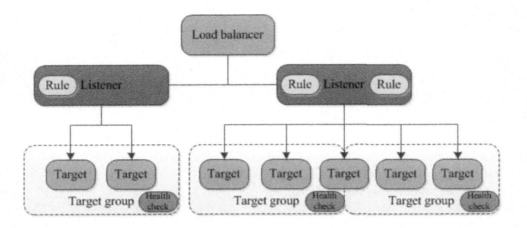

Target groups are used for registering instances against an ALB, NLB, or GLB.

Target groups are a regional construct (as are ELBs).

The following diagram shows how target groups can be used with an ALB using host-based and target-based routing to route traffic to multiple websites, running on multiple ports, on a single EC2 instance:

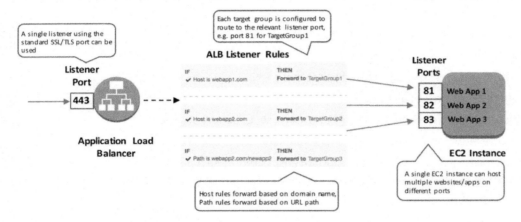

The following attributes can be defined:

- Deregistration delay – the amount of time for Elastic Load Balancing to wait before deregistering a target.
- Slow start duration – the time, in seconds, during which the load balancer sends a newly registered target a linearly increasing share of the traffic to the target group.
- Stickiness – indicates whether sticky sessions are enabled.

The default settings for attributes are shown below:

Edit attributes   ✕

Deregistration delay ⓘ	300	seconds
	Specify a value from 0-3600.	
Slow start duration ⓘ	0	seconds
	Specify a value from 30-900 or 0 to disable.	
Stickiness ⓘ	◯ Enable	

Cancel **Save**

Auto Scaling groups can scale each target group individually.

You can only use Auto Scaling with the load balancer if using instance IDs in your target group.

Health checks are defined per target group.

ALB/NLB/GLB can route to multiple target groups.

You can register the same EC2 instance or IP address with the same target group multiple times using different ports (used for routing requests to microservices).

If you register by instance ID the traffic is routed using the primary private IP address of the primary network interface.

If you register by IP address you can route traffic to an instance using any private address from one or more network interfaces.

You cannot mix different types within a target group (EC2, ECS, IP, Lambda function).

IP addresses can be used to register:

- Instances in a peered VPC.
- AWS resources that are addressable by IP address and port.
- On-premises resources linked to AWS through Direct Connect or a VPN connection.

APPLICATION LOAD BALANCER (ALB)

The Application Load Balancer operates at the request level (layer 7), routing traffic to targets – EC2 instances, containers and IP addresses based on the content of the request.

You can load balance HTTP/HTTPS applications and use layer 7-specific features, such as X-Forwarded-For headers.

The ALB supports HTTPS termination between the clients and the load balancer.

The ALB supports management of SSL certificates through AWS IAM and AWS Certificate Manager for predefined security policies.

The ALB supports Server Name Indication (SNI) which allows multiple secure websites to use a single secure listener.

With Server Name Indication (SNI) a client indicates the hostname to which it wants to connect.

IP addresses can be configured as targets which allows load balancing to applications hosted in AWS or on-premises using the IP addresses of the back-end instances/servers as targets.

You need at least two Availability Zones, and you can distribute incoming traffic across your targets in multiple Availability Zones.

The ALB automatically scales its request handling capacity in response to incoming application traffic.

You can configure an ALB to be Internet facing or create a load balancer without public IP addresses to serve as an internal (non-Internet-facing) load balancer.

The ALB supports content-based routing which allows the routing of requests to a service based on the content of the request. For example:

- **Host-based routing** routes client requests based on the Host field of the HTTP header allowing you to route to multiple domains from the same load balancer.
- **Path-based routing** routes a client request based on the URL path of the HTTP header (e.g. /images or /orders).

Support for microservices and containers with load balancing across multiple ports on a single EC2 instance.

Integration with Amazon Cognito for user authentication.

The slow start mode allows targets to "warm up" with a ramp-up period.

Health Checks:

- Can have custom response codes in health checks (200-399).
- Details provided in the API and management console for health check failures.
- Reason codes are returned with failed health checks.
- Health checks do not support WebSockets.
- Fail open means that if no AZ contains a healthy target the load balancer nodes route requests to all targets.

Detailed access log information is provided and saved to an S3 bucket every 5 or 6 minutes.

Deletion protection is possible.

Deregistration delay is like connection draining.

Sticky Sessions:

- Uses cookies to ensure a client is bound to an individual back-end instance for the duration of the cookie lifetime.
- ALB supports duration-based cookies and application-based cookies.
- For application-based cookies the cookie name is specified for each target group.
- For duration-based cookies the name of the cookie is always AWSALB.
- Sticky sessions are enabled at the target group level.
- WebSockets connections are inherently sticky (following the upgrade process).

Listeners and Rules

Listeners:

- Each ALB needs at least one listener and can have up to 10.
- Listeners define the port and protocol to listen on.
- Can add one or more listeners.
- Cannot have the same port in multiple listeners.

Listener rules:

- Rules determine how the load balancer routes requests to the targets in one or more target groups.
- Each rule consists of a priority, one or more actions, an optional host condition, and an optional path condition.
- Only one action can be configured per rule.
- One or more rules are required.
- Each listener has a default rule, and you can optionally define additional rules.
- Rules determine what action is taken when the rule matches the client request.
- Rules are defined on listeners.
- You can add rules that specify different target groups based on the content of the request (content-based routing).
- If no rules are found the default rule will be followed which directs traffic to the default target groups.

The image below shows a ruleset with a host-based and path-based entry and a default rule at the end:

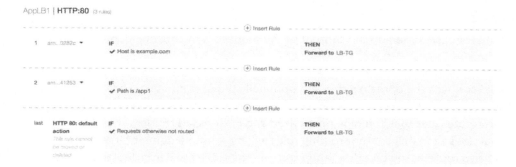

Default rules:
- When you create a listener you define an action for the default rule.
- Default rules cannot have conditions.
- You can delete the non-default rules for a listener at any time.
- You cannot delete the default rule for a listener.
- When you delete a listener all its rules are deleted.
- If no conditions for any of a listener's rules are met, the action for the default rule is taken.

Rule priority:
- Each rule has a priority, and they are evaluated in order of lowest to highest.
- The default rule is evaluated last.
- You can change the value of a non-default rule at any time.
- You cannot change the value of the default rule.

Rule action:
- Only one target group per action.
- Each rule has a type and a target group.
- The only supported action type is forward, which forwards requests to the target group.

- You can change the target group for a rule at any time.

Rule conditions:

- There are two types of rule condition: host and path.
- When the conditions for a rule are met the action is taken.
- Each rule can have up to 2 conditions, 1 path condition and 1 host condition.
- Optional condition is the path pattern you want the ALB to evaluate for it to route requests.

Request routing:

- After the load balancer receives a request it evaluates the listener rules in priority order to determine which rule to apply, and then selects a target from the target group for the rule action using the round robin routing algorithm.
- Routing is performed independently for each target group even when a target is registered with multiple target groups.
- You can configure listener rules to route requests to different target groups based on the content of the application traffic.

Content-based routing:

- ALB can route requests based on the content of the request in the host field: host-based or path-based.
- Host-based is domain name-based routing e.g. example.com or app1.example.com.
- The host field contains the domain name and optionally the port number.
- Path-based is URL based routing e.g. example.com/images, example.com/app1.
- You can also create rules that combine host-based and path-based routing.
- Anything that doesn't match content routing rules will be sent to a default target group.
- The ALB can also route based on other information in the HTTP header including query string parameters, request method, and source IP addresses

ALB and ECS

ECS service maintains the "desired count" of instances.

Optionally a load balancer can distribute traffic across tasks.

All containers in a single task definition are placed on a single EC2 container instance.

ECS service can only use a single load balancer.

ALB does not support multiple listeners in a single task definition.

ALB supports dynamic host-port mapping which means that multiple ports from the same service are allowed on the same container host.

ALB supports path-based routing and priority rules.

The ALB integrates with the EC2 container service using service load balancing.

Federated authentication:

- ALB supports authentication from OIDC compliant identity providers such as Google, Facebook, and Amazon.
- Implemented through an authentication action on a listener rule that integrates with Amazon

Cognito to create user pools.
- AWS SAM can also be used with Amazon Cognito.

NETWORK LOAD BALANCER

Network Load Balancer operates at the connection level (Layer 4), routing connections to targets – Amazon EC2 instances, containers and IP addresses based on IP protocol data.

The NLB is designed to handle millions of requests/sec and to support sudden volatile traffic patterns at extremely low latencies.

The NLB can be configured with a single static/Elastic IP address for each Availability Zone.

You can load balance any application hosted in AWS or on-premises using IP addresses of the application back-ends as targets.

The NLB supports connections from clients to IP-based targets in peered VPCs across different AWS Regions.

NLB supports both network and application target health checks.

NLB supports long-running/lived connections (ideal for WebSocket applications).

NLB supports failover between IP addresses within and across AWS Regions (uses Amazon Route 53 health checks).

The integration with Amazon Route 53 enables the removal of a failed load balancer IP address from service and subsequent redirection of traffic to an alternate NLB in another region.

NLB support cross-zone load balancing, but it is not enabled by default when the NLB is created through the console.

Target groups for NLBs support the following protocols and ports:
- **Protocols:** TCP, TLS, UDP, TCP_UDP.
- **Ports:** 1-65535.

The table below summarizes the supported listener and protocol combinations and target group settings:

Listener Protocol	Target Group Protocol	Target Group Type	Health Check Protocol
TCP	TCP | TCP_UDP	instance | ip	HTTP | HTTPS | TCP
TLS	TCP | TLS	Instance | ip	HTTP | HTTPS | TCP
UDP	UDP | TCP_UDP	instance	HTTP | HTTPS | TCP
TCP_UDP	TCP_UDP	instance	HTTP | HTTPS | TCP

Amazon CloudWatch reports Network Load Balancer metrics.

You can use VPC Flow Logs to record all requests sent to your load balancer.

MONITORING

AWS CloudTrail captures API calls for auditing.

You only pay for the S3 storage charges.

CloudTrail only monitors API calls.

Access logs can be used to monitor other actions such as the time the request was received, the client's IP address, request paths etc.

Access logging is optional and disabled by default.

You are only charged for the S3 storage with access logging.

With access logging, the ALB logs requests sent to the load balancer including requests that never reached targets.

The ALB does not log health check requests.

AMAZON EC2 AUTO SCALING

AMAZON EC2 AUTO SCALING FEATURES

AWS Auto Scaling monitors your applications and automatically adjusts capacity to maintain steady, predictable performance at the lowest possible cost.

AWS Auto Scaling refers to a collection of Auto Scaling capabilities across several AWS services.

The services within the AWS Auto Scaling family include:

- Amazon EC2 (known as Amazon EC2 Auto Scaling).
- Amazon ECS.
- Amazon DynamoDB.
- Amazon Aurora.

This page is specifically for Amazon EC2 Auto Scaling – Auto Scaling will also be discussed for the other services on their respective pages.

AMAZON EC2 AUTO SCALING FEATURES

Amazon EC2 Auto Scaling helps you ensure that you have the correct number of Amazon EC2 instances available to handle the load for your application.

You create collections of EC2 instances, called Auto Scaling groups.

Automatically provides horizontal scaling (scale-out) for your instances.

Triggered by an event of scaling action to either launch or terminate instances.

Availability, cost, and system metrics can all factor into scaling.

Auto Scaling is a region-specific service.

Auto Scaling can span multiple AZs within the same AWS region.

Auto Scaling can be configured from the Console, CLI, SDKs and APIs.

There is no additional cost for Auto Scaling, you just pay for the resources (EC2 instances) provisioned.

Auto Scaling works with ELB, CloudWatch and CloudTrail.

You can determine which subnets Auto Scaling will launch new instances into.

Auto Scaling will try to distribute EC2 instances evenly across AZs.

Launch configuration is the template used to create new EC2 instances and includes parameters such as instance family, instance type, AMI, key pair, and security groups.

You cannot edit a launch configuration once defined.

A launch configuration:

- Can be created from the AWS console or CLI.
- You can create a new launch configuration, or.
- You can use an existing running EC2 instance to create the launch configuration.
  - The AMI must exist on EC2.
  - EC2 instance tags and any additional block store volumes created after the instance launch will not be considered.
- If you want to change your launch configurations you have to create a new one, make the required changes, and use that with your auto scaling groups.

You can use a launch configuration with multiple Auto Scaling Groups (ASG).

Launch templates are similar to launch configurations and offer more options (more below).

An Auto Scaling Group (ASG) is a logical grouping of EC2 instances managed by an Auto Scaling Policy.

An ASG can be edited once defined.

You can attach one or more classic ELBs to your existing ASG.

You can attach one or more Target Groups to your ASG to include instances behind an ALB.

The ELBs must be in the same region.

Once you do this any EC2 instance existing or added by the ASG will be automatically registered with the ASG defined ELBs.

If adding an instance to an ASG would result in exceeding the maximum capacity of the ASG the request will fail.

You can add a running instance to an ASG if the following conditions are met:

- The instance is in a running state.
- The AMI used to launch the instance still exists.
- The instance is not part of another ASG.
- The instance is in the same AZs for the ASG.

SCALING OPTIONS

The scaling options define the triggers and when instances should be provisioned/de-provisioned.

There are four scaling options:

- Maintain – keep a specific or minimum number of instances running.
- Manual – use maximum, minimum, or a specific number of instances.
- Scheduled – increase or decrease the number of instances based on a schedule.
- Dynamic – scale based on real-time system metrics (e.g. CloudWatch metrics).

- Predictive - machine learning to schedule the right number of EC2 instances in anticipation of approaching traffic changes.

The following table describes the scaling options available and when to use them:

Scaling	Description	When to use
Maintain	Ensures the required number of instances are running	Use when you always need a known number of instances running at all times
Manual	Manually change desired capacity	Use when your needs change rarely enough that you're ok the make manual changes
Scheduled	Adjust min/max on specific dates/times or recurring time periods	Use when you know when your busy and quiet times are. Useful for ensuring enough instances are available before very busy times
Dynamic	Scale in response to system load or other triggers using metrics	Useful for changing capacity based on system utilization, e.g. CPU hits 80%.
Predictive	predict capacity required ahead of time using ML	Useful for when capacity, and number of instances is unknown.

Scheduled Scaling

Scaling based on a schedule allows you to scale your application ahead of predictable load changes.

For example, you may know that traffic to your application is highest between 9am and 12pm Monday-Friday.

Dynamic Scaling

Amazon EC2 Auto Scaling enables you to follow the demand curve for your applications closely, reducing the need to manually provision Amazon EC2 capacity in advance.

For example, you can track the CPU utilization of your EC2 instances or the "Request Count Per Target" to track the number of requests coming through an Application Load Balancer.

Amazon EC2 Auto Scaling will then automatically adjust the number of EC2 instances as needed to maintain your target.

Predictive Scaling

Predictive Scaling uses machine learning to schedule the optimum number of EC2 instances in anticipation of upcoming traffic changes.

Predictive Scaling predicts future traffic, including regularly occurring spikes, and provisions the right number of EC2 instances in advance.

Predictive Scaling uses machine learning algorithms to detect changes in daily and weekly patterns and then automatically adjust forecasts.

You can configure the scaling options through Scaling Policies which determine when, if, and how the ASG scales out and in.

The following table describes the scaling policy types available for dynamic scaling policies and when to use them (more detail further down the page):

Scaling Policy	What it is	When to use
Target Tracking Policy	Adds or removes capacity as required to keep the metric at or close to the specific target value.	You want to keep the CPU usage of your ASG at 70%
Simple Scaling Policy	Waits for the health check and cool down periods to expire before re-evaluating	Useful when load is erratic. AWS recommends step scaling instead of simple in most cases.
Step Scaling Policy	Increases or decreases the configured capacity of the Auto Scaling group based on a set of scaling adjustments, known as step adjustments.	You want to vary adjustments based on the size of the alarm breach

The diagram below depicts an Auto Scaling group with a Scaling policy set to a minimum size of 1 instance, a desired capacity of 2 instances, and a maximum size of 4 instances:

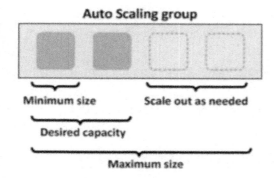

Scaling based on Amazon SQS

Can also scale based on an Amazon Simple Queue Service (SQS) queue.

This comes up as an exam question for SAA-C02.

Uses a custom metric that's sent to Amazon CloudWatch that measures the number of messages in the queue per EC2 instance in the Auto Scaling group.

A target tracking policy configures your Auto Scaling group to scale based on the custom metric and a set target value. CloudWatch alarms invoke the scaling policy.

A custom "backlog per instance" metric is used to track the number of messages in the queue and also the number available for retrieval.

Can base the adjustments off the SQS Metric "ApproximateNumberOfMessages".

LAUNCH TEMPLATES VS LAUNCH CONFIGURATIONS

Launch templates are like launch configurations in that they specify the instance configuration information.

Information includes the ID of the Amazon Machine Image (AMI), the instance type, a key pair, security groups, and the other parameters that you use to launch EC2 instances.

Launch templates include additional features such as supporting multiple versions of a template.

With versioning, you can create a subset of the full set of parameters and then reuse it to create other templates or template versions.

EC2 AUTO SCALING LIFECYCLE HOOKS

Lifecycle pause EC2 instances as an Auto Scaling group launches or terminates them so you can perform custom actions.

Paused instances remain in a wait state either until you complete the lifecycle action using the complete-lifecycle-action command or the CompleteLifecycleAction operation, or until the timeout period ends (one hour by default).

Lifecycle hooks provide greater control over how instances launch and terminate.

You can send notifications when an instance enters a wait state using Amazon EventBridge, Amazon SNS, or Amazon SQS to receive the notifications.

HIGH AVAILABILITY

Amazon EC2 Auto Scaling offers high availability (HA) when instances are launched into at least two Availability Zones.

You can use an Amazon Elastic Load Balancer or Amazon Route 53 to direct incoming connections to your EC2 instances.

EC2 Auto Scaling cannot provide HA across multiple AWS Regions as it is a regional service.

MONITORING AND REPORTING

When Auto Scaling group metrics are enabled the Auto Scaling group sends sampled data to CloudWatch every minute (no charge).

You can enable and disable Auto Scaling group metrics using the AWS Management Console, AWS CLI, or AWS SDKs.

The AWS/AutoScaling namespace includes the following metrics which are sent to CloudWatch every 1 minute:

- GroupMinSize
- GroupMaxSize
- GroupDesiredCapacity
- GroupInServiceInstances
- GroupPendingInstances
- GroupStandbyInstances
- GroupTerminatingInstances
- GroupTotalInstances

Metrics are also sent from the Amazon EC2 instances to Amazon CloudWatch:

- Basic monitoring sends EC2 metrics to CloudWatch about ASG instances every 5 minutes.
- Detailed monitoring can be enabled and sends metrics every 1 minute (chargeable).
- If the launch configuration is created from the console basic monitoring of EC2 instances is enabled by default.
- If the launch configuration is created from the CLI detailed monitoring of EC2 instances is enabled by default.

EC2 Auto Scaling uses health checks to check if instances are healthy and available.

- By default Auto Scaling uses EC2 status checks.
- Auto Scaling supports ELB health checks and custom health checks in addition to the EC2 status checks.
- If any of the configured health checks returns an unhealthy status the instance will be terminated.
- With ELB health checks enabled an instance is marked as unhealthy if the ELB reports it as OutOfService.
- A healthy instance enters the InService state.
- If an EC2 instance is marked as unhealthy it will be scheduled for replacement.
- If connection draining is enabled, EC2 Auto Scaling will wait for any in-flight requests to complete or timeout before terminating instances.
- The health check grace period is a period of time in which a new instance is allowed to warm up before health check are performed (300 seconds by default).

Note: *When using Elastic Load Balancers it is an AWS best practice to enable the ELB health checks. If you don't, EC2 status checks may show an instance as being healthy that the ELB has determined is unhealthy. In this case the instance will be removed from service by the ELB but will not be terminated by Auto Scaling.*

LOGGING AND AUDITING

AWS CloudTrail captures all API calls for AWS Auto Scaling as events.

The API calls that are captured include calls from the Amazon EC2 Auto Scaling console and code calls to the AWS Auto Scaling API.

If you create a trail, you can enable continuous delivery of CloudTrail events to an Amazon S3 bucket, including events for AWS Auto Scaling.

If you don't configure a trail, you can still view the most recent (up to 90 days) events in the CloudTrail console in the **Event history**.

CloudTrail events include the calls made to AWS Auto Scaling, the IP address from which the requests were made, who made the requests, when they were made, and additional details.

AUTHORIZATION AND ACCESS CONTROL

EC2 Auto Scaling support identity-based IAM policies.

Amazon EC2 Auto Scaling does not support resource-based policies.

Amazon EC2 Auto Scaling uses service-linked roles for the permissions that it requires to call other AWS services on your behalf.

A service-linked role is a unique type of IAM role that is linked directly to an AWS service.

There is a default service-linked role for your account, named **AWSServiceRoleForAutoScaling**.

This role is automatically assigned to your Auto Scaling groups unless you specify a different service-linked role.

Amazon EC2 Auto Scaling also does not support Access Control Lists (ACLs).

You can apply tag-based, resource-level permissions in the identity-based policies that you create for Amazon EC2 Auto Scaling.

This offers better control over which resources a user can create, modify, use, or delete.

ASG BEHAVIOR AND CONFIGURATION

EC2 Auto Scaling – Termination Policy:

- Termination policies control the instances which are terminated first when a scale-in event occurs.
- There is a default termination policy configured and you can create your own customized termination policies.
- The default termination policy helps to ensure that EC2 instances span Availability Zones evenly for high availability.
- The default policy is fairly generic and flexible to cover a range of scenarios.

You can enable Instance Protection which prevents Auto Scaling from scaling in and terminating the EC2 instances.

If Auto Scaling fails to launch instances in a specific AZ it will try other AZs until successful.

The default health check grace period is 300 seconds.

"Scaling out" is the process in which EC2 instances are launched by the scaling policy.

"Scaling in" is the process in which EC2 instances are terminated by the scaling policy.

It is recommended to create a scale-in event for every configured scale-out event.

An imbalance may occur due to:

- Manually removing AZs/subnets from the configuration.

- Manually terminating EC2 instances.
- EC2 capacity issues.
- Spot price is reached.

All Elastic IPs and EBS volumes are detached from terminated EC2 instances and will need to be manually reattached.

Using custom health checks a CLI command can be issued to set the instance's status to unhealthy, e.g.:

aws autoscaling set–instance-health –instance-id i-123abc45d –health-status Unhealthy

Once an EC2 instance enters the terminating state it cannot be put back into service again.

However, there is a short period of time in which an AWS CLI command can be run to change an instance to healthy.

Termination of unhealthy instances happens first, then Auto Scaling attempts to launch new instances to replace terminated instances. This is different to AZ rebalancing.

You can use the AWS Console or AWS CLI to manually remove (detach) instances from an ASG.

When detaching an EC2 instance you can optionally decrement the ASG's desired capacity (to prevent it from launching another instance).

An instance can only be attached to one Auto Scaling group at a time.

You can suspend and then resume one or more of the scaling processes for your ASG at any time.

This can be useful when if want to investigate an issue with an application and make changes without invoking the scaling processes.

You can manually move an instance from an ASG and put it in the standby state.

Instances in the standby state are still managed by Auto Scaling, are charged as normal, and do not count towards available EC2 instance for workload/application use.

Auto scaling does not perform any health checks on EC2 instances in the standby state.

Standby state can be used for performing updates/changes/troubleshooting etc. without health checks being performed or replacement instances being launched.

When you delete an Auto Scaling group all EC2 instances will be terminated.

You can select to use Spot instances in launch configurations.

The ASG treats spot instances the same as on-demand instances.

You can mix Spot instances with on-demand (when using launch templates).

The ASG can be configured to send an Amazon SNS notification when:

- An instance is launched.
- An instance is terminated.
- An instance fails to launch.
- An instance fails to terminate.

Merging ASGs.

- Can merge multiple single AZ Auto Scaling Groups into a single multi-AZ ASG.
- Merging can only be performed by using the CLI.
- The process is to rezone one of the groups to cover/span the other AZs for the other ASGs and

then delete the other ASGs.
- This can be performed on ASGs with or without ELBs attached to them.

Cooldown Period:

- The cooldown period is a setting you can configure for your Auto Scaling group that helps to ensure that it doesn't launch or terminate additional instances before the previous scaling activity takes effect.
- A default cooldown period of 300 seconds is applied when you create your Auto Scaling group.
- You can configure the cooldown period when you create the Auto Scaling group.
- You can override the default cooldown via scaling-specific cooldown.

The warm-up period is the period in which a newly launched EC2 instance in an ASG that uses step scaling is not considered toward the ASG metrics.

AWS LAMBDA

AWS LAMBDA FEATURES

AWS Lambda lets you run code as functions without provisioning or managing servers.

Lambda-based applications are composed of functions triggered by events.

With serverless computing, your application still runs on servers, but all the server management is done by AWS.

You cannot log in to the compute instances that run Lambda functions or customize the operating system or language runtime.

Lambda functions:

- Consist of code and any associated dependencies.
- Configuration information is associated with the function.
- You specify the configuration information when you create the function.
- API provided for updating configuration data.

You specify the amount of memory you need allocated to your Lambda functions.

AWS Lambda allocates CPU power proportional to the memory you specify using the same ratio as a general purpose EC2 instance type.

Functions can access:

- AWS services or non-AWS services.
- AWS services running in VPCs (e.g. RedShift, Elasticache, RDS instances).
- Non-AWS services running on EC2 instances in an AWS VPC.

To enable your Lambda function to access resources inside your private VPC, you must provide additional VPC-specific configuration information that includes VPC subnet IDs and security group IDs.

AWS Lambda uses this information to set up elastic network interfaces (ENIs) that enable your function.

You can request additional memory in 1 MB increments from 128 MB to 10240 MB.

There is a maximum execution timeout.

- Max is 15 minutes (900 seconds), default is 3 seconds.

- You pay for the time it runs.
- Lambda terminates the function at the timeout.

Code is invoked using API calls made using AWS SDKs.

Lambda assumes an IAM role when it executes the function.

AWS Lambda stores code in Amazon S3 and encrypts it at rest.

Lambda provides continuous scaling – scales out not up.

Lambda scales concurrently executing functions up to your default limit (1000).

Lambda can scale up to tens of thousands of concurrent executions.

Lambda functions are serverless and independent, 1 event = 1 function.

Functions can trigger other functions so 1 event can trigger multiple functions.

Use cases fall within the following categories:

- Using Lambda functions with AWS services as event sources.
- On-demand Lambda function invocation over HTTPS using Amazon API Gateway (custom REST API and endpoint).
- On-demand Lambda function invocation using custom applications (mobile, web apps, clients) and AWS SDKs, AWS Mobile SDKs, and the AWS Mobile SDK for Android.
- Scheduled events can be configured to run code on a scheduled basis through the AWS Lambda Console.

EVENT SOURCE MAPPINGS

Lambda is an event-driven compute service where AWS Lambda runs code in response to events such as changes to data in an S3 bucket or a DynamoDB table.

An event source is an AWS service or developer-created application that produces events that trigger an AWS Lambda function to run.

You can use event source mappings to process items from a stream or queue in services that don't invoke Lambda functions directly.

Supported AWS event sources include:

- Amazon S3.
- Amazon DynamoDB.
- Amazon Kinesis Data Streams.
- Amazon Simple Notification Service.
- Amazon Simple Email Service.
- Amazon Simple Queue Service.
- Amazon Cognito.
- AWS CloudFormation.
- Amazon CloudWatch Logs.
- Amazon CloudWatch Events.
- AWS CodeCommit.
- AWS Config.
- Amazon Alexa.

- Amazon Lex.
- Amazon API Gateway.
- AWS IoT Button.
- Amazon CloudFront.
- Amazon Kinesis Data Firehose.
- Other Event Sources: Invoking a Lambda Function On Demand.

Other event sources can invoke Lambda functions on-demand.

Applications need permissions to invoke Lambda functions.

Lambda can run code in response to HTTP requests using Amazon API gateway or API calls made using the AWS SDKs.

Services that Lambda reads events from:

- Amazon Kinesis
- Amazon DynamoDB
- Amazon Simple Queue Service

An event source mapping uses permissions in the function's execution role to read and manage items in the event source.

Permissions, event structure, settings, and polling behavior vary by event source.

To process items from a stream or queue, you can create an event source mapping.

Each event that your function processes can contain hundreds or thousands of items.

The configuration of the event source mapping for stream-based services (DynamoDB, Kinesis), and Amazon SQS, is made on the Lambda side.

Note: for other services such as Amazon S3 and SNS, the function is invoked asynchronously, and the configuration is made on the source (S3/SNS) rather than Lambda.

LAMBDA@EDGE

Lambda@Edge allows you to run code across AWS locations globally without provisioning or managing servers, responding to end users at the lowest network latency.

Lambda@Edge lets you run Node.js and Python Lambda functions to customize content that CloudFront delivers, executing the functions in AWS locations closer to the viewer.

The functions run in response to CloudFront events, without provisioning or managing servers. You can use Lambda functions to change CloudFront requests and responses at the following points:

- After CloudFront receives a request from a viewer (viewer request).
- Before CloudFront forwards the request to the origin (origin request).
- After CloudFront receives the response from the origin (origin response).
- Before CloudFront forwards the response to the viewer (viewer response).

You just upload your Node.js code to AWS Lambda and configure your function to be triggered in response to an Amazon CloudFront request.

The code is then ready to execute across AWS locations globally when a request for content is received, and scales with the volume of CloudFront requests globally.

LAMBDA AND AMAZON VPC

You can connect a Lambda function to private subnets in a VPC.

Lambda needs the following VPC configuration information so that it can connect to the VPC:

- Private subnet ID.
- Security Group ID (with required access).

Lambda uses this information to setup an Elastic Network Interface (ENI) using an available IP address from your private subnet.

Lambda functions provide access only to a single VPC. If multiple subnets are specified, they must all be in the same VPC.

Lambda functions configured to access resources in a particular VPC will not have access to the Internet as a default configuration.

If you need access to the internet, you will need to create a NAT in your VPC to forward this traffic and configure your security group to allow this outbound traffic.

Careful with DNS resolution of public hostnames as it could add to function running time (cost).

Cannot connect to a dedicated tenancy VPC.

Exam tip: *If a Lambda function needs to connect to a VPC and needs Internet access, make sure you connect to a private subnet that has a route to a NAT Gateway (the NAT Gateway will be in a public subnet).*

Lambda uses your function's permissions to create and manage network interfaces. To connect to a VPC, your function's execution role must have the following permissions:

- ec2:CreateNetworkInterface
- ec2:DescribeNetworkInterfaces
- ec2:DeleteNetworkInterface

These permissions are included in the AWSLambdaVPCAccessExecutionRole managed policy.

Only connect to a VPC if you need to as it can slow down function execution.

BUILDING LAMBDA APPS

You can deploy and manage your serverless applications using the AWS Serverless Application Model (AWS SAM).

AWS SAM is a specification that prescribes the rules for expressing serverless applications on AWS.

This specification aligns with the syntax used by AWS CloudFormation today and is supported natively within AWS CloudFormation as a set of resource types (referred to as "serverless resources").

You can automate your serverless application's release process using AWS CodePipeline and AWS CodeDeploy.

You can enable your Lambda function for tracing with AWS X-Ray.

ELASTIC LOAD BALANCING

Application Load Balancers (ALBs) support AWS Lambda functions as targets.

You can register your Lambda functions as targets and configure a listener rule to forward requests to the target group for your Lambda function.

Exam tip: Functions can be registered to target groups using the API, AWS Management Console or the CLI.

When the load balancer forwards the request to a target group with a Lambda function as a target, it invokes your Lambda function and passes the content of the request to the Lambda function, in JSON format.

Limits:

- The Lambda function and target group must be in the same account and in the same Region.
- The maximum size of the request body that you can send to a Lambda function is 1 MB.
- The maximum size of the response JSON that the Lambda function can send is 1 MB.
- WebSockets are not supported. Upgrade requests are rejected with an HTTP 400 code.

By default, health checks are disabled for target groups of type lambda.

You can enable health checks to implement DNS failover with Amazon Route 53. The Lambda function can check the health of a downstream service before responding to the health check request.

If you create the target group and register the Lambda function using the AWS Management Console, the console adds the required permissions to your Lambda function policy on your behalf.

Otherwise, after you create the target group and register the function using the AWS CLI, you must use the add-permission command to grant Elastic Load Balancing permission to invoke your Lambda function.

LAMBDA LIMITS

Memory – minimum 128 MB, maximum 10,240 MB in 1 MB increments.

Ephemeral disk capacity (/tmp space) per invocation – 512 MB.

Size of environment variables maximum 4 KB.

Number of file descriptors – 1024.

Number of processes and threads (combined) – 1024.

Maximum execution duration per request – 900 seconds.

Concurrent executions per account – 1000 (soft limit).

Function burst concurrency 500 -3000 (region dependent).

Invocation payload:

- Synchronous 6 MB.
- Asynchronous 256 KB

Lambda function deployment size is 50 MB (zipped), 250 MB unzipped.

OPERATIONS AND MONITORING

Lambda automatically monitors Lambda functions and reports metrics through CloudWatch.

Lambda tracks the number of requests, the latency per request, and the number of requests resulting in an error.

You can view the request rates and error rates using the AWS Lambda Console, the CloudWatch console, and other AWS resources.

You can use AWS X-Ray to visualize the components of your application, identify performance bottlenecks, and troubleshoot requests that resulted in an error.

Your Lambda functions send trace data to X-Ray, and X-Ray processes the data to generate a service map and searchable trace summaries.

The AWS X-Ray Daemon is a software application that gathers raw segment data and relays it to the AWS X-Ray service.

The daemon works in conjunction with the AWS X-Ray SDKs so that data sent by the SDKs can reach the X-Ray service.

When you trace your Lambda function, the X-Ray daemon automatically runs in the Lambda environment to gather trace data and send it to X-Ray.

Must have permissions to write to X-Ray in the execution role.

CHARGES

Priced based on:

- Number of requests.
- Duration of the request calculated from the time your code begins execution until it returns or terminates.
- The amount of memory allocated to the function.

AWS ELASTIC BEANSTALK

AWS ELASTIC BEANSTALK FEATURES

AWS Elastic Beanstalk can be used to quickly deploy and manage applications in the AWS Cloud.

Developers upload applications and Elastic Beanstalk handles the deployment details of capacity provisioning, load balancing, auto-scaling, and application health monitoring.

You can use multiple availability zones to improve application reliability and availability.

Considered a Platform as a Service (PaaS) solution.

Supports the following platforms:

- Docker
- Multicontainer Docker
- Preconfigured Docker
- Go
- Java SE
- Tomcat
- .NET Core on Linux
- .NET on Windows Server
- Node.js
- PHP
- Python
- Ruby

Developers can focus on writing code and don't need to worry about deploying infrastructure.

You pay only for the resources provisioned, not for Elastic Beanstalk itself.

Elastic Beanstalk automatically scales your application up and down.

You can select the EC2 instance type that is optimal for your application.

Can retain full administrative control or have Elastic Beanstalk do it for you.

The Managed Platform Updates feature automatically applies updates for your operating system and platform.

Elastic Beanstalk monitors and manages application health and information is viewable via a dashboard.

Integrated with CloudWatch and X-Ray for performance data and metrics.

Integrates with Amazon VPC and AWS IAM.

Can provision most database instances.

Stores your application files and, optionally, server log files in Amazon S3.

Application data can also be stored on S3.

Multiple environments are supported to enable versioning.

Changes from Git repositories are replicated.

Linux and Windows AMI support.

Code is deployed using a WAR file or Git repository.

Can use the AWS toolkit for Visual Studio and the AWS toolkit for Eclipse to deploy Elastic Beanstalk.

Fault tolerance within a single region.

By default applications are publicly accessible.

Can access logs without logging into application servers.

Provides ISO, PCI, SOC 1, SOC 2, and SOC 3 compliance along with the criteria for HIPAA eligibility.

Supports AWS Graviton arm64-based processors.

ELASTIC BEANSTALK LAYERS

There are several layers that make up Elastic Beanstalk and each layer is described below:

Application:

- Within Elastic Beanstalk, an application is a collection of different elements, such as environments, environment configurations, and application versions.
- You can have multiple application versions held within an application.

Application version:

- An application version is a very specific reference to a section of deployable code.
- The application version will point typically to an Amazon s3 bucket containing the code.

Environment:

- An environment refers to an application version that has been deployed on AWS resources.

- The resources are configured and provisioned by AWS Elastic Beanstalk.
- The environment is comprised of all the resources created by Elastic Beanstalk and not just an EC2 instance with your uploaded code.

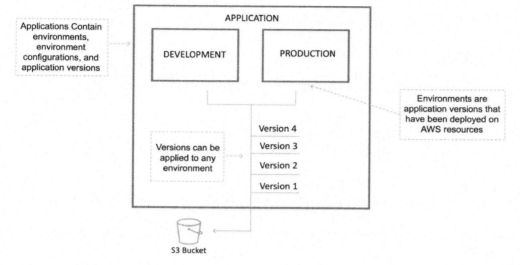

Environment tier:

- Determines how Elastic Beanstalk provisions resources based on what the application is designed to do.
- **Web servers** are standard applications that listen for and then process HTTP requests, typically over port 80.
- **Workers** are specialized applications that have a background processing task that listens for messages on an Amazon SQS queue.

Environment configurations:

- An environment configuration is a collection of parameters and settings that dictate how an environment will have its resources provisioned by Elastic Beanstalk and how these resources will behave.

Configuration template:

- This is a template that provides the baseline for creating a new, unique environment configuration.

DEPLOYMENT OPTIONS

AWS Elastic Beanstalk provides several options for how deployments are processed, including deployment policies and options that let you configure batch size and health check behavior during deployments.

Deployment options

Single instance: great for development.

High availability with load balancer: great for production.

Deployment policies

The deployment policies are: All at once, Rolling, Rolling with additional batch, and Immutable.

All at once:

- Deploys the new version to all instances simultaneously.
- All your instances are out of service while the deployment takes place.
- Fastest deployment.
- Good for quick iterations in the development environment.
- You will experience an outage while the deployment is taking place – not ideal for mission-critical systems.
- If the update fails, you need to roll back the changes by re-deploying the original version to all your instances.
- No additional cost.

Rolling:

- Update a few instances at a time (batch), and then move onto the next batch once the first batch is healthy (downtime for 1 batch at a time).
- The application is running both versions simultaneously.
- Each batch of instances is taken out of service while the deployment takes place.
- Your environment capacity will be reduced by the number of instances in a batch while the deployment takes place.
- Not ideal for performance-sensitive systems.
- If the update fails, you need to perform an additional rolling update to roll back the changes.
- No additional cost.
- Long deployment time.

Rolling with additional batch:

- Like Rolling but launches new instances in a batch ensuring that there is full availability.
- The application is running at capacity.
- You can set the bucket size.
- The application is running both versions simultaneously.
- Small additional cost.
- Additional batch is removed at the end of the deployment.
- Longer deployment.
- Good for production environments.

Immutable:

- Launches new instances in a new ASG and deploys the version update to these instances before swapping traffic to these instances once healthy.

- Zero downtime.
- New code is deployed to new instances using an ASG.
- High cost as double the number of instances running during updates.
- Longest deployment.
- Quick rollback in case of failures.
- Great for production environments.

Additionally, Elastic Beanstalk supports blue/green deployment.

Blue / Green deployment:

- This is not a feature within Elastic Beanstalk
- You create a new "staging" environment and deploy updates there.
- The new environment (green) can be validated independently, and you can roll back if there are issues.
- Route 53 can be set up using weighted policies to redirect a percentage of traffic to the staging environment.
- Using Elastic Beanstalk, you can "swap URLs" when done with the environment test.
- Zero downtime.

The following tables summarizes the different deployment policies:

Deployment Policy	Deploy Time	Zero Downtime	Rollback	Extra Cost	Reduction in capacity
All at once	🕐	NO	Manual redeploy	NONE	YES (total)
Rolling	🕐🕐	YES	Manual redeploy	NONE	YES (batch size)
Rolling with additional batch	🕐🕐🕐	YES	Manual redeploy	YES (batch size)	NO
Immutable	🕐🕐🕐🕐	YES	Terminate new instances	YES (total)	NO
Blue/green	🕐🕐🕐🕐	YES	Swap URL	YES (varies)	NO

GOLDEN AMIS

When deploying code to Amazon EC2 using Beanstalk, Elastic Beanstalk must resolve application dependencies which can take a long time.

A golden AMI is a method of reducing this time by packaging all dependencies, configuration, and software into the AMI before deploying.

WORKER ENVIRONMENTS

If an application performs tasks that take a long time to complete (long-running tasks), offload to a worker environment.

It allows you to decouple your application tiers.

Can define periodic tasks in the cron.yaml file.

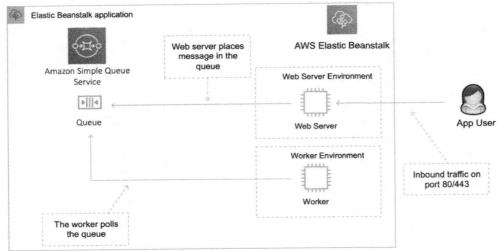

ELASTIC BEANSTALK WITH AMAZON RELATIONAL DATABASE SERVICE (RDS)

You can deploy Amazon RDS within an Elastic Beanstalk environment as in the diagram below:

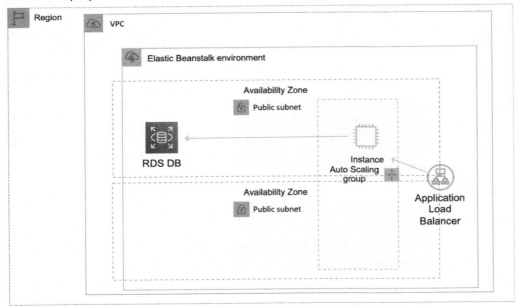

However, if you terminate your Elastic Beanstalk environment you also lose the database.

The use case is only for development environments, typically not suitable for production.

For production, it is preferable to create the Amazon RDS database outside of Elastic Beanstalk as in the diagram below:

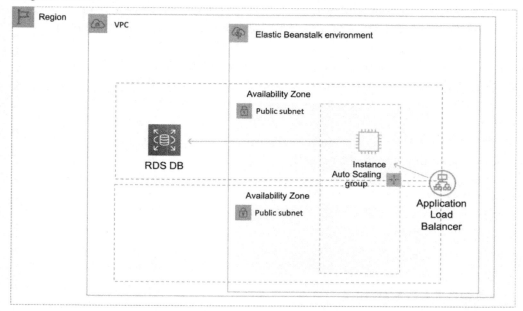

Steps to migrate from RDS within a Beanstalk environment to standalone RDS:

- Take a snapshot of the RDS DB.
- Enable deletion protection on the RDS DB.
- Create a new environment without an RDS DB and point applications to the existing RDS DB.
- Perform a blue/green deployment and swap the new and old environments.
- Terminate the old environment (RDS will not be deleted due to termination protection).
- Delete the CloudFormation stack (will be in the DELETE_FAILED state).

Connecting to an Amazon RDS database

When the environment update is complete, the DB instance's hostname and other connection information are available to your application through the following environment properties:

- RDS_HOSTNAME – The hostname of the DB instance.
- RDS_PORT – The port on which the DB instance accepts connections. The default value varies among DB engines.
- RDS_DB_NAME – The database name, ebdb.
- RDS_USERNAME – The user name that you configured for your database.
- RDS_PASSWORD – The password that you configured for your database.

CUSTOM DOMAIN NAMES

If you're using AWS Elastic Beanstalk to deploy and manage applications in the AWS Cloud, you can use Amazon Route 53 to route DNS traffic for your domain, such as example.com, to a new or an existing Elastic Beanstalk environment.

You create either a *CNAME record* or an *alias record*, depending on whether the domain name for the environment includes the Region, such as **us-east-2**, in which you deployed the environment. New environments include the Region in the domain name; environments that were created before early 2016 do not.

If the domain name does NOT include the Region: create a CNAME record.

If the domain name DOES include the Region: create an Alias record.

SECURITY

Elastic Beanstalk works with HTTPS:

- Load the SSL certificate onto the load balancer.
- Can be performed from the console or in code (.ebextensions/securelistener-alb.config).
- SSL certificate can be provisioned using ACM or CLI.

For redirecting HTTP to HTTPS:

- Configure in the application.
- Configure the ALB with a rule.
- Ensure health checks are not redirected.

MONITORING AND REPORTING

Elastic Beanstalk automatically uses Amazon CloudWatch to help you monitor your application and environment status.

You can navigate to the Amazon CloudWatch console to see your dashboard and get an overview of all your resources as well as your alarms.

You can also choose to view more metrics or add custom metrics.

LOGGING AND AUDITING

With CloudWatch Logs, you can monitor and archive your Elastic Beanstalk application, system, and custom log files from Amazon EC2 instances of your environments.

You can also configure alarms that make it easier for you to react to specific log stream events that your metric filters extract.

The CloudWatch Logs agent installed on each Amazon EC2 instance in your environment publishes metric data points to the CloudWatch service for each log group you configure.

Each log group applies its own filter patterns to determine what log stream events to send to CloudWatch as data points.

Log streams that belong to the same log group share the same retention, monitoring, and access control settings.

In addition to instance logs, if you enable enhanced health for your environment, you can configure the environment to stream health information to CloudWatch Logs.

AUTHORIZATION AND ACCESS CONTROL

AWS Elastic Beanstalk supports identity-based policies.

AWS Elastic Beanstalk does not support resource-based policies.

AWS Elastic Beanstalk has partial support for resource-level permissions.

When you create an environment, AWS Elastic Beanstalk prompts you to provide two AWS Identity and Access Management (IAM) roles: a service role and an instance profile.

The service role is assumed by Elastic Beanstalk to use other AWS services on your behalf.

The instance profile is applied to the instances in your environment and allows them to retrieve application versions from Amazon Simple Storage Service (Amazon S3), upload logs to Amazon S3, and perform other tasks that vary depending on the environment type and platform.

You can also create user policies and apply them to IAM users and groups in your account to allow users to create and manage Elastic Beanstalk applications and environments. Elastic Beanstalk provides managed policies for full access and read-only access.

STORAGE

AMAZON S3

AMAZON S3 FEATURES

Amazon S3 is object storage built to store and retrieve any amount of data from anywhere on the Internet.

It's a simple storage service that offers an extremely durable, highly available, and infinitely scalable data storage infrastructure at very low costs.

Amazon S3 is a distributed architecture and objects are redundantly stored on multiple devices across multiple facilities (AZs) in an Amazon S3 region.

Amazon S3 is a simple key-based object store.

Keys can be any string, and they can be constructed to mimic hierarchical attributes.

Alternatively, you can use S3 Object Tagging to organize your data across all your S3 buckets and/or prefixes.

Amazon S3 provides a simple, standards-based REST web services interface that is designed to work with any Internet-development toolkit.

Files can be from 0 bytes to 5TB.

The largest object that can be uploaded in a single PUT is 5 gigabytes.

For objects larger than 100 megabytes use the Multipart Upload capability.

Updates to an object are atomic – when reading an updated object you will either get the new object or the old one, you will never get partial or corrupt data.

There is unlimited storage available.

It is recommended to access S3 through SDKs and APIs (the console uses APIs).

Event notifications for specific actions, can send alerts or trigger actions.

Notifications can be sent to:

- SNS Topics.
- SQS Queue.
- Lambda functions.
- Need to configure SNS/SQS/Lambda before S3.
- No extra charges from S3 but you pay for SNS, SQS and Lambda.

Requester pays function causes the requester to pay (removes anonymous access).

Can provide time-limited access to objects.

Provides read after write consistency for PUTS of new objects.

Provides eventual consistency for overwrite PUTS and DELETES (takes time to propagate).

You can only store files (objects) on S3.

HTTP 200 code indicates a successful write to S3.

S3 data is made up of:

- Key (name).
- Value (data).
- Version ID.
- Metadata.
- Access Control Lists.

Amazon S3 automatically scales to high request rates.

For example, your application can achieve at least 3,500 PUT/POST/DELETE and 5,500 GET requests per second per prefix in a bucket.

There are no limits to the number of prefixes in a bucket.

For read intensive requests you can also use CloudFront edge locations to offload from S3.

ADDITIONAL CAPABILITIES

Additional capabilities offered by Amazon S3 include:

Additional S3 Capability	How it works
Transfer Acceleration	Speeds up data uploads using CloudFront in reverse
Requester Pays	The requester rather than the bucket owner pays for requests and data transfer
Tags	Assign tags to objects to use in hosting, billing, security etc.
Events	Trigger notifications to SNS, SQS, or Lambda when certain events happen in your bucket
Static Web Hosting	Simple and massively scalable static web hosting
BitTorrent	Use the BitTorrent protocol to retrieve any publicly available object by automatically generating a .torrent file.
Storage Class Analysis	Analyzes storage access patterns to help you decide when to transition the right data to the right storage class.
Storage Lens	Delivers organization-wide visibility into object storage usage, activity trends, and makes actionable recommendations to improve cost-efficiency

	and apply data protection best practices.
S3 Object Lambda	Add your own code to S3 GET requests to modify and process data as it is returned to an application.

BUCKETS

Files are stored in buckets:

- A bucket can be viewed as a container for objects.
- A bucket is a flat container of objects.
- It does not provide a hierarchy of objects.
- You can use an object key name (prefix) to mimic folders.

100 buckets per account by default.

You can store unlimited objects in your buckets.

You can create folders in your buckets (only available through the Console).

You cannot create nested buckets.

Bucket ownership is not transferable.

Bucket names cannot be changed after they have been created.

If a bucket is deleted its name becomes available again.

Bucket names are part of the URL used to access the bucket.

An S3 bucket is region specific.

S3 is a universal namespace so names must be unique globally.

URL is in this format: https://s3-**eu-west-1**.amazonaws.com/**<bucketname>.**

Can backup a bucket to another bucket in another account.

Can enable logging to a bucket.

Bucket naming:

- Bucket names must be at least 3 and no more than 63 characters in length.
- Bucket names must start and end with a lowercase character or a number.
- Bucket names must be a series of one or more labels which are separated by a period.
- Bucket names can contain lowercase letters, numbers, and hyphens.
- Bucket names cannot be formatted as an IP address.

For better performance, lower latency, and lower cost, create the bucket closer to your clients.

OBJECTS

Each object is stored and retrieved by a unique key (ID or name).

An object in S3 is uniquely identified and addressed through:

- Service endpoint.
- Bucket name.

- Object key (name).
- Optionally, an object version.

Objects stored in a bucket will never leave the region in which they are stored unless you move them to another region or enable cross-region replication.

You can define permissions on objects when uploading and at any time afterwards using the AWS Management Console.

SUBRESOURCES

Sub-resources are subordinate to objects, they do not exist independently but are always associated with another entity such as an object or bucket.

Sub-resources (configuration containers) associated with buckets include:

- Lifecycle – define an object's lifecycle.
- Website – configuration for hosting static websites.
- Versioning – retain multiple versions of objects as they are changed.
- Access Control Lists (ACLs) – control permissions access to the bucket.
- Bucket Policies – control access to the bucket.
- Cross Origin Resource Sharing (CORS).
- Logging.

Sub-resources associated with objects include:

- ACLs – define permissions to access the object.
- Restore – restoring an archive.

CROSS-ORIGIN-RESOURCE-SHARING (CORS)

Used to allow requests to a different origin when connected to the main origin.

The request will fail unless the origin allows the requests using CORS headers (e.g. Access-Control-Allow-Origin).

Must enable the correct CORS headers.

Specify a CORS configuration on the S3 bucket.

STORAGE CLASSES

There are six S3 storage classes.

- S3 Standard (durable, immediately available, frequently accessed).
- S3 Intelligent-Tiering (automatically moves data to the most cost-effective tier).
- S3 Standard-IA (durable, immediately available, infrequently accessed).
- S3 One Zone-IA (lower cost for infrequently accessed data with less resilience).
- S3 Glacier (archived data, retrieval times in minutes or hours).
- S3 Glacier Deep Archive (lowest cost storage class for long term retention).

The table below provides the details of each Amazon S3 storage class:

	S3 Standard	S3 Intelligent	S3 Standard-	S3 One	S3 Glacier Instant	S3 Glacier Flexible	S3 Glacier Deep

© 2023 Digital Cloud Training

		Tiering	IA	Zone-IA	Retrieval	Retrieval	Archive
Designed for durability	99.999999999% (11 9's)	99.999999999% (11 9's)	99.999999999% (11 9's)	99.999999999% (11 9's)	99.999999999% (11 9's)	99.999999999% (11 9's)	99.999999999% (11 9's)
Designed for availability	99.99%	99.9%	99.9%	99.5%	99.9%	99.99%	99.99%
Availability SLA	99.9%	99%	99%	99%	99%	99.%	99.9%
Availability Zones	≥3	≥3	≥3	1	≥3	≥3	≥3
Minimum capacity charge per object	N/A	N/A	128 KB	128 KB	128 KB	40 KB	40 KB
Minimum storage duration charge	N/A	N/A	30 days	30 days	90 days	90 days	180 days
Retrieval charge	N/A	N/A	per GB retrieved	per GB retrieved	per GB retrieved	per GB retrieved	per GB retrieved
First byte latency	milliseconds	milliseconds	milliseconds	milliseconds	milliseconds	minutes or hours	hours
Storage type	Object	Object	Object	Object	Object	Object	Object
Lifecycle transitions	Yes	Yes	Yes	Yes	Yes	Yes	Yes

Objects stored in the S3 One Zone-IA storage class are stored redundantly within a single Availability Zone in the AWS Region you select.

ACCESS AND ACCESS POLICIES

There are four mechanisms for controlling access to Amazon S3 resources:

- IAM policies.

- Bucket policies.
- Access Control Lists (ACLs).
- Query string authentication (URL to an Amazon S3 object which is only valid for a limited time).

Access auditing can be configured by configuring an Amazon S3 bucket to create access log records for all requests made against it.

For capturing IAM/user identity information in logs configure AWS CloudTrail Data Events.

By default a bucket, its objects, and related sub-resources are all private.

By default only a resource owner can access a bucket.

The resource owner refers to the AWS account that creates the resource.

With IAM the account owner rather than the IAM user is the owner.

Within an IAM policy you can grant either programmatic access or AWS Management Console access to Amazon S3 resources.

Amazon Resource Names (ARN) are used for specifying resources in a policy.

The format for any resource on AWS is:

arn:partition:service:region:namespace:relative-id.

For S3 resources:
- aws is a common partition name.
- s3 is the service.
- You don't specify Region and namespace.
- For Amazon S3, it can be a bucket-name or a bucket-name/object-key. You can use wild card.

The format for S3 resources is:
- arn:aws:s3:::bucket_name.
- arn:aws:s3:::bucket_name/key_name.

A bucket owner can grant cross-account permissions to another AWS account (or users in an account) to upload objects.
- The AWS account that uploads the objects owns them.
- The bucket owner does not have permissions on objects that other accounts own, however:
  - The bucket owner pays the charges.
  - The bucket owner can deny access to any objects regardless of ownership.
  - The bucket owner can archive any objects or restore archived objects regardless of ownership.

Access to buckets and objects can be granted to:
- Individual users.
- AWS accounts.
- Everyone (public/anonymous).
- All authenticated users (AWS users).

Access policies define access to resources and can be associated with resources (buckets and objects) and users.

You can use the AWS Policy Generator to create a bucket policy for your Amazon S3 bucket.

The categories of policy are resource-based policies and user policies.

Resource-based policies:

- Attached to buckets and objects.
- ACL-based policies define permissions.
- ACLs can be used to grant read/write permissions to other accounts.
- Bucket policies can be used to grant other AWS accounts or IAM users' permission to the bucket and objects.

User policies:

- Can use IAM to manage access to S3 resources.
- Using IAM you can create users, groups and roles and attach access policies to them granting them access to resources.
- You cannot grant anonymous permissions in an IAM user policy as the policy is attached to a user.
- User policies can grant permissions to a bucket and the objects in it.

ACLs:

- S3 ACLs enable you to manage access to buckets and objects.
- Each bucket and object has an ACL attached to it as a subresource.
- Bucket and object permissions are independent of each other.
- The ACL defines which AWS accounts (grantees) or pre-defined S3 groups are granted access and the type of access.
- A grantee can be an AWS account or one of the predefined Amazon S3 groups.
- When you create a bucket or an object, S3 creates a default ACL that grants the resource owner full control over the resource.

Cross account access:

- You grant permission to another AWS account using the email address or the canonical user ID.
- However, if you provide an email address in your grant request, Amazon S3 finds the canonical user ID for that account and adds it to the ACL.
- Grantee accounts can then then delegate the access provided by other accounts to their individual users.

PRE-DEFINED GROUPS

Authenticated Users group:

- This group represents all AWS accounts.
- Access permission to this group allows any AWS account access to the resource.
- All requests must be signed (authenticated).
- Any authenticated user can access the resource.

All Users group:

- Access permission to this group allows anyone in the world access to the resource.
- The requests can be signed (authenticated) or unsigned (anonymous).

- Unsigned requests omit the authentication header in the request.
- AWS recommends that you never grant the All Users group WRITE, WRITE_ACP, or FULL_CONTROL permissions.

Log Delivery group:

- Providing WRITE permission to this group on a bucket enables S3 to write server access logs.
- Not applicable to objects.

The following table lists the set of permissions that Amazon S3 supports in an ACL.

- The set of ACL permissions is the same for an object ACL and a bucket ACL.
- Depending on the context (bucket ACL or object ACL), these ACL permissions grant permissions for specific buckets or object operations.
- The table lists the permissions and describes what they mean in the context of objects and buckets.

Permission	When granted on a bucket	When granted on an object
READ	Allows grantee to list the objects in the bucket	Allows grantee to read the object data and its metadata
WRITE	Allows grantee to create, overwrite and delete any object in the bucket	N/A
READ_ACP	Allows grantee to read the bucket ACL	Allows grantee to read the object ACL
WRITE_ACP	Allows grantee to write the ACL for the applicable buckets	Allows grantee to write the ACL for the applicable object
FULL_CONTROL	Allows grantee the READ, WRITE, READ_ACP, WRITE_ACP permissions on the bucket	Allows grantee the READ, WRITE, READ_ACP, WRITE_ACP permissions on the object

Note the following:

- Permissions are assigned at the account level for authenticated users.
- You cannot assign permissions to individual IAM users.
- When Read is granted on a bucket it only provides the ability to list the objects in the bucket.
- When Read is granted on an object the data can be read.
- ACP means access control permissions and READ_ACP/WRITE_ACP control who can read/write the ACLs themselves.
- WRITE is only applicable to the bucket level (except for ACP).

© 2023 Digital Cloud Training

Bucket policies are limited to 20 KB in size.

Object ACLs are limited to 100 granted permissions per ACL.

The only recommended use case for the bucket ACL is to grant write permissions to the S3 Log Delivery group.

There are limits to managing permissions using ACLs:

- You cannot grant permissions to individual users.
- You cannot grant conditional permissions.
- You cannot explicitly deny access.

When granting other AWS accounts the permissions to upload objects, permissions to these objects can only be managed by the object owner using object ACLs.

You can use bucket policies for:

- Granting users permissions to a bucket owned by your account.
- Managing object permissions (where the object owner is the same account as the bucket owner).
- Managing cross-account permissions for all Amazon S3 permissions.

You can use user policies for:

- Granting permissions for all Amazon S3 operations.
- Managing permissions for users in your account.
- Granting object permissions to users within the account.

For an IAM user to access resources in another account the following must be provided:

- Permission from the parent account through a user policy.
- Permission from the resource owner to the IAM user through a bucket policy, or the parent account through a bucket policy, bucket ACL or object ACL.

If an AWS account owns a resource it can grant permissions to another account, that account can then delegate those permissions or a subset of them to users in the account (permissions delegation).

An account that receives permissions from another account cannot delegate permissions cross-account to a third AWS account.

MULTIPART UPLOAD

Can be used to speed up uploads to S3.

Multipart upload uploads objects in parts independently, in parallel and in any order.

Performed using the S3 Multipart upload API.

It is recommended for objects of 100MB or larger.

- Can be used for objects from 5MB up to 5TB.
- Must be used for objects larger than 5GB.

If transmission of any part fails it can be retransmitted.

Improves throughput.

Can pause and resume object uploads.

Can begin upload before you know the final object size.

S3 COPY

You can create a copy of objects up to 5GB in size in a single atomic operation.

For files larger than 5GB you must use the multipart upload API.

Can be performed using the AWS SDKs or REST API.

The copy operation can be used to:

- Generate additional copies of objects.
- Renaming objects.
- Changing the copy's storage class or encryption at rest status.
- Move objects across AWS locations/regions.
- Change object metadata.

Once uploaded to S3 some object metadata cannot be changed, copying the object can allow you to modify this information.

TRANSFER ACCELERATION

Amazon S3 Transfer Acceleration enables fast, easy, and secure transfers of files over long distances between your client and your Amazon S3 bucket.

S3 Transfer Acceleration leverages Amazon CloudFront's globally distributed AWS Edge Locations.

Used to accelerate object uploads to S3 over long distances (latency).

Transfer acceleration is as secure as a direct upload to S3.

You are charged only if there was a benefit in transfer times.

Need to enable transfer acceleration on the S3 bucket.

Cannot be disabled, can only be suspended.

May take up to 30 minutes to implement.

URL is: <bucketname>.s3-accelerate.amazonaws.com.

Bucket names must be DNS compliance and cannot have periods between labels.

Now HIPAA compliant.

You can use multipart uploads with transfer acceleration.

Must use one of the following endpoints:

- .s3-accelerate.amazonaws.com.
- .s3-accelerate.dualstack.amazonaws.com (dual-stack option).

S3 Transfer Acceleration supports all bucket level features including multipart uploads.

STATIC WEBSITES

S3 can be used to host static websites.

Cannot use dynamic content such as PHP, .Net etc.

Automatically scales.

You can use a custom domain name with S3 using a Route 53 Alias record.

When using a custom domain name the bucket name must be the same as the domain name.

Can enable redirection for the whole domain, pages, or specific objects.

URL is: <bucketname>.s3-website-.amazonaws.com.

Requester pays does not work with website endpoints.

Does not support HTTPS/SSL.

Returns an HTML document.

Supports object and bucket level redirects.

Only supports GET and HEAD requests on objects.

Supports publicly readable content only.

To enable website hosting on a bucket, specify:

- An Index document (default web page).
- Error document (optional).

Key Difference	REST API Endpoint	Website Endpoint
Access Control	Supports both public and private content	Supports only publicly readable content
Error message handling	Returns an XML-formatted error response	Returns an HTML document
Redirection support	Not applicable	Supports both object-level and bucket-level redirects
Requests support	Supports all bucket and object operations	Supports only GET and HEAD requests on objects
Responses to GET and HEAD requests at the root of the bucket	Returns a list of the object keys in the bucket	Returns the Index document that is specified in the website configuration
SSL support	Supports SSL connections	Does not support SSL connections

PRE-SIGNED URLS

Pre-signed URLs can be used to provide temporary access to a specific object to those who do not have AWS credentials.

By default all objects are private and can only be accessed by the owner.

To share an object you can either make it public or generate a pre-signed URL.

Expiration date and time must be configured.

These can be generated using SDKs for Java and .Net and AWS explorer for Visual Studio.

Can be used for downloading and uploading S3 objects.

VERSIONING

Versioning stores all versions of an object (including all writes and even if an object is deleted).

Versioning protects against accidental object/data deletion or overwrites.

Enables "roll-back" and "un-delete" capabilities.

Versioning can also be used for data retention and archive.

Old versions count as billable size until they are permanently deleted.

Enabling versioning does not replicate existing objects.

Can be used for backup.

Once enabled versioning cannot be disabled only suspended.

Can be integrated with lifecycle rules.

Multi-factor authentication (MFA) delete can be enabled.

MFA delete can also be applied to changing versioning settings.

MFA delete applies to:
- Changing the bucket's versioning state.
- Permanently deleting an object.

Cross Region Replication requires versioning to be enabled on the source and destination buckets.

Reverting to previous versions isn't replicated.

By default a HTTP GET retrieves the most recent version.

Only the S3 bucket owner can permanently delete objects once versioning is enabled.

When you try to delete an object with versioning enabled a DELETE marker is placed on the object.

You can delete the DELETE marker and the object will be available again.

Deletion with versioning replicates the delete marker. But deleting the delete marker is not replicated.

Bucket versioning states:
- Enabled.
- Versioned.
- Un-versioned.

Objects that existed before enabling versioning will have a version ID of NULL.

Suspension:
- If you suspend versioning the existing objects remain as they are however new versions will not be created.
- While versioning is suspended new objects will have a version ID of NULL and uploaded objects of the same name will overwrite the existing object.

OBJECT LIFECYCLE MANAGEMENT

Used to optimize storage costs, adhere to data retention policies and to keep S3 volumes well-maintained.

A *lifecycle configuration* is a set of rules that define actions that Amazon S3 applies to a group of objects. There are two types of actions:

- **Transition actions**—Define when objects transition to another storage class. For example, you might choose to transition objects to the STANDARD_IA storage class 30 days after you created them, or archive objects to the GLACIER storage class one year after creating them.

There are costs associated with the lifecycle transition requests. For pricing information, see Amazon S3 Pricing.

- **Expiration actions**—Define when objects expire. Amazon S3 deletes expired objects on your behalf.

Lifecycle configuration is an XML file applied at the bucket level as a subresource.

Can be used in conjunction with versioning or independently.

Can be applied to current and previous versions.

Can be applied to specific objects within a bucket: objects with a specific tag or objects with a specific prefix.

Supported Transitions and Related Constraints

Amazon S3 supports the following lifecycle transitions between storage classes using a lifecycle configuration:

- You can transition from the STANDARD storage class to any other storage class.
- You can transition from any storage class to the GLACIER or DEEP_ARCHIVE storage classes.
- You can transition from the STANDARD_IA storage class to the INTELLIGENT_TIERING or ONEZONE_IA storage classes.
- You can transition from the INTELLIGENT_TIERING storage class to the ONEZONE_IA storage class.
- You can transition from the GLACIER storage class to the DEEP_ARCHIVE storage class.

The following lifecycle transitions are not supported:

- You can't transition from any storage class to the STANDARD storage class.
- You can't transition from any storage class to the REDUCED_REDUNDANCY storage class.
- You can't transition from the INTELLIGENT_TIERING storage class to the STANDARD_IA storage class.
- You can't transition from the ONEZONE_IA storage class to the STANDARD_IA or INTELLIGENT_TIERING storage classes.
- You can transition from the GLACIER storage class to the DEEP_ARCHIVE storage class only.
- You can't transition from the DEEP_ARCHIVE storage class to any other storage class.

The lifecycle storage class transitions have the following constraints:

- From the STANDARD or STANDARD_IA storage class to INTELLIGENT_TIERING. The following constraints apply:
  - For larger objects, there is a cost benefit for transitioning to INTELLIGENT_TIERING. Amazon S3 does not transition objects that are smaller than 128 KB to the INTELLIGENT_TIERING

storage class because it's not cost effective.

- From the STANDARD storage classes to STANDARD_IA or ONEZONE_IA. The following constraints apply:
  - For larger objects, there is a cost benefit for transitioning to STANDARD_IA or ONEZONE_IA. Amazon S3 does not transition objects that are smaller than 128 KB to the STANDARD_IA or ONEZONE_IA storage classes because it's not cost effective.
  - Objects must be stored at least 30 days in the current storage class before you can transition them to STANDARD_IA or ONEZONE_IA. For example, you cannot create a lifecycle rule to transition objects to the STANDARD_IA storage class one day after you create them.
  - Amazon S3 doesn't transition objects within the first 30 days because newer objects are often accessed more frequently or deleted sooner than is suitable for STANDARD_IA or ONEZONE_IA storage.
  - If you are transitioning noncurrent objects (in versioned buckets), you can transition only objects that are at least 30 days noncurrent to STANDARD_IA or ONEZONE_IA storage.
- From the STANDARD_IA storage class to ONEZONE_IA. The following constraints apply:

Objects must be stored at least 30 days in the STANDARD_IA storage class before you can transition them to the ONEZONE_IA class.

ENCRYPTION

You can securely upload/download your data to Amazon S3 via SSL endpoints using the HTTPS protocol (In Transit – SSL/TLS).

Encryption options:

Encryption Option	How It Works
SSE-S3	Use S3's existing encryption key for AES-256
SSE-C	Upload your own AES-256 encryption key which S3 uses when it writes objects
SSE-KMS	Use a key generated and managed by AWS KMS
Client Side	Encrypt objects using your own local encryption process before uploading to S3

Server-side encryption options

Server-side encryption protects data at rest.

Amazon S3 encrypts each object with a unique key.

As an additional safeguard, it encrypts the key itself with a master key that it rotates regularly.

Amazon S3 server-side encryption uses one of the strongest block ciphers available to encrypt your data, 256-bit Advanced Encryption Standard (AES-256).

If you need server-side encryption for all the objects that are stored in a bucket, use a bucket policy.

To request server-side encryption using the object creation REST APIs, provide the x-amz-server-side-encryption request header.

Note: You need the kms:Decrypt permission when you upload or download an Amazon S3 object encrypted with an AWS Key Management Service (AWS KMS) customer master key (CMK), and that is in addition to kms:ReEncrypt, kms:GenerateDataKey, and kms:DescribeKey permissions.

There are three options for using server-side encryption: SSE-S3, SSE-KMS and SSE-C. These are detailed below,

SSE-S3 – Server-Side Encryption with S3 managed keys

When you use Server-Side Encryption with Amazon S3-Managed Keys (SSE-S3), each object is encrypted with a unique key.

As an additional safeguard, it encrypts the key itself with a master key that it regularly rotates.

Amazon S3 server-side encryption uses one of the strongest block ciphers available, 256-bit Advanced Encryption Standard (AES-256), to encrypt your data.

- Each object is encrypted with a unique key.
- Encryption key is encrypted with a master key.
- AWS regularly rotate the master key.
- Uses AES 256.

SSE-KMS – Server-Side Encryption with AWS KMS keys

Server-Side Encryption with Customer Master Keys (CMKs) Stored in AWS Key Management Service (SSE-KMS) is like SSE-S3, but with some additional benefits and charges for using this service.

There are separate permissions for the use of a CMK that provides added protection against unauthorized access of your objects in Amazon S3.

SSE-KMS also provides you with an audit trail that shows when your CMK was used and by whom.

Additionally, you can create and manage customer managed CMKs or use AWS managed CMKs that are unique to you, your service, and your Region.

- KMS uses Customer Master Keys (CMKs) to encrypt.
- Can use the automatically created CMK key.
- OR you can select your own key (gives you control for management of keys).
- An envelope key protects your keys.
- Chargeable.

SSE-C – Server-Side Encryption with client provided keys

With Server-Side Encryption with Customer-Provided Keys (SSE-C), you manage the encryption keys and

Amazon S3 manages the encryption, as it writes to disks, and decryption, when you access your objects.

- Client manages the keys, S3 manages encryption.
- AWS does not store the encryption keys.
- If keys are lost data cannot be decrypted.

When using server-side encryption with customer-provided encryption keys (SSE-C), you must provide encryption key information using the following request headers:

x-amz-server-side-encryption-customer-algorithm – Use this header to specify the encryption algorithm. The header value must be "AES256".

x-amz-server-side-encryption-customer-key – Use this header to provide the 256-bit, base64-encoded encryption key for Amazon S3 to use to encrypt or decrypt your data.

x-amz-server-side-encryption-customer-key-MD5 – Use this header to provide the base64-encoded 128-bit MD5 digest of the encryption key according to RFC 1321. Amazon S3 uses this header for a message integrity check to ensure that the encryption key was transmitted without error.

Client-side encryption

This is the act of encrypting data before sending it to Amazon S3.

To enable client-side encryption, you have the following options:

1. Use a customer master key (CMK) stored in AWS Key Management Service (AWS KMS).
2. Use a master key you store within your application.

Option 1. Use a customer master key (CMK) stored in AWS Key Management Service (AWS KMS)

When uploading an object—Using the customer master key (CMK) ID, the client first sends a request to AWS KMS for a CMK that it can use to encrypt your object data. AWS KMS returns two versions of a randomly generated data key:

- A plaintext version of the data key that the client uses to encrypt the object data.
- A cipher blob of the same data key that the client uploads to Amazon S3 as object metadata.

When downloading an object—The client downloads the encrypted object from Amazon S3 along with the cipher blob version of the data key stored as object metadata. The client then sends the cipher blob to AWS KMS to get the plaintext version of the data key so that it can decrypt the object data.

Option 2. Use a master key you store within your application

When uploading an object—You provide a client-side master key to the Amazon S3 encryption client. The client uses the master key only to encrypt the data encryption key that it generates randomly. The process works like this:

1. The Amazon S3 encryption client generates a one-time-use symmetric key (also known as a data encryption key or data key) locally. It uses the data key to encrypt the data of a single Amazon S3 object. The client generates a separate data key for each object.
2. The client encrypts the data encryption key using the master key that you provide. The client uploads the encrypted data key and its material description as part of the object metadata. The client uses the material description to determine which client-side master key to use for decryption.

3. The client uploads the encrypted data to Amazon S3 and saves the encrypted data key as object metadata (x-amz-meta-x-amz-key) in Amazon S3.

When downloading an object—The client downloads the encrypted object from Amazon S3. Using the material description from the object's metadata, the client determines which master key to use to decrypt the data key. The client uses that master key to decrypt the data key and then uses the data key to decrypt the object.

The following diagram depicts the options for enabling encryption and shows you where the encryption is applied and where the keys are managed:

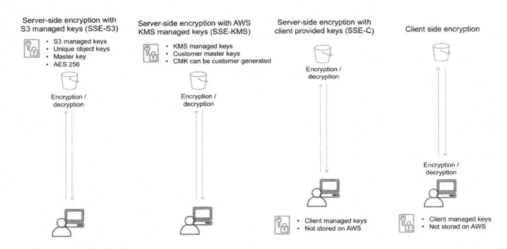

EVENT NOTIFICATIONS

Amazon S3 event notifications can be sent in response to actions in Amazon S3 like PUTs, POSTs, COPYs, or DELETEs.

Amazon S3 event notifications enable you to run workflows, send alerts, or perform other actions in response to changes in your objects stored in S3.

To enable notifications, you must first add a notification configuration that identifies the events you want Amazon S3 to publish and the destinations where you want Amazon S3 to send the notifications.

You can configure notifications to be filtered by the prefix and suffix of the key name of objects.

Amazon S3 can publish notifications for the following events:
- New object created events.
- Object removal events.
- Restore object events.
- Reduced Redundancy Storage (RRS) object lost events.
- Replication events.

Amazon S3 can send event notification messages to the following destinations:
- Publish event messages to an Amazon Simple Notification Service (Amazon SNS) topic.
- Publish event messages to an Amazon Simple Queue Service (Amazon SQS) queue.
- Publish event messages to AWS Lambda by invoking a Lambda function and providing the event

message as an argument.

Need to grant Amazon S3 permissions to post messages to an Amazon SNS topic or an Amazon SQS queue.

Need to also grant Amazon S3 permission to invoke an AWS Lambda function on your behalf. For information about granting these permissions.

OBJECT TAGS

S3 object tags are key-value pairs applied to S3 objects which can be created, updated, or deleted at any time during the lifetime of the object.

Allow you to create Identity and Access Management (IAM) policies, setup S3 Lifecycle policies, and customize storage metrics.

Up to ten tags can be added to each S3 object and you can use either the AWS Management Console, the REST API, the AWS CLI, or the AWS SDKs to add object tags.

AMAZON S3 CLOUDWATCH METRICS

You can use the AWS Management Console to enable the generation of 1-minute CloudWatch request metrics for your S3 bucket or configure filters for the metrics using a prefix or object tag.

Alternatively, you can call the S3 PUT Bucket Metrics API to enable and configure publication of S3 storage metrics.

CloudWatch Request Metrics will be available in CloudWatch within 15 minutes after they are enabled.

CloudWatch Storage Metrics are enabled by default for all buckets and reported once per day.

The S3 metrics that can be monitored include:

- S3 requests.
- Bucket storage.
- Bucket size.
- All requests.
- HTTP 4XX/5XX errors.

CROSS REGION REPLICATION

CRR is an Amazon S3 feature that automatically replicates data across AWS Regions.

With CRR, every object uploaded to an S3 bucket is automatically replicated to a destination bucket in a different AWS Region that you choose.

Provides automatic, asynchronous copying of objects between buckets in different regions.

CRR is configured at the S3 bucket level.

You enable a CRR configuration on your source bucket by specifying a destination bucket in a different Region for replication.

You can use either the AWS Management Console, the REST API, the AWS CLI, or the AWS SDKs to enable CRR.

Versioning must be enabled for both the source and destination buckets .

Source and destination buckets must be in different regions.

With CRR you can only replication between regions, not within a region (see SRR below for single region replication).

Replication is 1:1 (one source bucket, to one destination bucket).

You can configure separate S3 Lifecycle rules on the source and destination buckets.

You can replicate KMS-encrypted objects by providing a destination KMS key in your replication configuration.

You can set up CRR across AWS accounts to store your replicated data in a different account in the target region.

Provides low latency access for data by copying objects to buckets that are closer to users.

To activate CRR you need to configure the replication on the source bucket:

- Define the bucket in the other region to replicate to.
- Specify to replicate all objects or a subset of objects with specific key name prefixes.

The replicas will be exact replicas and share the same key names and metadata.

You can specify a different storage class (by default the source storage class will be used).

AWS S3 will encrypt data in-transit with SSL.

AWS S3 must have permission to replicate objects.

Bucket owners must have permission to read the object and object ACL.

Can be used across accounts but the source bucket owner must have permission to replicate objects into the destination bucket.

Triggers for replication are:

- Uploading objects to the source bucket.
- DELETE of objects in the source bucket.
- Changes to the object, its metadata, or ACL.

What is replicated:

- New objects created after enabling replication.
- Changes to objects.
- Objects created using SSE-S3 using the AWS managed key.
- Object ACL updates.

What isn't replicated:

- Objects that existed before enabling replication (can use the copy API).
- Objects created with SSE-C and SSE-KMS.
- Objects to which the bucket owner does not have permissions.
- Updates to bucket-level subresources.
- Actions from lifecycle rules are not replicated.
- Objects in the source bucket that are replicated from another region are not replicated.

Deletion behavior:

- If a DELETE request is made without specifying an object version ID a delete marker will be added and replicated.

- If a DELETE request is made specifying an object version ID the object is deleted but the delete marker is not replicated.

Charges:

- Requests for upload.
- Inter-region transfer.
- S3 storage in both regions.

SAME REGION REPLICATION (SRR)

As the name implies you can use SRR to replication objects to a destination bucket within the same region as the source bucket.

This feature was released in September 2018.

Replication is automatic and asynchronous.

New objects uploaded to an Amazon S3 bucket are configured for replication at the bucket, prefix, or object tag levels.

Replicated objects can be owned by the same AWS account as the original copy or by different accounts, to protect from accidental deletion.

Replication can be to any Amazon S3 storage class, including S3 Glacier and S3 Glacier Deep Archive to create backups and long-term archives.

When an S3 object is replicated using SRR, the metadata, Access Control Lists (ACL), and object tags associated with the object are also part of the replication.

Once SRR is configured on a source bucket, any changes to the object, metadata, ACLs, or object tags trigger a new replication to the destination bucket.

S3 ANALYTICS

Can run analytics on data stored on Amazon S3.

This includes data lakes, IoT streaming data, machine learning, and artificial intelligence.

The following strategies can be used:

S3 Analytics Strategies	Service Used
Data Lake Concept	Athena, Redshift Spectrum, QuickSight
IoT Streaming Data Repository	Kinesis Firehose
ML and AI Storage	Rekognition, Lex, MXNet
Storage Class Analysis	S3 Management Analytics

S3 INVENTORY

You can use S3 Inventory to audit and report on the replication and encryption status of your objects for business, compliance, and regulatory needs.

Amazon S3 inventory provides comma-separated values (CSV), Apache optimized row columnar (ORC) or Apache Parquet (Parquet) output files that list your objects and their corresponding metadata on a daily or weekly basis for an S3 bucket or a shared prefix (that is, objects that have names that begin with a common string).

MONITORING AND REPORTING

Amazon CloudWatch metrics for Amazon S3 can help you understand and improve the performance of applications that use Amazon S3. There are several ways that you can use CloudWatch with Amazon S3.

- **Daily storage metrics for buckets** - Monitor bucket storage using CloudWatch, which collects and processes storage data from Amazon S3 into readable, daily metrics. These storage metrics for Amazon S3 are reported once per day and are provided to all customers at no additional cost.
- **Request metrics** - Monitor Amazon S3 requests to quickly identify and act on operational issues. The metrics are available at 1-minute intervals after some latency to process. These CloudWatch metrics are billed at the same rate as the Amazon CloudWatch custom metrics.
- **Replication metrics** - Monitor the total number of S3 API operations that are pending replication, the total size of objects pending replication, and the maximum replication time to the destination Region. Only replication rules that have S3 Replication Time Control (S3 RTC) enabled will publish replication metrics.

LOGGING AND AUDITING

You can record the actions that are taken by users, roles, or AWS services on Amazon S3 resources and maintain log records for auditing and compliance purposes.

To do this, you can use Amazon S3 server access logging, AWS CloudTrail logs, or a combination of both.

AWS recommend that you use AWS CloudTrail for logging bucket and object-level actions for your Amazon S3 resources.

Server access logging provides detailed records for the requests that are made to a bucket.

This information can be used for auditing.

You must not set the bucket being logged to be the destination for the logs as this creates a logging loop and the bucket will grow exponentially.

GLACIER

Glacier is an archiving storage solution for infrequently accessed data.

There are three storage tiers:

S3 Glacier Instant Retrieval

- Data retrieval in milliseconds with the same performance as S3 Standard
- Designed for durability of 99.999999999% of objects across multiple Availability Zones
- Data is resilient in the event of the destruction of one entire Availability Zone

- Designed for 99.9% data availability each year
- 128 KB minimum object size
- Backed with the Amazon S3 Service Level Agreement for availability
- S3 PUT API for direct uploads to S3 Glacier Instant Retrieval, and S3 Lifecycle management for automatic migration of objects

S3 Glacier Flexible Retrieval (Formerly S3 Glacier)

- Designed for durability of 99.999999999% of objects across multiple Availability Zones
- Data is resilient in the event of one entire Availability Zone destruction
- Supports SSL for data in transit and encryption of data at rest
- Ideal for backup and disaster recovery use cases when large sets of data occasionally need to be retrieved in minutes, without concern for costs

- Configurable retrieval times, from minutes to hours, with free bulk retrievals
- S3 PUT API for direct uploads to S3 Glacier Flexible Retrieval, and S3 Lifecycle management for automatic migration of objects

Amazon S3 Glacier Deep Archive (S3 Glacier Deep Archive)

- Designed for durability of 99.999999999% of objects across multiple Availability Zones
- Lowest cost storage class designed for long-term retention of data that will be retained for 7-10 years
- Ideal alternative to magnetic tape libraries
- Retrieval time within 12 hours
- S3 PUT API for direct uploads to S3 Glacier Deep Archive, and S3 Lifecycle management for automatic migration of objects

The key difference between the top tiers is that Deep Archive is lower cost, but retrieval times are much longer (12 hours).

The S3 Glacier tier has configurable retrieval times from minutes to hours (you pay accordingly).

Archived objects are not available for real time access and you need to submit a retrieval request.

Glacier must complete a job before you can get its output.

Requested archival data is copied to S3 One Zone-IA.

Following retrieval you have 24 hours to download your data.

You cannot specify Glacier as the storage class at the time you create an object.

Glacier is designed to sustain the loss of two facilities.

Glacier automatically encrypts data at rest using AES 256 symmetric keys and supports secure transfer of data over SSL.

Glacier may not be available in all AWS regions.

Glacier objects are visible through S3 only (not Glacier directly).

Glacier does not archive object metadata; you need to maintain a client-side database to maintain this information.

Archives can be 1 byte up to 40TB.

Glacier file archives of 1 byte – 4 GB can be performed in a single operation.

Glacier file archives from 100MB up to 40TB can be uploaded to Glacier using the multipart upload API.

Uploading archives is synchronous.

Downloading archives is asynchronous.

The contents of an archive that has been uploaded cannot be modified.

You can upload data to Glacier using the CLI, SDKs or APIs – you cannot use the AWS Console.

Glacier adds 32-40KB (indexing and archive metadata) to each object when transitioning from other classes using lifecycle policies.

AWS recommends that if you have lots of small objects they are combined in an archive (e.g. zip file) before uploading.

A description can be added to archives, no other metadata can be added.

Glacier archive IDs are added upon upload and are unique for each upload.

Archive retrieval:

- Expedited is 1-5 minutes retrieval (most expensive).
- Standard is 3.5 hours retrieval (cheaper, 10GB data retrieval free per month).
- Bulk retrieval is 5-12 hours (cheapest, use for large quantities of data).

You can retrieve parts of an archive.

When data is retrieved it is copied to S3 and the archive remains in Glacier and the storage class therefore does not change.

AWS SNS can send notifications when retrieval jobs are complete.

Retrieved data is available for 24 hours by default (can be changed).

To retrieve specific objects within an archive you can specify the byte range (Range) in the HTTP GET request (need to maintain a DB of byte ranges).

Glacier Charges:

There is no charge for data transfer between EC2 and Glacier in the same region.

There is a charge if you delete data within 90 days.

When you restore you pay for:

- The Glacier archive.
- The requests.
- The restored data on S3.

AMAZON EFS

AMAZON EFS FEATURES

Amazon EFS is a fully managed service for hosting Network File System (NFS) filesystems in the cloud.

It is an implementation of a NFS file share and is accessed using the NFS protocol.

It provides elastic storage capacity and pay for what you use (in contrast to Amazon EBS with which you pay for what you provision).

You can configure mount-points in one, or many, AZs.

You can mount an AWS EFS filesystem from on-premises systems ONLY if you are using AWS Direct Connect or a VPN connection.

Typical use cases include big data and analytics, media processing workflows, content management, web serving, home directories etc.

Uses a pay for what you use model with no pre-provisioning required.

AWS EFS can scale up to petabytes.

AWS EFS is elastic and grows and shrinks as you add and remove data.

You can concurrently connect up to thousands of Amazon EC2 instances, from multiple AZs.

A file system can be accessed concurrently from all AZs in the region where it is located.

The following diagram depicts the various options for mounting an EFS filesystem:

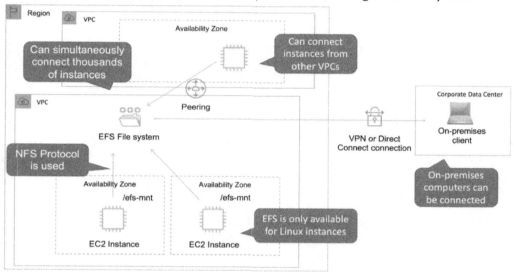

Access to AWS EFS file systems from on-premises servers can be enabled via AWS Direct Connect or AWS VPN.

You mount an AWS EFS file system on your on-premises Linux server using the standard Linux mount command for mounting a file system via the NFS protocol.

The Amazon VPC of the connecting instance must have DNS hostnames enabled.

EFS provides a file system interface, file system access semantics (such as strong consistency and file locking).

Data is stored across multiple AZs within a region.

Read after write consistency.

Need to create mount targets and choose AZs to include (recommended to include all AZ's).

Instances can be behind an Elastic Load Balancer (ELB).

Amazon EFS is compatible with all Linux-based AMIs for Amazon EC2.

Using the EFS-to-EFS Backup solution, you can schedule automatic incremental backups of your Amazon EFS file system.

The following table provides a comparison of the storage characteristics of EFS vs EBS:

	Amazon EFS	Amazon EBS Provisioned IOPS
Availability and durability	Data is stored redundantly across multiple AZs	Data is stored redundantly in a single AZ
Access	Up to thousands of Amazon EC2 instances, from multiple AZs, can connect concurrently to a file system	A single Amazon EC2 instance in a single AZ can connect to a file system
Use cases	Big data and analytics, media processing and workflows, content management, web serving and home directories	Boot volumes, transactional and NoSQL databases, data warehousing and ETL

BACKUPS AND LIFECYCLE MANAGEMENT

Automatic backups are enabled by default and use AWS Backup.

Lifecycle management moves files that have not been accessed for a period of time to the EFS Infrequent Access Storage class.

Amazon EFS Performance

There are two performance modes:

- "General Purpose" performance mode is appropriate for most file systems.
- "Max I/O" performance mode is optimized for applications where tens, hundreds, or thousands of EC2 instances are accessing the file system.

Amazon EFS is designed to burst to allow high throughput levels for periods of time.

There are two throughput modes:

- "Bursting" – throughput scales with file system size.
- "Provisioned" – Throughput is fixed at the specified amount.

Amazon EFS file systems are distributed across an unconstrained number of storage servers, enabling file systems to grow elastically to petabyte scale and allowing massively parallel access from Amazon EC2 instances to your data.

This distributed data storage design means that multithreaded applications and applications that concurrently access data from multiple Amazon EC2 instances can drive substantial levels of aggregate throughput and IOPS.

The table below compares high-level performance and storage characteristics for AWS's file (EFS) and block (EBS) cloud storage offerings:

	Amazon EFS	Amazon EBS Provisioned IOPS

Per-operation latency	Low, consistent latency	Lowest, consistent latency
Throughput scale	10+ GB per second	Up to 2 GB per second

AMAZON EFS ENCRYPTION

EFS offers the ability to encrypt data at rest and in transit.

Encryption keys are managed by the AWS Key Management Service (KMS).

Encryption in transit:

- Data encryption in transit uses Transport Layer Security (TLS) 1.2 to encrypt data sent between your clients and EFS file systems.
- Encryption in transit is enabled when mounting the file system.

Encryption at rest:

- Enable encryption at rest in the EFS console or by using the AWS CLI or SDKs.
- Encryption at rest MUST be enabled at file system creation time.
- Data encrypted at rest is transparently encrypted while being written, and transparently decrypted while being read.

Encryption of data at rest and of data in transit can be configured together or separately.

AMAZON EFS ACCESS CONTROL

When you create a file system, you create endpoints in your VPC called "mount targets".

When mounting from an EC2 instance, your file system's DNS name, which you provide in your mount command, resolves to a mount target's IP address.

You can control who can administer your file system using IAM (user-based and resource-based policies)

You can control the NFS clients that can access your file systems (resource-based policies).

You can control access to files and directories with POSIX-compliant user and group-level permissions.

POSIX permissions allow you to restrict access from hosts by user and group.

EFS Security Groups act as a firewall, and the rules you add define the traffic flow.

Monitoring and Reporting

The Amazon EFS console shows the following monitoring information for your file systems:

- The current metered size.
- The number of mount targets.
- The lifecycle state.

Amazon EFS reports metrics for Amazon CloudWatch. A few useful metrics are:

- TotalIOBytes – use the daily Sum statistic to determine throughput.
- ClientConnections – use the daily Sum statistic to track the number of connections from EC2 instances.
- BurstCreditBalance – monitor the burst credit balance.

© 2023 Digital Cloud Training

LOGGING AND AUDITING

Amazon EFS is integrated with AWS CloudTrail.

CloudTrail captures all API calls for Amazon EFS as events, including calls from the Amazon EFS console and from code calls to Amazon EFS API operations.

AWS STORAGE GATEWAY

AWS STORAGE GATEWAY FEATURES

The AWS Storage Gateway service enables hybrid storage between on-premises environments and the AWS Cloud.

It provides low-latency performance by caching frequently accessed data on premises, while storing data securely and durably in Amazon cloud storage services.

Implemented using a virtual machine that you run on-premises (VMware or Hyper-V virtual appliance).

Provides local storage resources backed by Amazon S3 and Glacier.

Often used in disaster recovery preparedness to sync data to AWS.

AWS Storage Gateway supports three storage interfaces: file, volume, and tape.

The table below shows the different gateways available and the interfaces and use cases:

New Name	Old Name	Interface	Use Case
File Gateway	None	NFS, SMB	Allow on-prem or EC2 instances to store objects in S3 via NFS or SMB mount points
Volume Gateway Stored Mode	Gateway-Stored Volumes	iSCSI	Asynchronous replication of on-prem data to S3
Volume Gateway Cached Mode	Gateway-Cached Volumes	iSCSI	Primary data stored in S3 with frequently accessed data cached locally on-prem
Tape Gateway	Gateway-Virtual Tape Library	ISCSI	Virtual media changer and tape library for use with existing backup software

Each gateway you have can provide one type of interface.

All data transferred between any type of gateway appliance and AWS storage is encrypted using SSL.

By default, all data stored by AWS Storage Gateway in S3 is encrypted server-side with Amazon S3-Managed Encryption Keys (SSE-S3).

When using the file gateway, you can optionally configure each file share to have your objects encrypted with AWS KMS-Managed Keys using SSE-KMS.

FILE GATEWAY

File gateway provides a virtual on-premises file server, which enables you to store and retrieve files as objects in Amazon S3.

Can be used for on-premises applications, and for Amazon EC2-resident applications that need file storage in S3 for object-based workloads.

Used for flat files only, stored directly on S3.

File gateway offers SMB or NFS-based access to data in Amazon S3 with local caching.

File gateway supports Amazon S3 Standard, S3 Standard – Infrequent Access (S3 Standard – IA) and S3 One Zone – IA.

File gateway supports clients connecting to the gateway using NFS v3 and v4.1.

Microsoft Windows clients that support SMB can connect to file gateway.

The maximum size of an individual file is 5 TB.

VOLUME GATEWAY

The volume gateway represents the family of gateways that support block-based volumes, previously referred to as gateway-cached and gateway-stored modes.

Block storage – iSCSI based.

Cached Volume mode – the entire dataset is stored on S3, and a cache of the most frequently accessed data is cached on-site.

Stored Volume mode – the entire dataset is stored on-site and is asynchronously backed up to S3 (EBS point-in-time snapshots). Snapshots are incremental and compressed.

Each volume gateway can support up to 32 volumes.

In cached mode, each volume can be up to 32 TB for a maximum of 1 PB of data per gateway (32 volumes, each 32 TB in size).

In stored mode, each volume can be up to 16 TB for a maximum of 512 TB of data per gateway (32 volumes, each 16 TB in size).

GATEWAY VIRTUAL TAPE LIBRARY

Used for backup with popular backup software.

Each gateway is preconfigured with a media changer and tape drives. Supported by NetBackup, Backup Exec, Veeam etc.

When creating virtual tapes, you select one of the following sizes: 100 GB, 200 GB, 400 GB, 800 GB, 1.5 TB, and 2.5 TB.

A tape gateway can have up to 1,500 virtual tapes with a maximum aggregate capacity of 1 PB.

Managing AWS Storage Gateway

You might need to shut down or reboot your VM for maintenance, such as when applying a patch to your hypervisor. Before you shut down the VM, you must first stop the gateway.

- For file gateway, you just shut down your VM.
- For volume and tape gateways, stop the gateway, reboot the VM, then start the gateway.

MONITORING AWS STORAGE GATEWAY

The following metrics are useful when monitoring cache usage for file, cached-volume, and tape gateways.

Metric	Description	Applies to
CacheHitPercent	Percent of application reads served from the cache. The sample is taken at the end of the reporting period. Unit: Percent	File, cached-volume, and tape gateways.
CacheUsed	The total number of bytes being used in the gateway's cache storage. The sample is taken at the end of the reporting period. Unit: Bytes	File, cached-volume, and tape gateways.

NETWORKING & CONTENT DELIVERY

AMAZON VPC

AMAZON VPC FEATURES

Amazon VPC lets you provision a logically isolated section of the Amazon Web Services (AWS) cloud where you can launch AWS resources in a virtual network that you define.

Analogous to having your own DC inside AWS.

Provides complete control over the virtual networking environment including selection of IP ranges, creation of subnets, and configuration of route tables and gateways.

A VPC is logically isolated from other VPCs on AWS.

Possible to connect the corporate data center to a VPC using a hardware VPN (site-to-site).

VPCs are region wide.

A default VPC is created in each region with a subnet in each AZ.

By default you can create up to 5 VPCs per region.

You can define dedicated tenancy for a VPC to ensure instances are launched on dedicated hardware (overrides the configuration specified at launch).

A default VPC is automatically created for each AWS account the first time Amazon EC2 resources are provisioned.

The default VPC has all-public subnets.

Public subnets are subnets that have:

- "Auto-assign public IPv4 address" set to "Yes".
- The subnet route table has an attached Internet Gateway.

Instances in the default VPC always have both a public and private IP address.

AZs names are mapped to different zones for different users (i.e. the AZ "ap-southeast-2a" may map to a different physical zone for a different user).

Components of a VPC:

- **A Virtual Private Cloud:** A logically isolated virtual network in the AWS cloud. You define a VPC's IP address space from ranges you select.
- **Subnet:** A segment of a VPC's IP address range where you can place groups of isolated resources (maps to an AZ, 1:1).
- **Internet Gateway:** The Amazon VPC side of a connection to the public Internet.
- **NAT Gateway:** A highly available, managed Network Address Translation (NAT) service for your resources in a private subnet to access the Internet.
- **Hardware VPN Connection:** A hardware-based VPN connection between your Amazon VPC and your datacenter, home network, or co-location facility.
- **Virtual Private Gateway:** The Amazon VPC side of a VPN connection.
- **Customer Gateway:** Your side of a VPN connection.

- **Router:** Routers interconnect subnets and direct traffic between Internet gateways, virtual private gateways, NAT gateways, and subnets.
- **Peering Connection:** A peering connection enables you to route traffic via private IP addresses between two peered VPCs.
- **VPC Endpoints:** Enables private connectivity to services hosted in AWS, from within your VPC without using an Internet Gateway, VPN, Network Address Translation (NAT) devices, or firewall proxies.
- **Egress-only Internet Gateway:** A stateful gateway to provide egress only access for IPv6 traffic from the VPC to the Internet.

Options for connecting to a VPC are:

- Hardware based VPN.
- Direct Connect.
- VPN CloudHub.
- Software VPN.

Want to learn how to create a VPC hands-on? In the AWS Hands-On Labs video tutorial below, we' show you how to create a Custom Amazon Virtual Private Cloud (VPC) on AWS. You will also learn how to create subnets, route tables, and Internet Gateways. We launch some EC2 instances into the new VPC and test connectivity.

ROUTING

The VPC router performs routing between AZs within a region.

The VPC router connects different AZs together and connects the VPC to the Internet Gateway.

Each subnet has a route table the router uses to forward traffic within the VPC.

Route tables also have entries to external destinations.

Up to 200 route tables per VPC.

Up to 50 route entries per route table.

Each subnet can only be associated with one route table.

Can assign one route table to multiple subnets.

If no route table is specified a subnet will be assigned to the main route table at creation time.

Cannot delete the main route table.

You can manually set another route table to become the main route table.

There is a default rule that allows all VPC subnets to communicate with one another – this cannot be deleted or modified.

Routing between subnets is always possible because of this rule – any problems communicating is more likely to be security groups or NACLs.

SUBNETS AND SUBNET SIZING

Types of subnet:

- If a subnet's traffic is routed to an internet gateway, the subnet is known as a **public subnet.**
- If a subnet doesn't have a route to the internet gateway, the subnet is known as a **private**

subnet.

- If a subnet doesn't have a route to the internet gateway, but has its traffic routed to a virtual private gateway for a VPN connection, the subnet is known as a **VPN-only subnet.**

The VPC is created with a master address range (CIDR block, can be anywhere from 16-28 bits), and subnet ranges are created within that range.

New subnets are always associated with the default route table.

Once the VPC is created you cannot change the CIDR block.

You cannot create additional CIDR blocks that overlap with existing CIDR blocks.

You cannot create additional CIDR blocks in a different RFC 1918 range.

Subnets with overlapping IP address ranges cannot be created.

The first 4 and last 1 IP addresses in a subnet are reserved.

Subnets are created within availability zones (AZs).

Each subnet must reside entirely within one Availability Zone and cannot span zones.

Availability Zones are distinct locations that are engineered to be isolated from failures in other Availability Zones.

Availability Zones are connected with low latency, high throughput, and highly redundant networking.

Can create private, public or VPN subnets.

Subnets map 1:1 to AZs and cannot span AZs.

You can only attach one Internet gateway to a custom VPC.

IPv6 addresses are all public and the range is allocated by AWS.

It is recommended these come from the private IP ranges specified in RFC 1918:

- 10.0.0.0 – 10.255.255.255 (10/8 prefix)
- 172.16.0.0 – 172.31.255.255 (172.16/12 prefix)
- 192.168.0.0 – 192.168.255.255 (192.168/16 prefix)

However, it is possible to create a VPC with publicly routable CIDR block.

The allowed block size is between a /28 netmask and /16 netmask.

The CIDR blocks of the subnets within a VPC cannot overlap.

The first four IP addresses and the last IP address in each subnet CIDR block are not available for you to use

For example, in a subnet with CIDR block 10.0.0.0/24, the following five IP addresses are reserved:

- 10.0.0.0: Network address.
- 10.0.0.1: Reserved by AWS for the VPC route.
- 10.0.0.2: Reserved by AWS.
- 10.0.0.3: Reserved by AWS for future use.
- 10.0.0.255: Network broadcast address (broadcast not supported).

For further information, check out this AWS article.

INTERNET GATEWAYS

An Internet Gateway is a horizontally scaled, redundant, and highly available VPC component that allows communication between instances in your VPC and the internet.

An Internet Gateway serves two purposes: .

- To provide a target in your VPC route tables for internet-routable traffic.
- To perform network address translation (NAT) for instances that have been assigned public IPv4 addresses.

Internet Gateways (IGW) must be created and then attached to a VPC, be added to a route table, and then associated with the relevant subnet(s).

No availability risk or bandwidth constraints.

If your subnet is associated with a route to the Internet, then it is a public subnet.

You cannot have multiple Internet Gateways in a VPC.

IGW is horizontally scaled, redundant and HA.

IGW performs NAT between private and public IPv4 addresses.

IGW supports IPv4 and IPv6.

IGWs must be detached before they can be deleted.

Can only attach 1 IGW to a VPC at a time.

Gateway terminology:

- Internet gateway (IGW) – AWS VPC side of the connection to the public Internet.
- Virtual private gateway (VPG) – VPC endpoint on the AWS side.
- Customer gateway (CGW) – representation of the customer end of the connection.

To enable access to or from the Internet for instances in a VPC subnet, you must do the following:

- Attach an Internet Gateway to your VPC.
- Ensure that your subnet's route table points to the Internet Gateway (see below).
- Ensure that instances in your subnet have a globally unique IP address (public IPv4 address, Elastic IP address, or IPv6 address).
- Ensure that your network access control and security group rules allow the relevant traffic to flow to and from your instance.

Must update subnet route table to point to IGW, either:

- To all destinations, e.g. 0.0.0.0/0 for IPv4 or ::/0for IPv6.
- To specific public IPv4 addresses, e.g. your company's public endpoints outside of AWS.

Egress-only Internet Gateway:

- Provides outbound Internet access for IPv6 addressed instances.
- Prevents inbound access to those IPv6 instances.
- IPv6 addresses are globally unique and are therefore public by default.
- Stateful – forwards traffic from instance to Internet and then sends back the response.
- Must create a custom route for ::/0 to the Egress-Only Internet Gateway.
- Use Egress-Only Internet Gateway instead of NAT for IPv6.

VPC WIZARD

VPC with a Single Public Subnet:

- Your instances run in a private, isolated section of the AWS cloud with direct access to the Internet.
- Network access control lists and security groups can be used to provide strict control over inbound and outbound network traffic to your instances.
- Creates a /16 network with a /24 subnet. Public subnet instances use Elastic IPs or Public IPs to access the Internet.

VPC with Public and Private Subnets:

- In addition to containing a public subnet, this configuration adds a private subnet whose instances are not addressable from the Internet.
- Instances in the private subnet can establish outbound connections to the Internet via the public subnet using Network Address Translation (NAT).
- Creates a /16 network with two /24 subnets.
- Public subnet instances use Elastic IPs to access the Internet.
- Private subnet instances access the Internet via Network Address Translation (NAT).

VPC with Public and Private Subnets and Hardware VPN Access:

- This configuration adds an IPsec Virtual Private Network (VPN) connection between your Amazon VPC and your data center – effectively extending your data center to the cloud while also providing direct access to the Internet for public subnet instances in your Amazon VPC.
- Creates a /16 network with two /24 subnets.
- One subnet is directly connected to the Internet while the other subnet is connected to your corporate network via an IPsec VPN tunnel.

VPC with a Private Subnet Only and Hardware VPN Access:

- Your instances run in a private, isolated section of the AWS cloud with a private subnet whose instances are not addressable from the Internet.
- You can connect this private subnet to your corporate data center via an IPsec Virtual Private Network (VPN) tunnel.
- Creates a /16 network with a /24 subnet and provisions an IPsec VPN tunnel between your Amazon VPC and your corporate network.

NAT INSTANCES

NAT instances are managed **by** you.

Used to enable private subnet instances to access the Internet.

NAT instance must live on a public subnet with a route to an Internet Gateway.

Private instances in private subnets must have a route to the NAT instance, usually the default route destination of 0.0.0.0/0.

When creating NAT instances always disable the source/destination check on the instance.

NAT instances must be in a single public subnet.

NAT instances need to be assigned to security groups.

Security groups for NAT instances must allow HTTP/HTTPS inbound from the private subnet and outbound to 0.0.0.0/0.

There needs to be a route from a private subnet to the NAT instance for it to work.

The amount of traffic a NAT instance can support is based on the instance type.

Using a NAT instance can lead to bottlenecks (not HA).

HA can be achieved by using Auto Scaling groups, multiple subnets in different AZ's and a script to automate failover.

Performance is dependent on instance size.

Can scale up instance size or use enhanced networking.

Can scale out by using multiple NATs in multiple subnets.

Can use as a bastion (jump) host.

Can monitor traffic metrics.

Not supported for IPv6 (use Egress-Only Internet Gateway).

NAT GATEWAYS

NAT gateways are managed **for** you by AWS.

Fully managed NAT service that replaces the need for NAT instances on EC2.

Must be created in a public subnet.

Uses an Elastic IP address for the public IP.

Private instances in private subnets must have a route to the NAT instance, usually the default route destination of 0.0.0.0/0.

Created in a specified AZ with redundancy in that zone.

For multi-AZ redundancy, create NAT Gateways in each AZ with routes for private subnets to use the local gateway.

Up to 5 Gbps bandwidth that can scale up to 45 Gbps.

Can't use a NAT Gateway to access VPC peering, VPN or Direct Connect, so be sure to include specific routes to those in your route table.

NAT gateways are highly available in each AZ into which they are deployed.

They are preferred by enterprises.

No need to patch.

Not associated with any security groups.

Automatically assigned a public IP address.

Remember to update route tables and point towards your gateway.

More secure (e.g. you cannot access with SSH and there are no security groups to maintain).

No need to disable source/destination checks.

Egress only Internet gateways operate on IPv6 whereas NAT gateways operate on IPv4.

Port forwarding is not supported.

Using the NAT Gateway as a Bastion host server is not supported.

Traffic metrics are not supported.

The table below highlights the key differences between both types of gateway:

	NAT Gateway	NAT Instance
Managed	Managed by AWS	Managed
Availability	Highly available within an AZ	Not highly available (would require scripting)
Bandwidth	Up to 45 GPS	Depends on the bandwidth of the EC2 instance you selected
Maintenance	Managed by AWS	Managed by you
Performance	Optimized for NAT	Amazon Linux 2 AMI configured to perform NAT
Public IP	Elastic IP cannot be detached	Elastic IP that can be detached
Security Groups	Cannot associate with a security group	Can associate with a security group
Bastion Host	Not supported	Can be used as a bastion host

SECURITY GROUPS

Security groups act like a firewall at the instance level.

Specifically security groups operate at the network interface level.

Can only assign permit rules in a security group, cannot assign deny rules.

There is an implicit deny rule at the end of the security group.

All rules are evaluated until a permit is encountered or continues until the implicit deny.

Can control ingress and egress traffic.

Security groups are stateful.

By default, custom security groups do not have inbound allow rules (all inbound traffic is denied by default).

By default, default security groups do have inbound allow rules (allowing traffic from within the group).

All outbound traffic is allowed by default in custom and default security groups.

You cannot delete the security group that's created by default within a VPC.

You can use security group names as the source or destination in other security groups.

You can use the security group name as a source in its own inbound rules.

Security group members can be within any AZ or subnet within the VPC.

Security group membership can be changed whilst instances are running.

Any changes made will take effect immediately.

Up to 5 security groups can be added per EC2 instance interface.

There is no limit on the number of EC2 instances within a security group.

You cannot block specific IP addresses using security groups, use NACLs instead.

NETWORK ACL'S

Network ACL's function at the subnet level.

The VPC router hosts the network ACL function.

With NACLs you can have permit and deny rules.

Network ACLs contain a numbered list of rules that are evaluated in order from the lowest number until the explicit deny.

Recommended to leave spacing between network ACL numbers.

Network ACLs have separate inbound and outbound rules and each rule can allow or deny traffic.

Network ACLs are stateless, so responses are subject to the rules for the direction of traffic.

NACLs only apply to traffic that is ingress or egress to the subnet not to traffic within the subnet.

A VPC automatically comes with a default network ACL which allows all inbound/outbound traffic.

A custom NACL denies all traffic both inbound and outbound by default.

All subnets must be associated with a network ACL.

You can create custom network ACL's. By default, each custom network ACL denies all inbound and outbound traffic until you add rules.

Each subnet in your VPC must be associated with a network ACL. If you don't do this manually it will be associated with the default network ACL.

You can associate a network ACL with multiple subnets; however a subnet can only be associated with one network ACL at a time.

Network ACLs do not filter traffic between instances in the same subnet.

NACLs are the preferred option for blocking specific IPs or ranges.

Security groups cannot be used to block specific ranges of IPs.

NACL is the first line of defense, the security group is the second line.

Also recommended to have software firewalls installed on your instances.

Changes to NACLs take effect immediately.

Security Group	Network ACL
Operates at the instance (interface level)	Operates at the subnet level
Supports allow rules only	Supports allow and deny rules
Stateful	Stateless
Evaluates all rules	Processes rules in order
Applies to an instance only if associated with a group	Automatically applies to all instances in the subnet it is associated with

VPC CONNECTIVITY

There are several methods of connecting to a VPC. These include:

- AWS Managed VPN.
- AWS Direct Connect.
- AWS Direct Connect plus a VPN.
- AWS VPN CloudHub.
- Software VPN.
- Transit VPC.
- VPC Peering.
- AWS PrivateLink.
- VPC Endpoints.

Each of these will be further detailed below.

AWS Managed VPN

What	AWS-provided network connectivity between two VPCs
When	Multiple VPCs need to communicate or access each other's resources
Pros	Uses AWS backbone without traversing the public internet

Cons	Transitive peering is not supported
How	VPC Peering request made; acceptor accepts request (either within or across accounts)

VPNs are quick, easy to deploy, and cost effective.

A Virtual Private Gateway (VGW) is required on the AWS side.

A Customer Gateway is required on the customer side.

The diagram below depicts an AWS S2S VPN configuration:

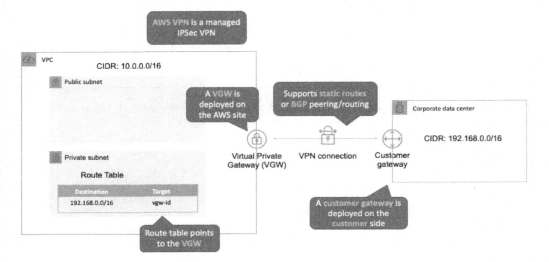

An Internet routable IP address is required on the customer gateway.

Two tunnels per connection must be configured for redundancy.

You cannot use a NAT gateway in AWS for clients coming in via a VPN.

For route propagation you need to point your VPN-only subnet's route tables at the VGW.

Must define the IP prefixes that can send/receive traffic through the VGW.

VGW does not route traffic destined outside of the received BGP advertisements, static route entries, or its attached VPC CIDR.

Cannot access Elastic IPs on your VPC via the VPN – Elastic IPs can only be connected to via the Internet.

AWS Direct Connect

What	Dedicated network connection over private line straight into the AWS backbone
When	Requires a large network link into AWS; lots of resources and services being provided

	on AWS to your corporate users
Pros	More predictable network performance; potential bandwidth cost reduction; up to 10 Gbps provisioned connections; supports BGP peering and routing
Cons	May require additional telecom and hosting provider relationships and/or network circuits; costly
How	Work with your existing data networking provider; create Virtual Interfaces (VIFs) to connect to VPCs (private VIFs) or other AWS services like S3 or Glacier (public VIFs)

AWS Direct Connect makes it easy to establish a dedicated connection from an on-premises network to Amazon VPC.

Using AWS Direct Connect, you can establish private connectivity between AWS and your data center, office, or collocated environment.

This private connection can reduce network costs, increase bandwidth throughput, and provide a more consistent network experience than internet-based connections.

AWS Direct Connect lets you establish 1 Gbps or 10 Gbps dedicated network connections (or multiple connections) between AWS networks and one of the AWS Direct Connect locations.

It uses industry standard VLANs to access Amazon Elastic Compute Cloud (Amazon EC2) instances running within an Amazon VPC using private IP addresses.

AWS Direct Connect does not encrypt your traffic that is in transit.

You can use the encryption options for the services that traverse AWS Direct Connect.

The diagram below depicts an AWS Direct Connect configuration:

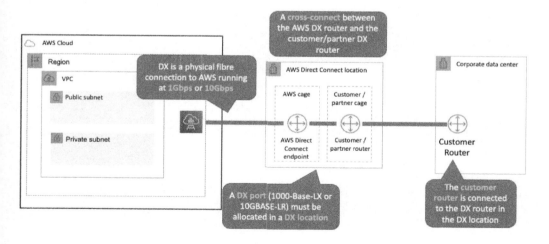

© 2023 Digital Cloud Training

AWS Direct Connect Plus VPN

What	IPSec VPN connection over private lines (Direct Connect)
When	Need the added security of encrypted tunnels over Direct Connect
Pros	More secure (in theory) than Direct Connect alone
Cons	More complexity introduced by VPN layer
How	Work with your existing data networking provider

With AWS Direct Connect plus VPN, you can combine one or more AWS Direct Connect dedicated network connections with the Amazon VPC VPN.

This combination provides an IPsec-encrypted private connection that also reduces network costs, increases bandwidth throughput, and provides a more consistent network experience than internet-based VPN connections.

You can use AWS Direct Connect to establish a dedicated network connection between your network create a logical connection to public AWS resources, such as an Amazon virtual private gateway IPsec endpoint.

This solution combines the AWS managed benefits of the VPN solution with low latency, increased bandwidth, more consistent benefits of the AWS Direct Connect solution, and an end-to-end, secure IPsec connection.

The diagram below depicts an AWS Direct Connect plus VPN configuration:

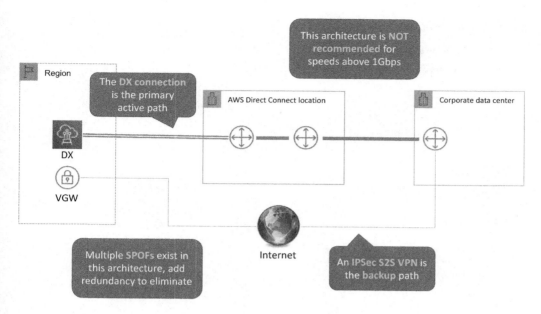

This architecture is NOT recommended for speeds above 1Gbps

The DX connection is the primary active path

Multiple SPOFs exist in this architecture, add redundancy to eliminate

An IPSec S2S VPN is the backup path

Region

AWS Direct Connect location

Corporate data center

DX

VGW

Internet

AWS VPN CloudHub

What	Connect locations in a hub and spoke manner using AWSs Virtual Private Gateway
When	Link remote offices for backup or primary WAN access to AWS resources and each other
Pros	Reuses existing Internet connections; supports BGP routes to direct traffic
Cons	Dependent on Internet connections; no inherent redundancy
How	Assign multiple Customer Gateways to a Virtual Private Gateway, each with their own BGP ASN and unique IP ranges

The AWS VPN CloudHub operates on a simple hub-and-spoke model that you can use with or without a VPC.

Use this design if you have multiple branch offices and existing internet connections and would like to implement a convenient, potentially low-cost hub-and-spoke model for primary or backup connectivity between these remote offices.

VPN CloudHub is used for hardware-based VPNs and allows you to configure your branch offices to go into a VPC and then connect that to the corporate DC (hub and spoke topology with AWS as the hub).

Can have up to 10 IPSec tunnels on a VGW by default.

Uses eBGP.

Branches can talk to each other (and provides redundancy).

Can have Direct Connect connections.

Hourly rates plus data egress charges.

The diagram below depicts an AWS VPN CloudHub configuration:

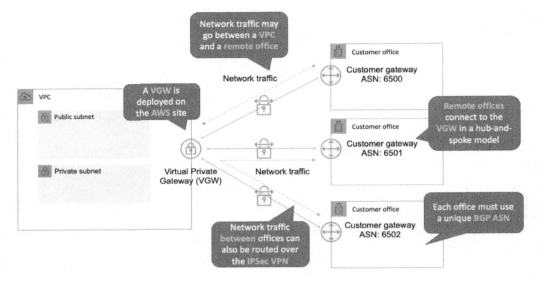

Software VPN

What	You must provide your own endpoint and software
When	You must manage both ends of the VPN connection for compliance reasons or you want to use a VPN option not supported by AWS
Pros	Ultimate flexibility and manageability
Cons	You must design for any needed redundancy across the whole chain
How	Install VPN software via Marketplace on an EC2 instance

Amazon VPC offers you the flexibility to fully manage both sides of your Amazon VPC connectivity by creating a VPN connection between your remote network and a software VPN appliance running in your Amazon VPC network.

This option is recommended if you must manage both ends of the VPN connection either for compliance purposes or for leveraging gateway devices that are not currently supported by Amazon VPC's VPN solution.

Transit VPC

What	Common strategy for connecting geographically dispersed VPCs and locations to create a global network transit center
When	Locations and VPC-deployed assets across multiple regions that need to communicate with one another
Pros	Ultimate flexibility and manageability but also AWS-managed VPN hub-and-spoke between VPCs
Cons	You must design for any redundancy across the whole chain
How	Providers like Cisco, Juniper Networks, and Riverbed have offerings which work with their equipment and AWS VPC

Building on the Software VPN design mentioned above, you can create a global transit network on AWS.

A transit VPC is a common strategy for connecting multiple, geographically disperse VPCs and remote networks to create a global network transit center.

A transit VPC simplifies network management and minimizes the number of connections required to connect multiple VPCs and remote networks.

VPC Peering

What	AWS-provided network connectivity between VPCs
When	Multiple VPCs need to connect with one another and access their resources
Pros	Uses AWS backbone without traversing the internet
Cons	Transitive peering is not supported
How	VPC Peering request made; accepter request (either within or across accounts)

A VPC peering connection is a networking connection between two VPCs that enables you to route traffic between them using private IPv4 addresses or IPv6 addresses.

Instances in either VPC can communicate with each other as if they are within the same network.

You can create a VPC peering connection between your own VPCs, or with a VPC in another AWS account.

The VPCs can be in different regions (also known as an inter-region VPC peering connection).

Data sent between VPCs in different regions is encrypted (traffic charges apply).

For inter-region VPC peering there are some limitations:

- You cannot create a security group rule that references a peer security group.
- Cannot enable DNS resolution.
- Maximum MTU is 1500 bytes (no jumbo frames support).
- Limited region support.

AWS uses the existing infrastructure of a VPC to create a VPC peering connection.

It is neither a gateway nor a VPN connection and does not rely on a separate piece of physical hardware.

There is no single point of failure for communication or a bandwidth bottleneck.

A VPC peering connection helps you to facilitate the transfer of data.

Can only have one peering connection between any two VPCs at a time.

Can peer with other accounts (within or between regions).

Cannot have overlapping CIDR ranges.

A VPC peering connection is a one-to-one relationship between two VPCs.

You can create multiple VPC peering connections for each VPC that you own, but transitive peering relationships are not supported.

You do not have any peering relationship with VPCs that your VPC is not directly peered with.

Limits are 50 VPC peers per VPC, up to 125 by request.

DNS is supported.

Must update route tables to configure routing.

Must update the inbound and outbound rules for VPC security group to reference security groups in the peered VPC.

When creating a VPC peering connection with another account you need to enter the account ID and VPC ID from the other account.

Need to accept the pending access request in the peered VPC.

The VPC peering connection can be added to route tables – shows as a target starting with "pcx-".

AWS PrivateLink

AWS PrivateLink simplifies the security of data shared with cloud-based applications by eliminating the exposure of data to the public Internet.

AWS PrivateLink provides private connectivity between VPCs, AWS services, and on-premises applications, securely on the Amazon network.

AWS PrivateLink makes it easy to connect services across different accounts and VPCs to significantly simplify the network architecture.

The table below provides more information on AWS PrivateLink and when to use it:

What	AWS-provided connectivity between VPCs and/or AWS services using interface endpoints
When	Keep private subnets truly private by using the AWS backbone rather than using the public internet
Pros	Redundant; uses AWS backbone
Cons	
How	Create endpoint for required AWS or Marketplace service in all required subnets; access via the provided DNS hostname

EXAM TIP: Know the difference between AWS PrivateLink and ClassicLink. ClassicLink allows you to link EC2-Classic instances to a VPC in your account, within the same region. EC2-Classic is an old platform from before VPCs were introduced and is not available to accounts created after December 2013. However, ClassicLink may come up in exam questions as a possible (incorrect) answer, so you need to know what it is.

VPC Endpoints

An Interface endpoint uses AWS PrivateLink and is an elastic network interface (ENI) with a private IP address that serves as an entry point for traffic destined to a supported service.

Using PrivateLink you can connect your VPC to supported AWS services, services hosted by other AWS accounts (VPC endpoint services) and supported AWS Marketplace partner services.

AWS PrivateLink access over Inter-Region VPC Peering:

- Applications in an AWS VPC can securely access AWS PrivateLink endpoints across AWS Regions using Inter-Region VPC Peering.
- AWS PrivateLink allows you to privately access services hosted on AWS in a highly available and scalable manner, without using public IPs, and without requiring the traffic to traverse the Internet.
- Customers can privately connect to a service even if the service endpoint resides in a different AWS Region.
- Traffic using Inter-Region VPC Peering stays on the global AWS backbone and never traverses the public Internet.

A gateway endpoint is a gateway that is a target for a specified route in your route table, used for traffic destined to a supported AWS service.

An interface VPC endpoint (interface endpoint) enables you to connect to services powered by AWS PrivateLink.

© 2023 Digital Cloud Training

The table below highlights some key information about both types of endpoints:

	Interface Endpoint	Gateway Endpoint
What	Elastic Network Interface with a private IP	A gateway that is a target for a specific route
How	Uses DNS entries to redirect traffic	Use prefix lists in the route table to redirect traffic
Which Services	A large amount of AWS services, for full list follow this link	Amazon S3, DynamoDB
Security	Security Groups	VPC Endpoint Policies

By default, IAM users do not have permission to work with endpoints.

You can create an IAM user policy that grants users the permissions to create, modify, describe, and delete endpoints.

There's a long list of services that are supported by interface endpoints.

Gateway endpoints are only available for:

- Amazon DynamoDB
- Amazon S3

EXAM TIP: Know which services use interface endpoints and gateway endpoints. The easiest way to remember this is that Gateway Endpoints are for Amazon S3 and DynamoDB only.

Shared Services VPCs

You can allow other AWS accounts to create their application resources, such as EC2 instances, Relational Database Service (RDS) databases, Redshift clusters, and Lambda functions, into shared, centrally managed Amazon Virtual Private Clouds (VPCs).

VPC sharing enables subnets to be shared with other AWS accounts within the same AWS Organization. Benefits include:

- Separation of duties: centrally controlled VPC structure, routing, IP address allocation.
- Application owners continue to own resources, accounts, and security groups.
- VPC sharing participants can reference security group IDs of each other.
- Efficiencies: higher density in subnets, efficient use of VPNs and AWS Direct Connect.
- Hard limits can be avoided, for example, 50 VIFs per AWS Direct Connect connection through simplified network architecture.
- Costs can be optimized through reuse of NAT gateways, VPC interface endpoints, and intra-Availability Zone traffic.

You can create separate Amazon VPCs for each account with the account owner being responsible for connectivity and security of each Amazon VPC.

With VPC sharing, your IT team can own and manage your Amazon VPCs and your application developers no longer must manage or configure Amazon VPCs, but they can access them as needed.

Can also share Amazon VPCs to leverage the implicit routing within a VPC for applications that require a high degree of interconnectivity and are within the same trust boundaries.

This reduces the number of VPCs that need to be created and managed, while you still benefit from using separate accounts for billing and access control.

Customers can further simplify network topologies by interconnecting shared Amazon VPCs using connectivity features, such as AWS PrivateLink, AWS Transit Gateway, and Amazon VPC peering.

Can also be used with AWS PrivateLink to secure access to resources shared such as applications behind a Network Load Balancer.

VPC FLOW LOGS

Flow Logs capture information about the IP traffic going to and from network interfaces in a VPC.

Flow log data is stored using Amazon CloudWatch Logs.

Flow logs can be created at the following levels:

- VPC.
- Subnet.
- Network interface.

You can't enable flow logs for VPC's that are peered with your VPC unless the peer VPC is in your account.

You can't tag a flow log.

You can't change the configuration of a flow log after it's been created.

After you've created a flow log, you cannot change its configuration (you need to delete and re-create).

Not all traffic is monitored, e.g. the following traffic is excluded:

- Traffic that goes to Route53.
- Traffic generated for Windows license activation.
- Traffic to and from 169.254.169.254 (instance metadata).
- Traffic to and from 169.254.169.123 for the Amazon Time Sync Service.
- DHCP traffic.
- Traffic to the reserved IP address for the default VPC router.

AMAZON CLOUDFRONT

AMAZON CLOUDFRONT FEATURES

CloudFront is a web service that gives businesses and web application developers an easy and cost-effective way to distribute content with low latency and high data transfer speeds.

CloudFront is a good choice for distribution of frequently accessed static content that benefits from edge delivery—like popular website images, videos, media files or software downloads.

Used for dynamic, static, streaming, and interactive content.

CloudFront is a global service:

- Ingress to upload objects.
- Egress to distribute content.

Amazon CloudFront provides a simple API that lets you:

- Distribute content with low latency and high data transfer rates by serving requests using a network of edge locations around the world.
- Get started without negotiating contracts and minimum commitments.

You can use a zone apex name on CloudFront.

CloudFront supports wildcard CNAME.

Supports wildcard SSL certificates, Dedicated IP, Custom SSL and SNI Custom SSL (cheaper).

Supports Perfect Forward Secrecy which creates a new private key for each SSL session.

EDGE LOCATIONS AND REGIONAL EDGE CACHES

An edge location is the location where content is cached (separate to AWS regions/AZs).

Requests are automatically routed to the nearest edge location.

Edge locations are not tied to Availability Zones or regions.

Regional Edge Caches are located between origin web servers and global edge locations and have a larger cache.

Regional Edge Caches have larger cache-width than any individual edge location, so your objects remain in cache longer at these locations.

Regional Edge caches aim to get content closer to users.

Proxy methods PUT/POST/PATCH/OPTIONS/DELETE go directly to the origin from the edge locations and do not proxy through Regional Edge caches.

Dynamic content goes straight to the origin and does not flow through Regional Edge caches.

Edge locations are not just read only, you can write to them too.

The diagram below shows where Regional Edge Caches and Edge Locations are placed in relation to end users:

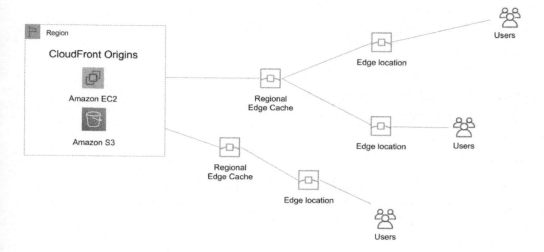

ORIGINS

An origin is the origin of the files that the CDN will distribute.

Origins can be either an S3 bucket, an EC2 instance, an Elastic Load Balancer, or Route 53 – can also be external (non-AWS).

When using Amazon S3 as an origin you place all your objects within the bucket.

You can use an existing bucket and the bucket is not modified in any way.

By default all newly created buckets are private.

You can setup access control to your buckets using:

- Bucket policies.
- Access Control Lists.

You can make objects publicly available or use CloudFront signed URLs.

A custom origin server is a HTTP server which can be an EC2 instance or an on-premises/non-AWS based web server.

When using an on-premises or non-AWS based web server you must specify the DNS name, ports, and protocols that you want CloudFront to use when fetching objects from your origin.

Most CloudFront features are supported for custom origins except RTMP distributions (must be an S3 bucket).

When using EC2 for custom origins Amazon recommend:

- Use an AMI that automatically installs the software for a web server.
- Use ELB to handle traffic across multiple EC2 instances.
- Specify the URL of your load balancer as the domain name of the origin server.

S3 static website:

- Enter the S3 static website hosting endpoint for your bucket in the configuration.
- Example: http://<bucketname>.s3-website-<region>.amazonaws.com.

Objects are cached for 24 hours by default.

The expiration time is controlled through the TTL.

The minimum expiration time is 0.

Static websites on Amazon S3 are considered custom origins.

AWS origins are Amazon S3 buckets (not a static website).

CloudFront keeps persistent connections open with origin servers.

Files can also be uploaded to CloudFront.

High availability with Origin Failover:

- Can set up CloudFront with origin failover for scenarios that require high availability.
- Uses an origin group in which you designate a primary origin for CloudFront plus a second origin that CloudFront automatically switches to when the primary origin returns specific HTTP status code failure responses.
- For more info, check this **article**.
- Also works with Lambda@Edge functions.

DISTRIBUTIONS

To distribute content with CloudFront you need to create a distribution.

The distribution includes the configuration of the CDN including:

- Content origins.
- Access (public or restricted).
- Security (HTTP or HTTPS).
- Cookie or query-string forwarding.
- Geo-restrictions.
- Access logs (record viewer activity).

There are two types of distribution.

Web Distribution:

- Static and dynamic content including .html, .css, .php, and graphics files.
- Distributes files over HTTP and HTTPS.
- Add, update, or delete objects, and submit data from web forms.
- Use live streaming to stream an event in real time.

RTMP:

- Distribute streaming media files using Adobe Flash Media Server's RTMP protocol.
- Allows an end user to begin playing a media file before the file has finished downloading from a CloudFront edge location.
- Files must be stored in an S3 bucket.

To use CloudFront live streaming, create a web distribution.

For serving both the media player and media files you need two types of distributions:

- A web distribution for the media player.

- An RTMP distribution for the media files.

S3 buckets can be configured to create access logs and cookie logs which log all requests made to the S3 bucket.

Amazon Athena can be used to analyze access logs.

CloudFront is integrated with CloudTrail.

CloudTrail saves logs to the S3 bucket you specify.

CloudTrail captures information about all requests whether they were made using the CloudFront console, the CloudFront API, the AWS SDKs, the CloudFront CLI, or another service.

CloudTrail can be used to determine which requests were made, the source IP address, who made the request etc.

To view CloudFront requests in CloudTrail logs you must update an existing trail to include global services.

To delete a distribution it must first be disabled (can take up to 15 minutes).

The diagram below depicts Amazon CloudFront Distributions and Origins:

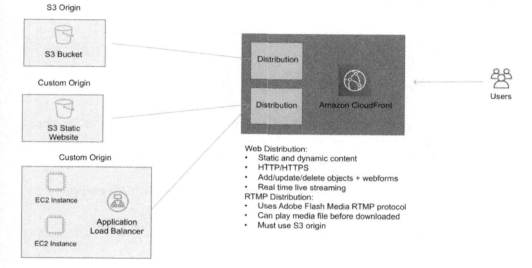

CACHE BEHAVIOR

Allows you to configure a variety of CloudFront functionality for a given URL path pattern.

For each cache behavior you can configure the following functionality:

- The path pattern (e.g. /images/*.jpg, /images*.php).
- The origin to forward requests to (if there are multiple origins).
- Whether to forward query strings.
- Whether to require signed URLs.
- Allowed HTTP methods.
- Minimum amount of time to retain the files in the CloudFront cache (regardless of the values of any cache-control headers).

The default cache behavior only allows a path pattern of /*.

Additional cache behaviors need to be defined to change the path pattern following creation of the distribution.

You can restrict access to content using the following methods:

- Restrict access to content using signed cookies or signed URLs.
- Restrict access to objects in your S3 bucket.

A special type of user called an Origin Access Identity (OAI) can be used to restrict access to content in an Amazon S3 bucket.

By using an OAI you can restrict users so they cannot access the content directly using the S3 URL, they must connect via CloudFront.

You can define the viewer protocol policy:

- HTTP and HTTPS.
- Redirect HTTP to HTTPS.
- HTTPS only.

You can define the Allowed HTTP Methods:

- GET, HEAD.
- GET, HEAD, OPTIONS.
- GET, HEAD, OPTIONS, PUT, POST, PATCH, DELETE.

For web distributions you can configure CloudFront to require that viewers use HTTPS.

Field-Level Encryption:

- Field-level encryption adds an additional layer of security on top of HTTPS that lets you protect specific data so that it is only visible to specific applications.
- Field-level encryption allows you to securely upload user-submitted sensitive information to your web servers.
- The sensitive information is encrypted at the edge closer to the user and remains encrypted throughout application processing.

Origin policy:

- HTTPS only.
- Match viewer – CloudFront matches the protocol with your custom origin.
- Use match viewer only if you specify Redirect HTTP to HTTPS or HTTPS only for the viewer protocol policy.
- CloudFront caches the object once even if viewers make requests using HTTP and HTTPS.

Object invalidation:

- You can remove an object from the cache by invalidating the object.
- You cannot cancel an invalidation after submission.
- You cannot invalidate media files in the Microsoft Smooth Streaming format when you have enabled Smooth Streaming for the corresponding cache behavior.

Objects are cached for the TTL (always recorded in seconds, default is 24 hours, default max is 1 year).

Only caches for GET requests (not PUT, POST, PATCH, DELETE).

Dynamic content is cached.

Consider how often your files change when setting the TTL.

Invalidation can be used to immediately revoke cached objects – chargeable.

Deletions propagate.

CACHE HIT RATIO

A good cache hit ratio means more requests are served from the cache.

Methods of improving the cache hit ratio include:

- Use the Cache-Control max-age directive to increase the time objects remain in the cache
- Use Origin Shield.
- Forward only the query string parameters for which your origin will return unique objects.
- Configure CloudFront to forward only specified cookies instead of forwarding all cookies.
- Configure CloudFront to forward and cache based on only specified headers instead of forwarding and caching based on all headers.

RESTRICTIONS

Blacklists and whitelists can be used for geography – you can only use one at a time.

There are two options available for geo-restriction (geo-blocking):

- Use the CloudFront geo-restriction feature (use for restricting access to all files in a distribution and at the country level).
- Use a 3rd party geo-location service (use for restricting access to a subset of the files in a distribution and for finer granularity at the country level).

SIGNED URLS AND SIGNED COOKIES

A signed URL includes additional information, for example, an expiration date and time, that gives you more control over access to your content. This additional information appears in a policy statement, which is based on either a canned policy or a custom policy.

CloudFront signed cookies allow you to control who can access your content when you don't want to change your current URLs or when you want to provide access to multiple restricted files, for example, all the files in the subscribers' area of a website.

Application must authenticate user and then send three Set-Cookie headers to the viewer; the viewer stores the name-value pair and adds them to the request in a Cookie header when requesting access to content.

Use signed URLs in the following cases:

- You want to restrict access to individual files, for example, an installation download for your application.
- Your users are using a client (for example, a custom HTTP client) that doesn't support cookies.

Use signed cookies in the following cases:

- You want to provide access to multiple restricted files, for example, all the files for a video in HLS format or all the files in the subscribers' area of website.

- You don't want to change your current URLs.

ORIGIN ACCESS IDENTITY

Used in combination with signed URLs and signed cookies to restrict direct access to an S3 bucket (prevents bypassing the CloudFront controls).

An origin access identity (OAI) is a special CloudFront user that is associated with the distribution.

Permissions must then be changed on the Amazon S3 bucket to restrict access to the OAI.

If users request files directly by using Amazon S3 URLs, they're denied access.

The origin access identity has permission to access files in your Amazon S3 bucket, but users don't.

AWS WAF

AWS WAF is a web application firewall that lets you monitor HTTP and HTTPS requests that are forwarded to CloudFront and lets you control access to your content.

With AWS WAF you can shield access to content based on conditions in a web access control list (web ACL) such as:

- Origin IP address.
- Values in query strings.

CloudFront responds to requests with the requested content or an HTTP 403 status code (forbidden).

CloudFront can also be configured to deliver a custom error page.

Need to associate the relevant distribution with the web ACL.

SECURITY

PCI DSS compliant but recommended not to cache credit card information at edge locations.

HIPAA compliant as a HIPAA eligible service.

Distributed Denial of Service (DDoS) protection:

- CloudFront distributes traffic across multiple edge locations and filters requests to ensure that only valid HTTP(S) requests will be forwarded to backend hosts. CloudFront also supports geo-blocking, which you can use to prevent requests from geographic locations from being served.

DOMAIN NAMES

CloudFront typically creates a domain name such as a232323.cloudfront.net.

Alternate domain names can be added using an alias record (Route 53).

For other service providers use a CNAME (cannot use the zone apex with CNAME).

Moving domain names between distributions:

- You can move subdomains yourself.
- For the root domain you need to use AWS support.

HIGH AVAILABILITY

CloudFront caches content at Edge Locations around the world. The more objects served by the cache, the fewer the requests to the origin. This reduces the load on your origin server and reduces latency.

You can set up CloudFront with __origin failover__ for scenarios that require high availability.

To set up origin failover, you must have a distribution with at least two origins. Next, you create an origin group for your distribution that includes two origins, setting one as the primary. Finally, you create or update a cache behavior to use the origin group.

MONITORING AND REPORTING

You can view __operational metrics__ about your CloudFront distributions and Lambda@Edge functions in the CloudFront console.

The following default metrics are included for all CloudFront distributions, at no additional cost:

Requests

The total number of viewer requests received by CloudFront, for all HTTP methods and for both HTTP and HTTPS requests.

Bytes downloaded

The total number of bytes downloaded by viewers for GET, HEAD, and OPTIONS requests.

Bytes uploaded

The total number of bytes that viewers uploaded to your origin with CloudFront, using POST and PUT requests.

4xx error rate

The percentage of all viewer requests for which the response's HTTP status code is 4xx.

5xx error rate

The percentage of all viewer requests for which the response's HTTP status code is 5xx.

Total error rate

The percentage of all viewer requests for which the response's HTTP status code is 4xx or 5xx.

In addition to the default metrics, you can enable additional metrics for an additional cost.

These additional metrics must be enabled for each distribution separately:

Cache hit rate

The percentage of all cacheable requests for which CloudFront served the content from its cache. HTTP POST and PUT requests, and errors, are not considered cacheable requests.

Origin latency

The total time spent from when CloudFront receives a request to when it starts providing a response to the network (not the viewer), for requests that are served from the origin, not the CloudFront cache. This is also known as *first byte latency*, or *time-to-first-byte*.

Error rate by status code

The percentage of all viewer requests for which the response's HTTP status code is a particular code in the 4xx or 5xx range. This metric is available for all the following error codes: 401, 403, 404, 502, 503, and 504.

LOGGING AND AUDITING

S3 buckets can be configured to create access logs and cookie logs which log all requests made to the S3 bucket.

Amazon Athena can be used to analyze access logs.

CloudFront is integrated with CloudTrail.

CloudTrail saves logs to the S3 bucket you specify.

CloudTrail captures information about all requests whether they were made using the CloudFront console, the CloudFront API, the AWS SDKs, the CloudFront CLI, or another service.

CloudTrail can be used to determine which requests were made, the source IP address, who made the request etc.

To view CloudFront requests in CloudTrail logs you must update an existing trail to include global services.

CHARGES

There is an option for reserved capacity over 12 months or longer (starts at 10TB of data transfer in a single region).

You pay for:

- Data Transfer Out to Internet.
- Data Transfer Out to Origin.
- Number of HTTP/HTTPS Requests.
- Invalidation Requests.
- Dedicated IP Custom SSL.
- Field level encryption requests.

You do not pay for:

- Data transfer between AWS regions and CloudFront.
- Regional edge cache.
- AWS ACM SSL/TLS certificates.
- Shared CloudFront certificates.

AMAZON ROUTE 53

AMAZON ROUTE 53 FEATURES

Amazon Route 53 is a highly available and scalable Domain Name System (DNS) service.

Amazon Route 53 offers the following functions:

- Domain name registry.
- DNS resolution.
- Health checking of resources.

Route 53 can perform any combination of these functions.

Route 53 provides a worldwide distributed DNS service.

Route 53 is located alongside all edge locations.

Health checks verify Internet connected resources are reachable, available, and functional.

Route 53 can be used to route Internet traffic for domains registered with another domain registrar (any domain).

When you register a domain with Route 53 it becomes the authoritative DNS server for that domain and creates a public hosted zone.

To make Route 53 the authoritative DNS for an existing domain without transferring the domain create a Route 53 public hosted zone and change the DNS Name Servers on the existing provider to the Route 53 Name Servers.

Changes to Name Servers may not take effect for up to 48 hours due to the DNS record Time To Live (TTL) values.

You can transfer domains to Route 53 only if the Top-Level Domain (TLD) is supported.

You can transfer a domain from Route 53 to another registrar by contacting AWS support.

You can transfer a domain to another account in AWS however it does not migrate the hosted zone by default (optional).

It is possible to have the domain registered in one AWS account and the hosted zone in another AWS account.

Primarily uses UDP port 53 (can use TCP).

AWS offer a 100% uptime SLA for Route 53.

You can control management access to your Amazon Route 53 hosted zone by using IAM.

There is a default limit of 50 domain names, but this can be increased by contacting support.

Private DNS is a Route 53 feature that lets you have authoritative DNS within your VPCs without exposing your DNS records (including the name of the resource and its IP address(es) to the Internet.

You can use the AWS Management Console or API to register new domain names with Route 53.

HOSTED ZONES

A hosted zone is a collection of records for a specified domain.

A hosted zone is analogous to a traditional DNS zone file; it represents a collection of records that can be managed together.

There are two types of zones:

- Public host zone – determines how traffic is routed on the Internet.
- Private hosted zone for VPC – determines how traffic is routed within VPC (resources are not accessible outside the VPC).

Amazon Route 53 automatically creates the Name Server (NS) and Start of Authority (SOA) records for the hosted zones.

Amazon Route 53 creates a set of 4 unique name servers (a delegation set) within each hosted zone.

You can create multiple hosted zones with the same name and different records.

NS servers are specified by Fully Qualified Domain Name (FQDN), but you can get the IP addresses from the command line (e.g. dig or nslookup).

For private hosted zones you can see a list of VPCs in each region and must select one.

For private hosted zones you must set the following VPC settings to "true":

- enableDnsHostname.
- enableDnsSupport.

You also need to create a DHCP options set.

You can extend an on-premises DNS to VPC.

You cannot extend Route 53 to on-premises instances.

You cannot automatically register EC2 instances with private hosted zones (would need to be scripted).

Health checks check the instance health by connecting to it.

Health checks can be pointed at:

- Endpoints.
- Status of other health checks.
- Status of a CloudWatch alarm.

Endpoints can be IP addresses or domain names.

HEALTH CHECKS

Health checks check the instance health by connecting to it.

Health checks can be pointed at:

- Endpoints.
- Status of other health checks.
- Status of a CloudWatch alarm.

Endpoints can be IP addresses or domain names.

You can create the following types of health checks:

- **HTTP**: Route 53 tries to establish a TCP connection. If successful, Route 53 submits an HTTP request and waits for an HTTP status code of 200 or greater and less than 400.
- **HTTPS**: Route 53 tries to establish a TCP connection. If successful, Route 53 submits an HTTPS request and waits for an HTTP status code of 200 or greater and less than 400.
- **HTTP_STR_MATCH**: Route 53 tries to establish a TCP connection. If successful, Route 53 submits an HTTP request and searches the first 5,120 bytes of the response body for the string that you specify in SearchString.
- **HTTPS_STR_MATCH**: Route 53 tries to establish a TCP connection. If successful, Route 53 submits an HTTPS request and searches the first 5,120 bytes of the response body for the string that you specify in SearchString.
- **TCP**: Route 53 tries to establish a TCP connection.
- **CLOUDWATCH_METRIC**: The health check is associated with a CloudWatch alarm. If the state of the alarm is OK, the health check is considered healthy. If the state is ALARM, the health check is

considered unhealthy. If CloudWatch doesn't have sufficient data to determine whether the state is OK or ALARM, the health check status depends on the setting for InsufficientDataHealthStatus: Healthy, Unhealthy, or LastKnownStatus.

- **CALCULATED**: For health checks that monitor the status of other health checks, Route 53 adds up the number of health checks that Route 53 health checkers consider to be healthy and compares that number with the value of HealthThreshold.

RECORDS

Amazon Route 53 currently supports the following DNS record types:

- A (address record).
- AAAA (IPv6 address record).
- CNAME (canonical name record).
- CAA (certification authority authorization).
- MX (mail exchange record).
- NAPTR (name authority pointer record).
- NS (name server record).
- PTR (pointer record).
- SOA (start of authority record).
- SPF (sender policy framework).
- SRV (service locator).
- TXT (text record).
- Alias (an Amazon Route 53-specific virtual record).

The Alias record is a Route 53 specific record type.

Alias records are used to map resource record sets in your hosted zone to Amazon Elastic Load Balancing load balancers, Amazon CloudFront distributions, AWS Elastic Beanstalk environments, or Amazon S3 buckets that are configured as websites.

You can use Alias records to map custom domain names (such as api.example.com) both to API Gateway custom regional APIs and edge-optimized APIs and to Amazon VPC interface endpoints.

The Alias is pointed to the DNS name of the service.

You cannot set the TTL for Alias records for ELB, S3, or Elastic Beanstalk environment (uses the service's default).

Alias records work like a CNAME record in that you can map one DNS name (e.g. example.com) to another 'target' DNS name (e.g. elb1234.elb.amazonaws.com).

An Alias record can be used for resolving apex / naked domain names (e.g. example.com rather than sub.example.com).

A CNAME record can't be used for resolving apex / naked domain names.

Generally use an Alias record where possible.

Route 53 supports wildcard entries for all record types, except NS records.

The following table details the differences between Alias and CNAME records:

CNAME Records	Alias Records

Route 53 charges for CNAME queries	Route 53 doesn't charge for alias queries to AWS resources
You can't create a CNAME record at the top node of a DNS namespace (zone apex)	You can create an alias record at the zone apex (however you can't route to a CNAME at the zone apex)
A CNAME record redirects queries for a domain name regardless of record type	Route 53 follows the pointer in an alias record only when the record type also matches
A CNAME can point to any DNS record that is hosted anywhere	An alias record can only point to a CloudFront distribution, Elastic Beanstalk environment, ELB, S3 bucket as a static website, or to another record in the same hosted zone that you're creating the alias record in
A CNAME record is visible in the answer section of a reply from a Route 53 DNS server	An alias record is only visible in the Route 53 console or the Route 53 API
A CNAME record is followed by a recursive resolver	An alias record is only followed inside Route 53. This means that both the alias record and its target must exist in Route 53

ROUTING POLICIES

Routing policies determine how Route 53 responds to queries.

The following table highlights the key function of each type of routing policy:

Policy	What it Does
Simple	Simple DNS response providing the IP address associated with a name
Failover	If primary is down (based on health checks), routes to secondary destination
Geolocation	Uses geographic location you're in (e.g. Europe) to route you to the closest region
Geoproximity	Routes you to the closest region within a geographic area
Latency	Directs you based on the lowest latency route to resources
Multivalue answer	Returns several IP addresses and functions as a basic load balancer

Weighted	Uses the relative weights assigned to resources to determine which to route to

Simple Routing Policy

- An A record is associated with one or more IP addresses.
- Uses round robin.
- Does not support health checks.

The following diagram depicts an Amazon Route 53 Simple routing policy configuration:

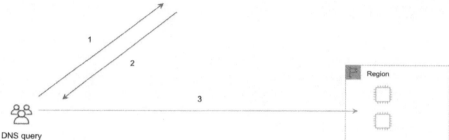

Name	Type	Value	TTL
simple.dctlabs.com	A	1.1.1.1 2.2.2.2	60
simpler.dctlabs.com	A	3.3.3.3	60

Amazon Route 53

Failover:

- Failover to a secondary IP address.
- Associated with a health check.
- Used for active-passive.
- Routes only when the resource is healthy.
- Can be used with ELB.
- When used with Alias records set Evaluate Target Health to "Yes" and do not use health checks.

The following diagram depicts an Amazon Route 53 Failover routing policy configuration:

© 2023 Digital Cloud Training

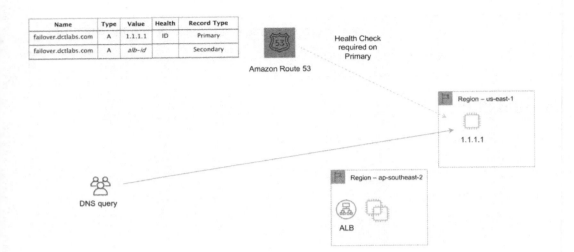

Name	Type	Value	Health	Record Type
failover.dctlabs.com	A	1.1.1.1	ID	Primary
failover.dctlabs.com	A	alb–id		Secondary

Geo-location Routing Policy

- Caters to different users in different countries and different languages.
- Contains users within a particular geography and offers them a customized version of the workload based on their specific needs.
- Geolocation can be used for localizing content and presenting some or all your website in the language of your users.
- Can also protect distribution rights.
- Can be used for spreading load evenly between regions.
- If you have multiple records for overlapping regions, Route 53 will route to the smallest geographic region.
- You can create a default record for IP addresses that do not map to a geographic location.

The following diagram depicts an Amazon Route 53 Geolocation routing policy configuration:

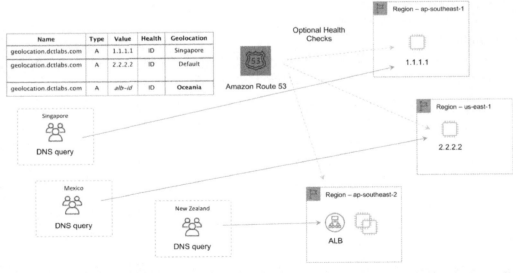

Name	Type	Value	Health	Geolocation
geolocation.dctlabs.com	A	1.1.1.1	ID	Singapore
geolocation.dctlabs.com	A	2.2.2.2	ID	Default
geolocation.dctlabs.com	A	alb–id	ID	Oceania

Geo-proximity routing policy (requires Route Flow):

- Use for routing traffic based on the location of resources and, optionally, shift traffic from resources in one location to resources in another.

Latency Routing Policy

AWS maintains a database of latency from different parts of the world.

- Focused on improving performance by routing to the region with the lowest latency.
- You create latency records for your resources in multiple EC2 locations.

The following diagram depicts an Amazon Route 53 Latency based routing policy configuration:

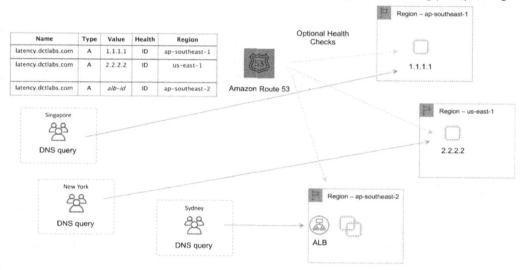

Multi-value Answer Routing Policy

- Use for responding to DNS queries with up to eight healthy records selected at random.

The following diagram depicts an Amazon Route 53 Multivalue routing policy configuration:

Weighted Routing Policy

- Like simple but you can specify a weight per IP address.
- You create records that have the same name and type and assign each record a relative weight.
- Numerical value that favors one IP over another.
- To stop sending traffic to a resource you can change the weight of the record to 0.

The following diagram depicts an Amazon Route 53 Weighted routing policy configuration:

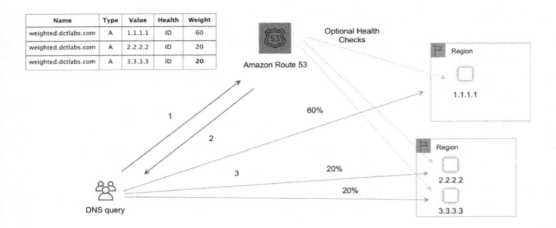

Name	Type	Value	Health	Weight
weighted.dctlabs.com	A	1.1.1.1	ID	60
weighted.dctlabs.com	A	2.2.2.2	ID	20
weighted.dctlabs.com	A	3.3.3.3	ID	20

TRAFFIC FLOW

Route 53 Traffic Flow provides Global Traffic Management (GTM) services.

Traffic flow policies allow you to create routing configurations for resources using routing types such as failover and geolocation.

Create policies that route traffic based on specific constraints, including latency, endpoint health, load, geo-proximity, and geography.

Scenarios include:

- Adding a simple backup page in Amazon S3 for a website.
- Building sophisticated routing policies that consider an end user's geographic location, proximity to an AWS region, and the health of each of your endpoints.

Amazon Route 53 Traffic Flow also includes a versioning feature that allows you to maintain a history of changes to your routing policies, and easily roll back to a previous policy version using the console or API.

ROUTE 53 RESOLVER

Route 53 Resolver is a set of features that enable bi-directional querying between on-premises and AWS over private connections.

Used for enabling DNS resolution for hybrid clouds.

Route 53 Resolver Endpoints.

- Inbound query capability is provided by Route 53 Resolver Endpoints, allowing DNS queries that originate on-premises to resolve AWS hosted domains.
- Connectivity needs to be established between your on-premises DNS infrastructure and AWS through a Direct Connect (DX) or a Virtual Private Network (VPN).
- Endpoints are configured through IP address assignment in each subnet for which you would like to provide a resolver.

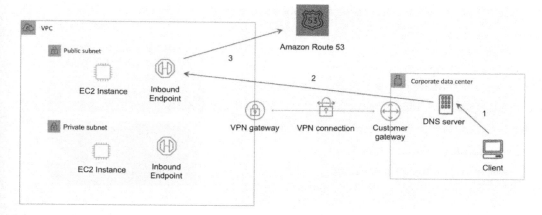

Conditional forwarding rules:

- Outbound DNS queries are enabled using Conditional Forwarding Rules. .
- Domains hosted within your on-premises DNS infrastructure can be configured as forwarding rules in Route 53 Resolver.
- Rules will trigger when a query is made to one of those domains and will attempt to forward DNS requests to your DNS servers that were configured along with the rules.
- Like the inbound queries, this requires a private connection over DX or VPN.

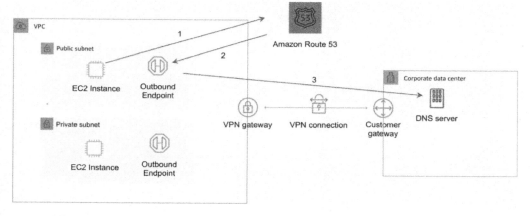

CHARGES

You pay per hosted zone per month (no partial months).

A hosted zone deleted within 12 hours of creation is not charged (queries are charged).

Additional charges for:

- Queries.
- Traffic Flow.
- Health Checks.
- Route 53 Resolver ENIs + queries.
- Domain names.

Alias records are free of charge when the records are mapped to one of the following:

- Elastic Load Balancers.
- Amazon CloudFront distributions.
- AWS Elastic Beanstalk environments.
- Amazon S3 buckets that are configured as website endpoints.

Health checks are charged with different prices for AWS vs non-AWS endpoints.

You do not pay for the records that you add to your hosted zones.

Latency-based routing queries are more expensive.

Geo DNS and geo-proximity also have higher prices.

DATABASE

AWS RDS

AMAZON RDS FEATURES

Amazon Relational Database Service (Amazon RDS) is a managed service that you can use to launch and manage relational databases on AWS.

Amazon RDS is an Online Transaction Processing (OLTP) type of database.

The primary use case is a transactional database (rather than an analytical database).

It is best suited to structured, relational data store requirements.

It aims to be drop-in replacement for existing on-premises instances of the same databases.

Automated backups and patching are applied in customer-defined maintenance windows.

Push-button scaling, replication, and redundancy.

Amazon RDS supports the following database engines:

- Amazon Aurora.
- MySQL.
- MariaDB.
- Oracle.
- SQL Server.
- PostgreSQL.

RDS is a managed service and you do not have access to the underlying EC2 instance (no root access).

The exception to the above rule is Amazon RDS Custom which allows access to the underlying operating system. This is new, available for limited DB engines, and does not appear on the exam yet.

The Amazon RDS managed service includes the following:

- Security and patching of the DB instances.
- Automated backup for the DB instances.
- Software updates for the DB engine.
- Easy scaling for storage and compute.
- Multi-AZ option with synchronous replication.
- Automatic failover for Multi-AZ option.
- Read replicas option for read heavy workloads.

A DB instance is a database environment in the cloud with the compute and storage resources you specify.

Database instances are accessed via endpoints.

Endpoints can be retrieved via the DB instance description in the AWS Management Console, **DescribeDBInstances** API or **describe-db-instances** command.

By default, customers are allowed to have up to a total of 40 Amazon RDS DB instances (only 10 of these can be Oracle or MS SQL unless you have your own licenses).

Maintenance windows are configured to allow DB instances modifications to take place such as scaling and software patching (some operations require the DB instance to be taken offline briefly).

You can define the maintenance window or AWS will schedule a 30-minute window.

Windows integrated authentication for SQL only works with domains created using the AWS directory service – need to establish a trust with an on-premises AD directory.

Events and Notifications:

- Amazon RDS uses AWS SNS to send RDS events via SNS notifications.
- You can use API calls to the Amazon RDS service to list the RDS events in the last 14 days (DescribeEvents API).
- You can view events from the last 14 days using the CLI.
- Using the AWS Console you can only view RDS events for the last 1 day.

ENCRYPTION

You can encrypt your Amazon RDS instances and snapshots at rest by enabling the encryption option for your Amazon RDS DB instance.

Encryption at rest is supported for all DB types and uses AWS KMS.

When using encryption at rest the following elements are also encrypted:

- All DB snapshots.
- Backups.
- DB instance storage.
- Read Replicas.

You cannot encrypt an existing DB, you need to create a snapshot, copy it, encrypt the copy, then build an encrypted DB from the snapshot.

Data that is encrypted at rest includes the underlying storage for a DB instance, its automated backups, Read Replicas, and snapshots.

A Read Replica of an Amazon RDS encrypted instance is also encrypted using the same key as the master instance when both are in the same region.

If the master and Read Replica are in different regions, you encrypt using the encryption key for that region.

You can't have an encrypted Read Replica of an unencrypted DB instance or an unencrypted Read Replica of an encrypted DB instance.

Encryption/decryption is handled transparently.

RDS supports SSL encryption between applications and RDS DB instances.

RDS generates a certificate for the instance.

DB SUBNET GROUPS

A DB subnet group is a collection of subnets (typically private) that you create in a VPC and that you then designate for your DB instances.

Each DB subnet group should have subnets in at least two Availability Zones in a given region.

It is recommended to configure a subnet group with subnets in each AZ (even for standalone instances).

During the creation of an RDS instance you can select the DB subnet group and the AZ within the group to place the RDS DB instance in.

You cannot pick the IP within the subnet that is allocated.

BILLING AND PROVISIONING

AWS Charge for:

- DB instance hours (partial hours are charged as full hours).
- Storage GB/month.
- I/O requests/month – for magnetic storage.
- Provisioned IOPS/month – for RDS provisioned IOPS SSD.
- Egress data transfer.
- Backup storage (DB backups and manual snapshots).

Backup storage for the automated RDS backup is free of charge up to the provisioned EBS volume size.

However, AWS replicate data across multiple AZs and so you are charged for the extra storage space on S3.

For multi-AZ you are charged for:

- Multi-AZ DB hours.
- Provisioned storage.
- Double write I/Os.

For multi-AZ you are not charged for DB data transfer during replication from primary to standby.

Oracle and Microsoft SQL licenses are included, or you can bring your own (BYO).

On-demand and reserved instance pricing available.

Reserved instances are defined based on the following attributes which must not be changed:

- DB engine.
- DB instance class.
- Deployment type (standalone, multi-AZ_.
- License model.
- Region.

Reserved instances:

- Can be moved between AZs in the same region.
- Are available for multi-AZ deployments.
- Can be applied to Read Replicas if DB instance class and region are the same.
- Scaling is achieved through changing the instance class for compute and modifying storage capacity for additional storage allocation.

SCALABILITY

You can only scale RDS up (compute and storage).

You cannot decrease the allocated storage for an RDS instance.

You can scale storage and change the storage type for all DB engines except MS SQL.

For MS SQL the workaround is to create a new instance from a snapshot with the new configuration.

Scaling storage can happen while the RDS instance is running without outage however there may be performance degradation.

Scaling compute will cause downtime.

You can choose to have changes take effect immediately, however the default is within the maintenance window.

Scaling requests are applied during the specified maintenance window unless "apply immediately" is used.

All RDS DB types support a maximum DB size of 64 TiB except for Microsoft SQL Server (16 TiB)

PERFORMANCE

Amazon RDS uses EBS volumes (never uses instance store) for DB and log storage.

There are three storage types available: General Purpose (SSD), Provisioned IOPS (SSD), and Magnetic.

General Purpose (SSD):

- Use for Database workloads with moderate I/O requirement.
- Cost effective.
- Also called gp2.
- 3 IOPS/GB.
- Burst up to 3000 IOPS.

Provisioned IOPS (SSD):

- Use for I/O intensive workloads.
- Low latency and consistent I/O.
- User specified IOPS (see table below).

For provisioned IOPS storage the table below shows the range of Provisioned IOPS and storage size range for each database engine.

Database Engine	Range of Provisioned IOPS	Range of Storage
MariaDB	1,000-80,000 IOPS	100 GiB-64TiB
SQL Server	1,000-64,000 IOPS	20 GiB-16TiB
MySQL	1,000-80,000 IOPS	100 GiB-64TiB
Oracle	1,000-256,000 IOPS	100 GiB-64TiB
PostgreSQL	1,000-80,000 IOPS	100 GiB-64TiB

Magnetic:

- Not recommended anymore, available for backwards compatibility.
- Doesn't allow you to scale storage when using the SQL Server database engine.
- Doesn't support elastic volumes.
- Limited to a maximum size of 4 TiB.
- Limited to a maximum of 1,000 IOPS.

MULTI-AZ AND READ REPLICAS

Multi-AZ and Read Replicas are used for high availability, fault tolerance and performance scaling.

The table below compares multi-AZ deployments to Read Replicas:

Multi-AZ Deployments	Read Replicas
Synchronous Replication - highly durable	Asynchronous replication - highly scalable
Only database engine on primary instance is active	All read replicas are accessible and can be used for read scaling
Automated backups are taken from standby	No backups configured by default
Always span two availability zones within a single region	Can be within an Availability Zone, Cross-AZ, or Cross-Region
Database engine version upgrades happen on primary	Database engine version upgrade is independent from source instance
Automatic failover to standby when a problem is detected	Can be manually promoted to a standalone database instance

Multi-AZ

Multi-AZ RDS creates a replica in another AZ and synchronously replicates to it (DR only).

There is an option to choose multi-AZ during the launch wizard.

AWS recommends the use of provisioned IOPS storage for multi-AZ RDS DB instances.

Each AZ runs on its own physically distinct, independent infrastructure, and is engineered to be highly reliable.

You cannot choose which AZ in the region will be chosen to create the standby DB instance.

You can view which AZ the standby DB instance is created in.

A failover may be triggered in the following circumstances:

- Loss of primary AZ or primary DB instance failure.
- Loss of network connectivity on primary.
- Compute (EC2) unit failure on primary.
- Storage (EBS) unit failure on primary.
- The primary DB instance is changed.
- Patching of the OS on the primary DB instance.
- Manual failover (reboot with failover selected on primary).

During failover RDS automatically updates configuration (including DNS endpoint) to use the second node.

Depending on the instance class it can take 1 to a few minutes to failover to a standby DB instance.

It is recommended to implement DB connection retries in your application.

Recommended to use the endpoint rather than the IP address to point applications to the RDS DB.

The method to initiate a manual RDS DB instance failover is to reboot selecting the option to failover.

A DB instance reboot is required for changes to take effect when you change the DB parameter group or when you change a static DB parameter.

The DB parameter group is a configuration container for the DB engine configuration.

You will be alerted by a DB instance event when a failover occurs.

The secondary DB in a multi-AZ configuration cannot be used as an independent read node (read or write).

There is no charge for data transfer between primary and secondary RDS instances.

System upgrades like OS patching, DB Instance scaling and system upgrades, are applied first on the standby, before failing over and modifying the other DB Instance.

In multi-AZ configurations snapshots and automated backups are performed on the standby to avoid I/O suspension on the primary instance.

Read Replica Support for Multi-AZ:

- Amazon RDS Read Replicas for MySQL, MariaDB, PostgreSQL, and Oracle support Multi-AZ deployments.
- Combining Read Replicas with Multi-AZ enables you to build a resilient disaster recovery strategy and simplify your database engine upgrade process.
- A Read Replica in a different region than the source database can be used as a standby database and promoted to become the new production database in case of a regional disruption.
- This allows you to scale reads whilst also having multi-AZ for DR.

The process for implementing maintenance activities is as follows:

- Perform operations on standby.
- Promote standby to primary.
- Perform operations on new standby (demoted primary).

You can manually upgrade a DB instance to a supported DB engine version from the AWS Console.

By default upgrades will take effect during the next maintenance window.

You can optionally force an immediate upgrade.

In multi-AZ deployments version upgrades will be conducted on both the primary and standby at the same time causing an outage of both DB instance.

Ensure security groups and NACLs will allow your application servers to communicate with both the primary and standby instances.

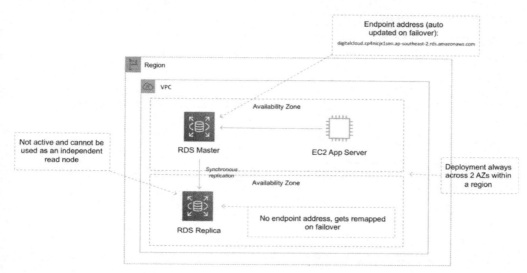

Read Replicas

Read replicas are used for read-heavy DBs and replication is asynchronous.

Read replicas are for workload sharing and offloading.

Read replicas provide read-only DR.

Read replicas are created from a snapshot of the master instance.

Must have automated backups enabled on the primary (retention period > 0).

Only supported for transactional database storage engines (InnoDB not MyISAM).

Read replicas are available for MySQL, PostgreSQL, MariaDB, Oracle, Aurora, and SQL Server.

For the MySQL, MariaDB, PostgreSQL, and Oracle database engines, Amazon RDS creates a second DB instance using a snapshot of the source DB instance.

It then uses the engines' native asynchronous replication to update the read replica whenever there is a change to the source DB instance.

Amazon Aurora employs an SSD-backed virtualized storage layer purpose-built for database workloads.

You can take snapshots of PostgreSQL read replicas but cannot enable automated backups.

You can enable automatic backups on MySQL and MariaDB read replicas.

You can enable writes to the MySQL and MariaDB Read Replicas.

You can have 5 read replicas of a production DB.

You cannot have more than four instances involved in a replication chain.

You can have read replicas of read replicas for MySQL and MariaDB but not for PostgreSQL.

Read replicas can be configured from the AWS Console or the API.

You can specify the AZ the read replica is deployed in.

The read replicas storage type and instance class can be different from the source but the compute should be at least the performance of the source.

You cannot change the DB engine.

In a multi-AZ failover the read replicas are switched to the new primary.

Read replicas must be explicitly deleted.

If a source DB instance is deleted without deleting the replicas each replica becomes a standalone single-AZ DB instance.

You can promote a read replica to primary.

Promotion of read replicas takes several minutes.

Promoted read replicas retain:

- Backup retention window.
- Backup window.
- DB parameter group.

Existing read replicas continue to function as normal.

Each read replica has its own DNS endpoint.

Read replicas can have multi-AZ enabled and you can create read replicas of multi-AZ source DBs.

Read replicas can be in another region (uses asynchronous replication).

This configuration can be used for centralizing data from across different regions for analytics.

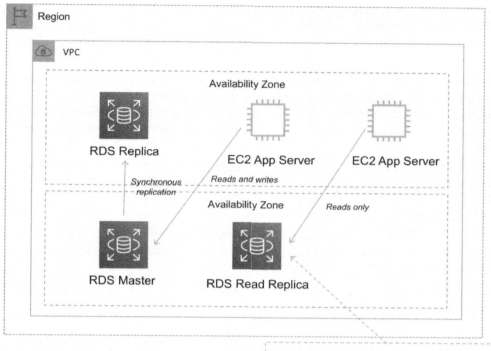

Replica has it's own DNS
endpoint:

ro-digitalcloud.cp4nicjx1son.ap-southeast-2.rds.amazonaws.com

DB SNAPSHOTS

DB Snapshots are user-initiated and enable you to back up your DB instance in a known state as frequently as you wish, and then restore to that specific state.

Cannot be used for point-in-time recovery.

Snapshots are stored on S3.

Snapshots remain on S3 until manually deleted.

Backups are taken within a defined window.

I/O is briefly suspended while backups initialize and may increase latency (applicable to single-AZ RDS).

DB snapshots that are performed manually will be stored even after the RDS instance is deleted.

Restored DBs will always be a new RDS instance with a new DNS endpoint.

Can restore up to the last 5 minutes.

Only default DB parameters and security groups are restored – you must manually associate all other DB parameters and SGs.

It is recommended to take a final snapshot before deleting an RDS instance.

Snapshots can be shared with other AWS accounts.

MONITORING, LOGGING AND REPORTING

You can use the following automated monitoring tools to watch Amazon RDS and report when something is wrong:

- **Amazon RDS Events** – Subscribe to Amazon RDS events to be notified when changes occur with a DB instance, DB snapshot, DB parameter group, or DB security group.
- **Database log files** – View, download, or watch database log files using the Amazon RDS console or Amazon RDS API operations. You can also query some database log files that are loaded into database tables.
- **Amazon RDS Enhanced Monitoring** — Look at metrics in real time for the operating system.
- **Amazon RDS Performance Insights** — Assess the load on your database and determine when and where to act.
- **Amazon RDS Recommendations** — Look at automated recommendations for database resources, such as DB instances, read replicas, and DB parameter groups.

In addition, Amazon RDS integrates with Amazon CloudWatch, Amazon EventBridge, and AWS CloudTrail for additional monitoring capabilities:

- **Amazon CloudWatch Metrics** – Amazon RDS automatically sends metrics to CloudWatch every minute for each active database. You don't get additional charges for Amazon RDS metrics in CloudWatch.
- **Amazon CloudWatch Alarms** – You can watch a single Amazon RDS metric over a specific time period. You can then perform one or more actions based on the value of the metric relative to a threshold that you set.
- **Amazon CloudWatch Logs** – Most DB engines enable you to monitor, store, and access your database log files in CloudWatch Logs.
- **Amazon CloudWatch Events and Amazon EventBridge** – You can automate AWS services and respond to system events such as application availability issues or resource changes. Events from AWS services are delivered to CloudWatch Events and EventBridge nearly in real time. You can write simple rules to indicate which events interest you and what automated actions to take when an event matches a rule
- **AWS CloudTrail** – You can view a record of actions taken by a user, role, or an AWS service in Amazon RDS. CloudTrail captures all API calls for Amazon RDS as events. These captures include calls from the Amazon RDS console and from code calls to the Amazon RDS API operations. If you create a trail, you can enable continuous delivery of CloudTrail events to an Amazon S3 bucket, including events for Amazon RDS. If you don't configure a trail, you can still view the most recent events in the CloudTrail console in **Event history**.

AUTHORIZATION AND ACCESS CONTROL

Amazon RDS supports identity-based policies.

RDS does not support resource-based policies.

The following AWS managed policies, which you can attach to users in your account, are specific to Amazon RDS:

- **AmazonRDSReadOnlyAccess** – Grants read-only access to all Amazon RDS resources for the AWS account specified.

- **AmazonRDSFullAccess** – Grants full access to all Amazon RDS resources for the AWS account specified.

You can authenticate to your DB instance using AWS Identity and Access Management (IAM) database authentication. IAM database authentication works with MySQL and PostgreSQL. With this authentication method, you don't need to use a password when you connect to a DB instance. Instead, you use an authentication token.

IAM database authentication provides the following benefits:

- Network traffic to and from the database is encrypted using Secure Sockets Layer (SSL).
- You can use IAM to centrally manage access to your database resources, instead of managing access individually on each DB instance.
- For applications running on Amazon EC2, you can use profile credentials specific to your EC2 instance to access your database instead of a password, for greater security.

AMAZON AURORA

AMAZON AURORA FEATURES

Amazon Aurora is a relational database service that combines the speed and availability of high-end commercial databases with the simplicity and cost-effectiveness of open-source databases.

Aurora is an AWS proprietary database.

Fully managed service.

High performance, low price.

2 copies of data are kept in each AZ with a minimum of 3 AZ's (6 copies).

Can handle the loss of up to two copies of data without affecting DB write availability and up to three copies without affecting read availability.

The following diagram depicts how Aurora Fault Tolerance and Replicas work:

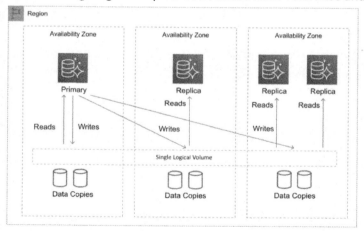

Aurora Fault Tolerance
- Fault tolerance across 3 AZs
- Single logical volume
- Aurora Replicas scale-out read requests
- Up to 15 Aurora Replicas with sub-10ms replica lag
- Aurora Replicas are independent endpoints
- Can promote Aurora Replica to be a new primary or create new primary
- Set priority (tiers) on Aurora Replicas to control order of promotion
- Can use Auto Scaling to add replicas

AURORA REPLICAS

There are two types of replication: Aurora replica (up to 15), MySQL Read Replica (up to 5).

The table below describes the differences between the two replica options:

Feature	Aurora Replica	MySQL Replica
Number of replicas	Up to 15	Up to 5
Replication type	Asynchronous (milliseconds)	Asynchronous (seconds)
Performance impact on primary	Low	High
Replica location	In-region	Cross-region
Act as failover target	Yes (no data loss)	Yes (potentially minutes of data loss)
Automated failover	Yes	No
Support for user-defined replication delay	No	Yes
Support for different data or schema vs. primary	No	Yes

You can create read replicas for an Amazon Aurora database in up to five AWS regions. This capability is available for Amazon Aurora with MySQL compatibility.

CROSS-REGION READ REPLICAS

Cross-region read replicas allow you to improve your disaster recovery posture, scale read operations in regions closer to your application users, and easily migrate from one region to another.

Cross-region replicas provide fast local reads to your users.

Each region can have an additional 15 Aurora replicas to further scale local reads.

You can choose between **Global Database**, which provides the best replication performance, and traditional binlog-based replication.

You can also set up your own binlog replication with external MySQL databases.

The following diagram depicts the Cross-Region Read Replica topology:

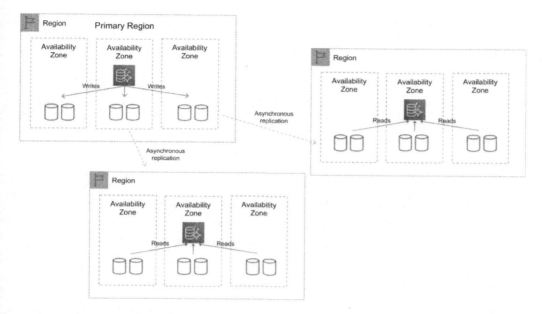

GLOBAL DATABASE

For globally distributed applications you can use **Global Database**, where a single Aurora database can span multiple AWS regions to enable fast local reads and quick disaster recovery.

Global Database uses storage-based replication to replicate a database across multiple AWS Regions, with typical latency of less than 1 second.

You can use a secondary region as a backup option in case you need to recover quickly from a regional degradation or outage.

A database in a secondary region can be promoted to full read/write capabilities in less than 1 minute.

The following table depicts the Aurora Global Database topology:

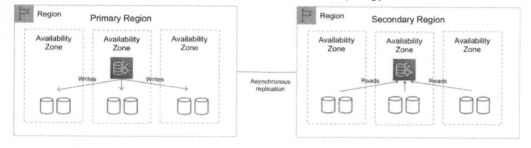

MULTI-MASTER

Amazon Aurora Multi-Master is a new feature of the Aurora MySQL-compatible edition that adds the ability to scale out write performance across multiple Availability Zones, allowing applications to direct read/write workloads to multiple instances in a database cluster and operate with higher availability.

Aurora Multi-Master is designed to achieve high availability and ACID transactions across a cluster of database nodes with configurable read after write consistency.

ARCHITECTURE

An Aurora cluster consists of a set of compute (database) nodes and a shared storage volume.

The storage volume consists of six storage nodes placed in three Availability Zones for high availability and durability of user data.

Every database node in the cluster is a writer node that can run read and write statements.

There is no single point of failure in the cluster.

Applications can use any writer node for their read/write and DDL needs.

A database change made by a writer node is written to six storage nodes in three Availability Zones, providing data durability and resiliency against storage node and Availability Zone failures.

The writer nodes are all functionally equal, and a failure of one writer node does not affect the availability of the other writer nodes in the cluster.

HIGH AVAILABILITY

Aurora Multi-Master improves upon the high availability of the single-master version of Amazon Aurora because all the nodes in the cluster are read/write nodes.

With single-master Aurora, a failure of the single writer node requires the promotion of a read replica to be the new writer.

In the case of Aurora Multi-Master, the failure of a writer node merely requires the application using the writer to open connections to another writer.

AURORA SERVERLESS

Amazon Aurora Serverless is an on-demand, auto-scaling configuration for Amazon Aurora.

Available for MySQL-compatible and PostgreSQL-compatible editions.

The database automatically starts up, shuts down, and scales capacity up or down based on application needs.

It enables you to run a database in the cloud without managing any database instances. It's a simple, cost-effective option for infrequent, intermittent, or unpredictable workloads.

You simply create a database endpoint and optionally specify the desired database capacity range and connect applications.

With Aurora Serverless, you only pay for database storage and the database capacity and I/O your database consumes while it is active.

Pay on a per-second basis for the database capacity you use when the database is active.

Can migrate between standard and serverless configurations with a few clicks in the Amazon RDS Management Console.

The table below provides a few example use cases for Amazon Aurora Serverless:

Use Case	Example

Infrequently Used Applications	Application that is only used for a few minutes several times per day or week. Need a cost-effective database that only requires you to pay when it's active. With Aurora Serverless, you only pay for the database resources you consume.
New Applications	Deploying a new application and are unsure which instance size you need. With Aurora Serverless, you simply create an endpoint and let the database auto-scale to the capacity requirements of your application.
Variable Workloads	Running a lightly used application, with peaks of 30 minutes to several hours a few times each day or several times per year. Now you only pay for what the resources needed based on load – avoiding paying for unused resources or risking poor performance.
Unpredictable Workloads	Running workloads where there is database usage throughout the day, and peaks of activity that are hard to predict. With Aurora Serverless, your database will auto-scale capacity to meet the needs of the application's peak load and scale back down when the surge of activity is over.
Development and Test Databases	Software development and QA teams are using databases during work hours, but don't need them on nights or weekends. With Aurora Serverless, your database automatically shuts down when not in use, and starts up much more quickly when work starts the next day.
Multitenant Applications	Web-based application with a database for each of your customers. Now you don't have to manage database capacity individually for each application in your fleet. Aurora manages individual database capacity for you, saving you valuable time.

FAULT-TOLERANT AND SELF-HEALING STORAGE

Each 10GB chunk of your database volume is replicated six ways, across three Availability Zones.

Amazon Aurora storage is fault-tolerant, transparently handling the loss of up to two copies of data without affecting database write availability and up to three copies without affecting read availability.

Amazon Aurora storage is also self-healing; data blocks and disks are continuously scanned for errors and replaced automatically.

AURORA AUTO SCALING

Aurora Auto Scaling dynamically adjusts the number of Aurora Replicas provisioned for an Aurora DB cluster using single-master replication.

Aurora Auto Scaling is available for both Aurora MySQL and Aurora PostgreSQL.

Aurora Auto Scaling enables your Aurora DB cluster to handle sudden increases in connectivity or workload.

When the connectivity or workload decreases, Aurora Auto Scaling removes unnecessary Aurora Replicas so that you don't pay for unused provisioned DB instances.

© 2023 Digital Cloud Training

BACKUP AND RESTORE

Amazon Aurora's backup capability enables point-in-time recovery for your instance.

This allows you to restore your database to any second during your retention period, up to the last five minutes.

Your automatic backup retention period can be configured up to thirty-five days.

Automated backups are stored in **Amazon S3**, which is designed for 99.999999999% durability. Amazon Aurora backups are automatic, incremental, and continuous and have no impact on database performance.

When automated backups are turned on for your DB Instance, Amazon RDS automatically performs a full daily snapshot of your data (during your preferred backup window) and captures transaction logs (as updates to your DB Instance are made).

Automated backups are enabled by default and data is stored on S3 and is equal to the size of the DB.

Amazon RDS retains backups of a DB Instance for a limited, user-specified period called the retention period, which by default is 7 days but can be up to 35 days.

There are two methods to backup and restore RDS DB instances:

- Amazon RDS automated backups.
- User initiated manual backups.

Both options back up the entire DB instance and not just the individual DBs.

Both options create a storage volume snapshot of the entire DB instance.

You can make copies of automated backups and manual snapshots.

Automated backups backup data to multiple AZs to provide for data durability.

Multi-AZ backups are taken from the standby instance (for MariaDB, MySQL, Oracle, and PostgreSQL).

The DB instance must be in an Active state for automated backups to happen.

Only automated backups can be used for point-in-time DB instance recovery.

The granularity of point-in-time recovery is 5 minutes.

Amazon RDS creates a daily full storage volume snapshot and captures transaction logs regularly.

You can choose the backup window.

There is no additional charge for backups, but you will pay for storage costs on S3.

You can disable automated backups by setting the retention period to zero (0).

An outage occurs if you change the backup retention period from zero to a non-zero value or the other way around.

The retention period is the period AWS keeps the automated backups before deleting them.

Retention periods:

- By default the retention period is 7 days if configured from the console for all DB engines except Aurora.
- The default retention period is 1 day if configured from the API or CLI.
- The retention period for Aurora is 1 day regardless of how it is configured.

- You can increase the retention period up to 35 days.

During the backup window I/O may be suspended.

Automated backups are deleted when you delete the RDS DB instance.

Automated backups are only supported for InnoDB storage engine for MySQL (not for myISAM).

When you restore a DB instance the default DB parameters and security groups are applied – you must then apply the custom DB parameters and security groups.

You cannot restore from a DB snapshot into an existing DB instance.

Following a restore the new DB instance will have a new endpoint.

The storage type can be changed when restoring a snapshot.

AMAZON ELASTICACHE

AMAZON ELASTICACHE FEATURES

Fully managed implementations of two popular in-memory data stores – Redis and Memcached.

ElastiCache is a web service that makes it easy to deploy and run Memcached or Redis protocol-compliant server nodes in the cloud.

The in-memory caching provided by ElastiCache can be used to significantly improve latency and throughput for many read-heavy application workloads or compute-intensive workloads.

Best for scenarios where the DB load is based on Online Analytics Processing (OLAP) transactions.

Push-button scalability for memory, writes and reads.

In-memory key/value store – not persistent in the traditional sense.

Billed by node size and hours of use.

ElastiCache EC2 nodes cannot be accessed from the Internet, nor can they be accessed by EC2 instances in other VPCs.

Cached information may include the results of I/O-intensive database queries or the results of computationally intensive calculations.

Can be on-demand or reserved instances too (but not Spot instances).

ElastiCache can be used for storing session state.

A node is a fixed-sized chunk of secure, network-attached RAM and is the smallest building block.

Each node runs an instance of the Memcached or Redis protocol-compliant service and has its own DNS name and port.

Failed nodes are automatically replaced.

Access to ElastiCache nodes is controlled by VPC security groups and subnet groups (when deployed in a VPC).

Subnet groups are a collection of subnets designated for your Amazon ElastiCache Cluster.

You cannot move an existing Amazon ElastiCache Cluster from outside VPC into a VPC.

You need to configure subnet groups for ElastiCache for the VPC that hosts the EC2 instances and the ElastiCache cluster.

© 2023 Digital Cloud Training

When not using a VPC, Amazon ElastiCache allows you to control access to your clusters through Cache Security Groups (you need to link the corresponding EC2 Security Groups).

ElastiCache nodes are deployed in clusters and can span more than one subnet of the same subnet group.

A cluster is a collection of one or more nodes using the same caching engine.

Applications connect to ElastiCache clusters using endpoints.

An endpoint is a node or cluster's unique address.

Maintenance windows can be defined and allow software patching to occur.

There are two types of ElastiCache engine:

- Memcached – simplest model, can run large nodes with multiple cores/threads, can be scaled in and out, can cache objects such as DBs.
- Redis – complex model, supports encryption, master / slave replication, cross AZ (HA), automatic failover and backup/restore.

USE CASES

The following table describes a few typical use cases for ElastiCache:

Use Case	Benefit
Web session store	In cases with load-balanced web servers, store web session information in Redis so if a server is lost, the session info is not lost, and another web server can pick it up
Database caching	Use Memcached in front of AWS RDS to cache popular queries to offload work from RDS and return results faster to users
Leaderboards	Use Redis to provide a live leaderboard for millions of users of your mobile app
Streaming data dashboards	Provide a landing spot for streaming sensor data on the factory floor, providing live real-time dashboard displays

Exam tip: the key use cases for ElastiCache are offloading reads from a database and storing the results of computations and session state. Also, remember that ElastiCache is an in-memory database and it's a managed service (so you can't run it on EC2).

The table below describes the requirements that would determine whether to use the Memcached or Redis engine:

Memcached	Redis
Simple, no-frills	You need encryption
You need to elasticity (scale out and in)	You need HIPAA compliance
You need to run multiple CPU cores and threads	Support for clustering
You need to cache objects (e.g. database queries)	You need complex data types

	You need HA (replication
	Pub/Sub capability

MEMCACHED

Simplest model and can run large nodes.

It can be scaled in and out and cache objects such as DBs.

Widely adopted memory object caching system.

Multi-threaded.

Scales out and in, by adding and removing nodes.

Ideal front-end for data stores (RDS, Dynamo DB etc.).

Use cases:

- Cache the contents of a DB.
- Cache data from dynamically generated web pages.
- Transient session data.
- High frequency counters for admission control in high volume web apps.

Max 100 nodes per region, 1-20 nodes per cluster (soft limits).

Can integrate with SNS for node failure/recovery notification.

Supports auto-discovery for nodes added/removed from the cluster.

Scales out/in (horizontally) by adding/removing nodes.

Scales up/down (vertically) by changing the node family/type.

Does not support multi-AZ failover or replication.

Does not support snapshots.

You can place nodes in different AZs.

With ElastiCache Memcached each node represents a partition of data and nodes in a cluster can span availability zones:

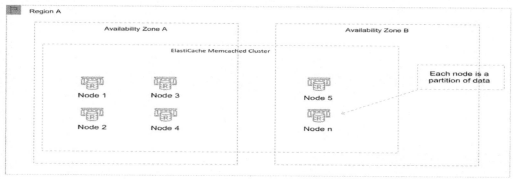

REDIS

Open-source in-memory key-value store.

Supports more complex data structures: sorted sets and lists.

Data is persistent and it can be used as a datastore.

Redis is not multi-threaded.

Scales by adding shards, not nodes.

Supports master / slave replication and multi-AZ for cross-AZ redundancy.

Supports automatic failover and backup/restore.

A Redis shard is a subset of the cluster's keyspace, that can include a primary node and zero or more read replicas.

Supports automatic and manual snapshots (S3).

Backups include cluster data and metadata.

You can restore your data by creating a new Redis cluster and populating it from a backup.

During backup you cannot perform CLI or API operations on the cluster.

Automated backups are enabled by default (automatically deleted with Redis deletion).

You can only move snapshots between regions by exporting them from ElastiCache before moving between regions (can then populate a new cluster with data).

Clustering mode disabled

You can only have one shard.

One shard can have one read/write primary node and 0-5 read only replicas.

You can distribute the replicas over multiple AZs in the same region.

Replication from the primary node is asynchronous.

A Redis cluster with cluster mode disabled is represented in the diagram below:

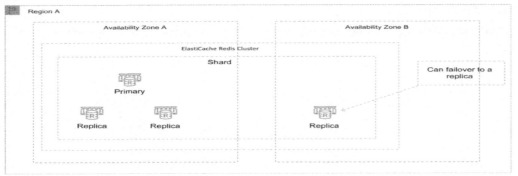

Clustering mode enabled

Can have up to 15 shards.

Each shard can have one primary node and 0-5 read only replicas.

Taking snapshots can slow down nodes, best to take from the read replicas.

A Redis cluster with cluster mode enabled is represented in the diagram below:

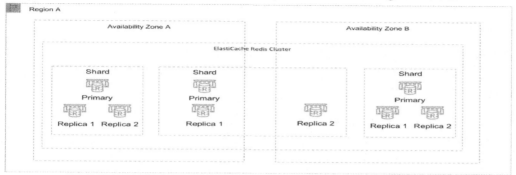

MULTI-AZ FAILOVER

Failures are detected by ElastiCache.

ElastiCache automatically promotes the replica that has the lowest replica lag.

DNS records remain the same but point to the IP of the new primary.

Other replicas start to sync with the new primary.

You can have a fully automated, fault tolerant ElastiCache-Redis implementation by enabling both cluster mode and multi-AZ failover.

The following table compares the Memcached and Redis engines:

Feature	Memcached	Redis (cluster mode disabled)	Redis (cluster mode enabled)
Data persistence	No	Yes	Yes
Data types	Simple	Complex	Complex
Data partitioning	Yes	No	Yes
Encryption	No	Yes	Yes
High availability (replication)	No	Yes	Yes
Multi-AZ	Yes, place nodes in multiple AZs. No failover or replication	Yes, with auto-failover. Uses read replicas (0-5 per shard)	Yes, with auto-failover. Uses read replicas (0-5 per shard)
Scaling	Up (node type); out (add nodes)	Single shard (can add replicas)	Add shards
Multithreaded	Yes	No	No

Backup and restore	No (and no snapshots)	Yes, automatic and manual snapshots	Yes, automatic and manual snapshots

CACHING STRATEGIES

There are two caching strategies available: Lazy Loading and Write-Through:

Lazy Loading

- Loads the data into the cache only when necessary (if a cache miss occurs).
- Lazy loading avoids filling up the cache with data that won't be requested.
- If requested data is in the cache, ElastiCache returns the data to the application.
- If the data is not in the cache or has expired, ElastiCache returns a null.
- The application then fetches the data from the database and writes the data received into the cache so that it is available for next time.
- Data in the cache can become stale if Lazy Loading is implemented without other strategies (such as TTL).

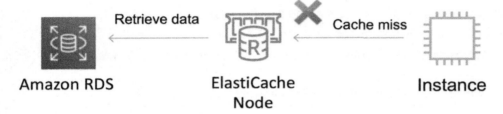

Write Through

- When using a write-through strategy, the cache is updated whenever a new write or update is made to the underlying database.
- Allows cache data to remain up to date.
- This can add wait time to write operations in your application.
- Without a TTL you can end up with a lot of cached data that is never read.

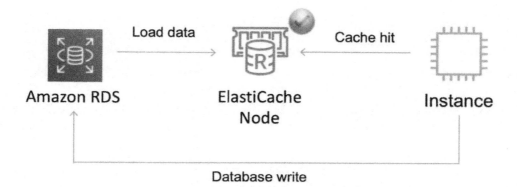

DEALING WITH STALE DATA – TIME TO LIVE (TTL)

- The drawbacks of lazy loading and write through techniques can be mitigated by a TTL.
- The TTL specifies the number of seconds until the key (data) expires to avoid keeping stale data in the cache.
- When reading an expired key, the application checks the value in the underlying database.
- Lazy Loading treats an expired key as a cache miss and causes the application to retrieve the data from the database and subsequently write the data into the cache with a new TTL.
- Depending on the frequency with which data changes this strategy may not eliminate stale data – but helps to avoid it.

Exam tip: Compared to DynamoDB Accelerator (DAX) remember that DAX is optimized for DymamoDB specifically and only supports the write-through caching strategy (does not use lazy loading).

MONITORING AND REPORTING

Memcached Metrics

The following CloudWatch metrics offer good insight into ElastiCache Memcached performance:

CPUUtilization – This is a host-level metric reported as a percent. Because Memcached is multi-threaded, this metric can be as high as 90%. If you exceed this threshold, scale your cache cluster up by using a larger cache node type, or scale out by adding more cache nodes.

SwapUsage – This is a host-level metric reported in bytes. This metric should not exceed 50 MB. If it does, we recommend that you increase the ConnectionOverhead parameter value.

Evictions – This is a cache engine metric. If you exceed your chosen threshold, scale your cluster up by using a larger node type, or scale out by adding more nodes.

CurrConnections – This is a cache engine metric. An increasing number of CurrConnections might indicate a problem with your application; you will need to investigate the application behavior to address this issue.

Redis Metrics

The following CloudWatch metrics offer good insight into ElastiCache Redis performance:

EngineCPUUtilization – Provides CPU utilization of the Redis engine thread. Since Redis is single threaded, you can use this metric to analyze the load of the Redis process itself.

MemoryFragmentationRatio – Indicates the efficiency in the allocation of memory of the Redis engine. Certain threshold will signify different behaviors. The recommended value is to have fragmentation above 1.0.

CacheHits – The number of successful read-only key lookups in the main dictionary.

CacheMisses – The number of unsuccessful read-only key lookups in the main dictionary.

CacheHitRate – Indicates the usage efficiency of the Redis instance. If the cache ratio is lower than ~0.8, it means that a significant number of keys are evicted, expired, or do not exist.

CurrConnections – The number of client connections, excluding connections from read replicas. ElastiCache uses two to four of the connections to monitor the cluster in each case.

LOGGING AND AUDITING

All Amazon ElastiCache actions are logged by AWS CloudTrail.

Every event or log entry contains information about who generated the request. The identity information helps you determine the following:

- Whether the request was made with root or IAM user credentials.
- Whether the request was made with temporary security credentials for a role or federated user.
- Whether the request was made by another AWS service.

AUTHORIZATION AND ACCESS CONTROL

Access to Amazon ElastiCache requires credentials that AWS can use to authenticate your requests. Those credentials must have permissions to access AWS resources, such as an ElastiCache cache cluster or an Amazon Elastic Compute Cloud (Amazon EC2) instance.

You can use **identity-based policies** with Amazon ElastiCache to provide the necessary access.

You can use **Redis Auth** to require a token with ElastiCache Redis.

The Redis authentication tokens enable Redis to require a token (password) before allowing clients to run commands, thereby improving data security.

CHARGES

Pricing is per Node-hour consumed for each Node Type.

Partial Node-hours consumed are billed as full hours.

There is no charge for data transfer between Amazon EC2 and Amazon ElastiCache within the same Availability Zone.

High Availability for ElastiCache

Memcached:

- Because Memcached does not support replication, a node failure will result in data loss.

- Use multiple nodes to minimize data loss on node failure.
- Launch multiple nodes across available AZs to minimize data loss on AZ failure.

Redis:

- Use multiple nodes in each shard and distribute the nodes across multiple AZs.
- Enable Multi-AZ on the replication group to permit automatic failover if the primary nodes fail.
- Schedule regular backups of your Redis cluster.

MANAGEMENT TOOLS

AWS ORGANIZATIONS

AWS ORGANIZATIONS FEATURES

AWS Organizations helps you centrally manage and govern your environment as you grow and scale your AWS resources.

AWS accounts are natural boundaries for permissions, security, costs, and workloads.

Using a multi-account environment is a recommended best-practice when scaling your cloud environment.

AWS Organizations provides many features for managing multi-account environments, including:

- Simplify account creation by programmatically creating new accounts using the AWS Command Line Interface (CLI), SDKs, or APIs.
- Group accounts into organizational units (OUs), or groups of accounts that serve a single application or service.
- Apply tag polices to classify or track resources in your organization and provide attribute-based access control for users or applications.
- Delegate responsibility for supported AWS services to accounts so users can manage them on behalf of your organization.
- Centrally provide tools and access for your security team to manage security needs on behalf of the organization.
- Set up Amazon Single Sign-On (SSO) to provide access to AWS accounts and resources using your active directory, and customize permissions based on separate job roles.
- Apply service control policies (SCPs) to users, accounts, or OUs to control access to AWS resources, services, and Regions within your organization.
- Share AWS resources within your organization using AWS Resource Allocation Management (RAM).
- Activate AWS CloudTrail across accounts, which creates a log of all activity in your cloud environment that cannot be turned off or modified by member accounts.
- Organizations provides you with a single consolidated bill.
- In addition, you can view usage from resources across accounts and track costs using AWS Cost Explorer and optimize your usage of compute resources using AWS Compute Optimizer.

AWS Organizations is available to all AWS customers at no additional charge.

The AWS Organizations API enables automation for account creation and management.

AWS Organizations is available in two feature sets:

- Consolidated billing.
- All features.

By default, organizations support consolidated billing features.

Consolidated billing separates paying accounts and linked accounts.

You can use AWS Organizations to set up a single payment method for all the AWS accounts in your organization through consolidated billing.

With consolidated billing, you can see a combined view of charges incurred by all your accounts.

Can also take advantage of pricing benefits from aggregated usage, such as volume discounts for Amazon EC2 and Amazon S3.

Limit of 20 linked accounts for consolidated billing (default).

Policies can be assigned at different points in the hierarchy.

Can help with cost control through volume discounts.

Unused reserved EC2 instances are applied across the group.

Paying accounts should be used for billing purposes only.

Billing alerts can be setup at the paying account which shows billing for all linked accounts.

KEY CONCEPTS

Some of the key concepts you need to understand are listed here:

AWS Organization – An organization is a collection of AWS accounts that you can organize into a hierarchy and manage centrally.

AWS Account – An AWS account is a container for your AWS resources.

Management Account – A management account is the AWS account you use to create your organization.

Member Account – A member account is an AWS account, other than the management account, that is part of an organization.

Administrative Root – An administrative root is the starting point for organizing your AWS accounts. The administrative root is the top-most container in your organization's hierarchy.

Organizational Unit (OU) – An organizational unit (OU) is a group of AWS accounts within an organization. An OU can also contain other OUs enabling you to create a hierarchy.

Policy – A policy is a "document" with one or more statements that define the controls that you want to apply to a group of AWS accounts. AWS Organizations supports a specific type of policy called a Service Control Policy (SCP). An SCP defines the AWS service actions, such as Amazon EC2 RunInstances, that are available for use in different accounts within an organization.

Best practices for the management account:

- Use the management account only for tasks that require the management account.
- Use a group email address for the management account's root user.
- Use a complex password for the management account's root user.
- Enable MFA for your root user credentials.
- Add a phone number to the account contact information.
- Review and keep track of who has access.
- Document the processes for using the root user credentials.
- Apply controls to monitor access to the root user credentials.

MIGRATING ACCOUNTS BETWEEN ORGANIZATIONS

Accounts can be migrated between organizations.

You must have root or IAM access to both the member and management accounts.

Use the AWS Organizations console for just a few accounts.

Use the AWS Organizations API or AWS Command Line Interface (AWS CLI) if there are many accounts to migrate.

Billing history and billing reports for all accounts stay with the management account in an organization.

Before migration download any billing or report history for any member accounts that you want to keep.

When a member account leaves an organization, all charges incurred by the account are charged directly to the standalone account.

Even if the account move only takes a minute to process, it is likely that some charges will be incurred by the member account.

SERVICE CONTROL POLICIES (SCPS)

Service control policies (SCPs) are a type of organization policy that you can use to manage permissions in your organization.

SCPs offer central control over the maximum available permissions for all accounts in your organization. SCPs help you to ensure your accounts stay within your organization's access control guidelines.

SCPs are available only in an organization that has all features enabled.

SCPs aren't available if your organization has enabled only the consolidated billing features.

SCPs alone are not sufficient to granting permissions to the accounts in your organization.

No permissions are granted by an SCP. An SCP defines a guardrail, or sets limits, on the actions that the account's administrator can delegate to the IAM users and roles in the affected accounts.

The administrator must still attach identity-based or resource-based policies to IAM users or roles, or to the resources in your accounts to grant permissions.

The effective permissions are the logical intersection between what is allowed by the SCP and what is allowed by the IAM and resource-based policies.

SCP Inheritance:

- SCPs **affect only IAM users and roles** that are managed by accounts that are part of the organization. SCPs don't affect resource-based policies directly. They also don't affect users or roles from accounts outside the organization.
- An SCP restricts permissions for IAM users and roles in member accounts, including the member account's root user.
- Any account has only those permissions permitted by **every** parent above it.
- If a permission is blocked at any level above the account, either implicitly (by not being included in an Allow policy statement) or explicitly (by being included in a Deny policy statement), a user or role in the affected account can't use that permission, even if the account administrator attaches the AdministratorAccess IAM policy with */* permissions to the user.

- SCPs affect only **member** accounts in the organization. They have no effect on users or roles in the management account.
- Users and roles must still be granted permissions with appropriate IAM permission policies. A user without any IAM permission policies has no access, even if the applicable SCPs allow all services and all actions.
- If a user or role has an IAM permission policy that grants access to an action that is also allowed by the applicable SCPs, the user or role can perform that action.
- If a user or role has an IAM permission policy that grants access to an action that is either not allowed or explicitly denied by the applicable SCPs, the user or role can't perform that action.
- SCPs affect all users and roles in attached accounts, **including the root user**. The only exceptions are those described in <u>Tasks and entities not restricted by SCPs</u>.
- SCPs **do not** affect any service-linked role. Service-linked roles enable other AWS services to integrate with AWS Organizations and can't be restricted by SCPs.
- When you disable the SCP policy type in a root, all SCPs are automatically detached from all AWS Organizations entities in that root. AWS Organizations entities include organizational units, organizations, and accounts.
- If you reenable SCPs in a root, that root reverts to only the default FullAWSAccess policy automatically attached to all entities in the root.
- Any attachments of SCPs to AWS Organizations entities from before SCPs were disabled are lost and aren't automatically recoverable, although you can manually reattach them.
- If both a permissions boundary (an advanced IAM feature) and an SCP are present, then the boundary, the SCP, and the identity-based policy must all allow the action.

You **can't** use SCPs to restrict the following tasks:

- Any action performed by the management account.
- Any action performed using permissions that are attached to a service-linked role.
- Register for the Enterprise support plan as the root user.
- Change the AWS support level as the root user.
- Provide trusted signer functionality for CloudFront private content.
- Configure reverse DNS for an Amazon Lightsail email server as the root user.
- Tasks on some AWS-related services:
  - Alexa Top Sites.
  - Alexa Web Information Service.
  - Amazon Mechanical Turk.
  - Amazon Product Marketing API.

RESOURCE GROUPS

You can use resource groups to organize your AWS resources.

In AWS, a resource is an entity that you can work with.

Resource groups make it easier to manage and automate tasks on large numbers of resources at one time.

Resource groups allow you to group resources and then tag them.

The Tag Editor assists with finding resources and adding tags.

You can access Resource Groups through any of the following entry points:

- On the navigation bar of the AWS Management Console.
- In the AWS Systems Manager console, from the left navigation pane entry for Resource Groups.
- By using the Resource Groups API, in AWS CLI commands or AWS SDK programming languages.

A resource group is a collection of AWS resources that are all in the same AWS region, and that match criteria provided in a query.

In Resource Groups, there are two types of queries on which you can build a group.

Both query types include resources that are specified in the format AWS::service::resource.

- **Tag-based** – Tag-based queries include lists of resources and tags. Tags are keys that help identify and sort your resources within your organization. Optionally, tags include values for keys.
- **AWS CloudFormation stack-based** – In an AWS CloudFormation stack-based query, you choose an AWS CloudFormation stack in your account in the current region, and then choose resource types within the stack that you want to be in the group. You can base your query on only one AWS CloudFormation stack.

Resource groups can be nested; a resource group can contain existing resource groups in the same region.

AMAZON CLOUDWATCH

AMAZON CLOUDWATCH FEATURES

Amazon CloudWatch is a monitoring service for AWS cloud resources and the applications you run on AWS.

CloudWatch is used to collect and track metrics, collect, and monitor log files, and set alarms.

With CloudWatch you can:

- Gain system-wide visibility into resource utilization.
- Monitor application performance.
- Monitor operational health.

CloudWatch alarms monitor metrics and can be configured to automatically initiate actions.

CloudWatch Logs centralizes logs from systems, applications, and AWS services.

CloudWatch Events delivers a stream of system events that describe changes in AWS resources.

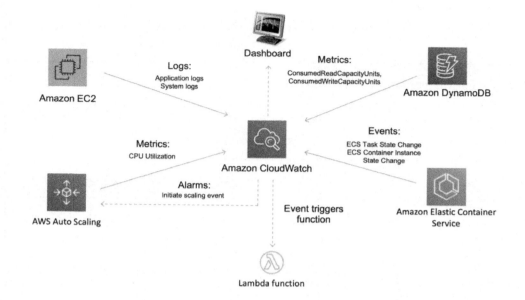

CloudWatch is accessed via API, command-line interface, AWS SDKs, and the AWS Management Console.

CloudWatch integrates with AWS IAM.

CloudWatch can automatically react to changes in your AWS resources.

With CloudWatch you can monitor resources such as:

- EC2 instances.
- DynamoDB tables.
- RDS DB instances.
- Custom metrics generated by applications and services.
- Any log files generated by your applications.

CloudWatch retains metric data as follows:

- Data points with a period of less than 60 seconds are available for 3 hours. These data points are high-resolution custom metrics.
- Data points with a period of 60 seconds (1 minute) are available for 15 days.
- Data points with a period of 300 seconds (5 minute) are available for 63 days.
- Data points with a period of 3600 seconds (1 hour) are available for 455 days (15 months).

AMAZON CLOUDWATCH VS AWS CLOUDTRAIL:

CloudWatch	CloudTrail
Performance monitoring	Auditing

Log events across AWS Services - think operations	Log API activity across AWS services - think activities, or who to blame
Higher-level comprehensive monitoring and event service	More low-level, granular
Log from multiple accounts	Log from multiple accounts
Logs stored indefinitely	Logs stored to S3 or CloudWatch indefinitely
Alarms history for 14 days	No native alarming; can use CloudWatch alarms

METRICS

Metrics are the fundamental concept in CloudWatch.

A metric represents a time-ordered set of data points that are published to CloudWatch.

AWS services send metrics to CloudWatch.

You can also send your own custom metrics to CloudWatch.

Metrics exist within a region.

Metrics cannot be deleted but automatically expire after 15 months.

Metrics are uniquely defined by a name, a namespace, and zero or more dimensions.

CloudWatch retains metric data as follows:

- Data points with a period of less than 60 seconds are available for 3 hours. These data points are high-resolution custom metrics.
- Data points with a period of 60 seconds (1 minute) are available for 15 days.
- Data points with a period of 300 seconds (5 minute) are available for 63 days.
- Data points with a period of 3600 seconds (1 hour) are available for 455 days (15 months).

CUSTOM METRICS

You can publish your own metrics to CloudWatch using the AWS CLI or an API.

You can view statistical graphs of your published metrics with the AWS Management Console.

CloudWatch stores data about a metric as a series of data points.

Each data point has an associated time stamp.

You can even publish an aggregated set of data points called a statistic set.

HIGH-RESOLUTION METRICS

Each metric is one of the following:

- Standard resolution, with data having a one-minute granularity
- High resolution, with data at a granularity of one second

Metrics produced by AWS services are standard resolution by default.

When you publish a custom metric, you can define it as either standard resolution or high resolution.

When you publish a high-resolution metric, CloudWatch stores it with a resolution of 1 second, and you can read and retrieve it with a period of 1 second, 5 seconds, 10 seconds, 30 seconds, or any multiple of 60 seconds.

High-resolution metrics can give you more immediate insight into your application's sub-minute activity.

Keep in mind that every PutMetricData call for a custom metric is charged, so calling PutMetricData more often on a high-resolution metric can lead to higher charges.

If you set an alarm on a high-resolution metric, you can specify a high-resolution alarm with a period of 10 seconds or 30 seconds, or you can set a regular alarm with a period of any multiple of 60 seconds.

There is a higher charge for high-resolution alarms with a period of 10 or 30 seconds.

NAMESPACE

A namespace is a container for CloudWatch metrics.

Metrics in different namespaces are isolated from each other, so that metrics from different applications are not mistakenly aggregated into the same statistics.

The following table provides some examples of namespaces for several AWS services:

Service	Namespace
Amazon API Gateway	AWS/ApiGateway
Amazon CloudFront	AWS/CloudFront
AWS CloudHSM	AWS/CloudHSM
Amazon CloudWatch Logs	AWS/Logs
AWS CodeBuild	AWS/CodeBuild
Amazon Cognito	AWS/Cognito
Amazon DynamoDB	AWS/DynamoDB
Amazon EC2	AWS/EC2
AWS Elastic Beanstalk	AWS/ElasticBeanstalk

DIMENSIONS

In custom metrics, the –dimensions parameter is common.

A dimension further clarifies what the metric is and what data it stores.

You can have up to 10 dimensions in one metric, and each dimension is defined by a name and value pair.

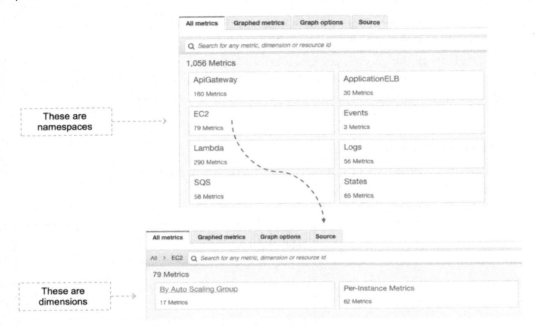

How you specify a dimension is different when you use different commands.

With put-metric-data, you specify each dimension as MyName=MyValue, and with get-metric-statistics or put-metric-alarm you use the format Name=MyName, Value=MyValue.

For example, the following command publishes a Buffers metric with two dimensions named InstanceId and InstanceType.

aws cloudwatch put-metric-data --metric-name Buffers --namespace MyNameSpace --unit Bytes --value 231434333 --dimensions InstanceId=1-23456789,InstanceType=m1.small

This command retrieves statistics for that same metric. Separate the Name and Value parts of a single dimension with commas, but if you have multiple dimensions, use a space between one dimension and the next.

aws cloudwatch get-metric-statistics --metric-name Buffers --namespace MyNameSpace --dimensions Name=InstanceId,Value=1-23456789 Name=InstanceType,Value=m1.small --start-time 2016-10-15T04:00:00Z --end-time 2016-10-19T07:00:00Z --statistics Average --period 60

If a single metric includes multiple dimensions, you must specify a value for every defined dimension when you use get-metric-statistics. For example, the Amazon S3 metric BucketSizeBytes includes the dimensions BucketName and StorageType, so you must specify both dimensions with get-metric-statistics.

aws cloudwatch get-metric-statistics --metric-name BucketSizeBytes --start-time 2017-01-23T14:23:00Z --end-time 2017-01-26T19:30:00Z --period 3600 --namespace AWS/S3 --statistics Maximum -- dimensions Name=BucketName,Value=MyBucketName Name=StorageType,Value=StandardStorage -- output table

Publishing Single Data Points

To publish a single data point for a new or existing metric, use the <u>put-metric-data</u> command with one value and time stamp.

For example, the following actions each publish one data point.

aws cloudwatch put-metric-data --metric-name PageViewCount --namespace MyService --value 2 -- timestamp 2016-10-20T12:00:00.000Z

aws cloudwatch put-metric-data --metric-name PageViewCount --namespace MyService --value 4 -- timestamp 2016-10-20T12:00:01.000Z

aws cloudwatch put-metric-data --metric-name PageViewCount --namespace MyService --value 5 -- timestamp 2016-10-20T12:00:02.000Z

STATISTICS

Statistics are metric data aggregations over specified periods of time.

CloudWatch provides statistics based on the metric data points provided by your custom data or provided by other AWS services to CloudWatch.

Statistic	Description
Minimum	The lowest value observed during the specified period. You can use this value to determine low volumes of activity for your application.
Maximum	The highest value observed during the specified period. You can use this value to determine high volumes of activity for your application.
Sum	All values submitted for the matching metric added together. This statistic can be useful for determining the total volume of a metric.
Average	The value Sum/SampleCount during the specific period. By comparing this statistic with the Minimum and Maximum you can determine the full scope of a metric and how close the average is to the Minimum and Maximum. This comparison helps you know when to increase or decrease your resources as needed.
SampleCount	The count (number) of data points used for the statistical calculation.

© 2023 Digital Cloud Training

pNN.NN	The value of the specified percentile. You can specify and percentile using up to two decimal places (e.. p45.45). Percentile statistics are not available for metric that include negative values. For more information see Percentiles.

CLOUDWATCH ALARMS

You can use an alarm to automatically initiate actions on your behalf.

An alarm watches a single metric over a specified time period, and performs one or more specified actions, based on the value of the metric relative to a threshold over time.

The action is a notification sent to an Amazon SNS topic or an Auto Scaling policy.

You can also add alarms to dashboards.

Alarms invoke actions for sustained state changes only.

CloudWatch alarms do not invoke actions simply because they are in a particular state.

The state must have changed and been maintained for a specified number of periods.

CLOUDWATCH LOGS

Amazon CloudWatch Logs lets you monitor and troubleshoot your systems and applications using your existing system, application, and custom log files.

You can use Amazon CloudWatch Logs to monitor, store, and access your log files from Amazon Elastic Compute Cloud (Amazon EC2) instances, AWS CloudTrail, Route 53, and other sources.

Features:

- **Monitor logs from Amazon EC2 instances** – monitors application and system logs and can trigger notifications.
- **Monitor CloudTrail Logged Events** – alarms can be created in CloudWatch based on API activity captured by CloudTrail.
- **Log retention** – by default, logs are retained indefinitely. Configurable per log group from 1 day to 10 years.

CloudWatch Logs can be used for real time application and system monitoring as well as long term log retention.

CloudTrail logs can be sent to CloudWatch Logs for real-time monitoring.

CloudWatch Logs metric filters can evaluate CloudTrail logs for specific terms, phrases, or values.

CLOUDWATCH LOGS AGENT

The CloudWatch Logs agent provides an automated way to send log data to CloudWatch Logs from Amazon EC2 instances.

There is now a unified CloudWatch agent that collects both logs and metrics.

The unified CloudWatch agent includes metrics such as memory and disk utilization.

The unified CloudWatch agent enables you to do the following:

- Collect more system-level metrics from Amazon EC2 instances across operating systems. The

metrics can include in-guest metrics, in addition to the metrics for EC2 instances.
- Collect system-level metrics from on-premises servers. These can include servers in a hybrid environment as well as servers not managed by AWS.
- Retrieve custom metrics from your applications or services using the StatsD and collectd protocols.

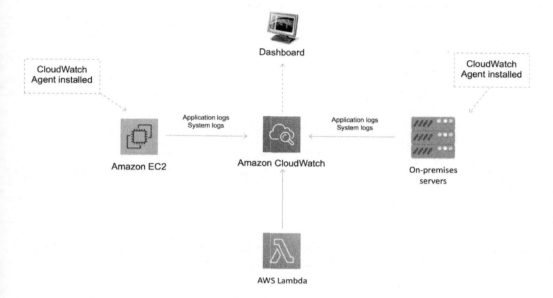

CLOUDWATCH EVENTS

Amazon CloudWatch Events delivers a near real-time stream of system events that describe changes in AWS resources.

Can use CloudWatch Events to schedule automated actions that self-trigger at certain times using cron or rate expressions

Can match events and route them to one or more target functions or streams.

Targets include:

- Amazon EC2 instances.
- AWS Lambda functions.
- Streams in Amazon Kinesis Data Streams.
- Delivery streams in Amazon Kinesis Data Firehose.
- Log groups in Amazon CloudWatch Logs.
- Amazon ECS tasks.
- Systems Manager Run Command.
- Systems Manager Automation.
- AWS Batch jobs.
- Step Functions state machines.
- Pipelines in CodePipeline.

- CodeBuild projects.
- Amazon Inspector assessment templates.
- Amazon SNS topics.
- Amazon SQS queues.

In the following example, an EC2 instance changes state (terminated) and the event is sent to CloudWatch Events which forwards the event to the target (SQS queue).

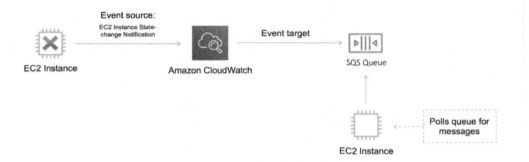

Useful API Actions

It is useful to understand the following API actions for the Developer Associate exam. You should check these out and other API actions on the AWS website as well prior to your exam.

GetMetricData

- Retrieve as many as 500 different metrics in a single request.

PutMetricData

- Publishes metric data points to Amazon CloudWatch.
- CloudWatch associates the data points with the specified metric.
- If the specified metric does not exist, CloudWatch creates the metric.

GetMetricStatistics

- Gets statistics for the specified metric.
- CloudWatch aggregates data points based on the length of the period that you specify.
- Maximum number of data points returned from a single call is 1,440.

PutMetricAlarm

- Creates or updates an alarm and associates it with the specified metric, metric math expression, or anomaly detection model.
- Alarms based on anomaly detection models cannot have Auto Scaling actions.

AWS CLOUDTRAIL

AWS CLOUDTRAIL FEATURES

AWS CloudTrail is a web service that records activity made on your account.

A CloudTrail trail can be created which delivers log files to an Amazon S3 bucket.

CloudTrail is about logging and saves a history of API calls for your AWS account.

CloudTrail enables governance, compliance, and operational and risk auditing of your AWS account.

Events include actions taken in the AWS Management Console, AWS Command Line Interface, and AWS SDKs and APIs.

CloudTrail provides visibility into user activity by recording actions taken on your account.

API history enables security analysis, resource change tracking, and compliance auditing.

Logs API calls made via:

- AWS Management Console.
- AWS SDKs.
- Command line tools.
- Higher-level AWS services (such as CloudFormation).

CloudTrail records account activity and service events from most AWS services and logs the following records:

- The identity of the API caller.
- The time of the API call.
- The source IP address of the API caller.
- The request parameters.
- The response elements returned by the AWS service.

CloudTrail is enabled on your AWS account when you create it.

CloudTrail is per AWS account.

You can create two types of trails for an AWS account:

- A trail that applies to all regions – records events in all regions and delivers to an S3 bucket.
- A trail that applies to a single region – records events in a single region and delivers to an S3 bucket. Additional single trails can use the same or a different S3 bucket.

Trails can be configured to log data events and management events:

- **Data events:** These events provide insight into the resource operations performed on or within a resource. These are also known as data plane operations.
- **Management events:** Management events provide insight into management operations that are performed on resources in your AWS account. These are also known as control plane operations. Management events can also include non-API events that occur in your account.

Example data events include:

- Amazon S3 object-level API activity (for example, GetObject, DeleteObject, and PutObject API operations).
- AWS Lambda function execution activity (the Invoke API).

Example management events include:

- Configuring security (for example, IAM AttachRolePolicy API operations).
- Registering devices (for example, Amazon EC2 CreateDefaultVpc API operations).
- Configuring rules for routing data (for example, Amazon EC2 CreateSubnet API operations).
- Setting up logging (for example, AWS CloudTrail CreateTrail API operations).

- CloudTrail log files are encrypted using S3 Server Side Encryption (SSE).

You can also enable encryption using SSE KMS for additional security.

A single KMS key can be used to encrypt log files for trails applied to all regions.

You can consolidate logs from multiple accounts using an S3 bucket:

1. Turn on CloudTrail in the paying account.
2. Create a bucket policy that allows cross-account access.
3. Turn on CloudTrail in the other accounts and use the bucket in the paying account.

You can integrate CloudTrail with CloudWatch Logs to deliver data events captured by CloudTrail to a CloudWatch Logs log stream.

CloudTrail log file integrity validation feature allows you to determine whether a CloudTrail log file was unchanged, deleted, or modified since CloudTrail delivered it to the specified Amazon S3 bucket.

CloudWatch vs CloudTrail:

CloudWatch	CloudTrail
Performance monitoring	Auditing
Log events across AWS services – think operations	Log API activity across AWS services – think activities
Higher-level comprehensive monitoring and events	More low-level granular
Log from multiple accounts	Log from multiple accounts
Logs stored indefinitely	Logs stored to S3 or CloudWatch indefinitely
Alarms history for 14 days	No native alarming; can use CloudWatch alarms

AWS OPSWORKS

AWS OPSWORKS FEATURES

AWS OpsWorks is a configuration management service that provides managed instances of Chef and Puppet two very popular automation platforms.

Automates how applications are configured, deployed, and managed.

Provide configuration management to deploy code, automate tasks, configure instances, perform upgrades etc.

OpsWorks lets you use Chef and Puppet to automate how servers are configured, deployed, and managed across your Amazon EC2 instances or on-premises compute environments.

OpsWorks is an automation platform that transforms infrastructure into code.

OpsWorks consists of Stacks and Layers:

- Stacks are collections of resources needed to support a service or application.

- Stacks are containers of resources (EC2, RDS etc.) that you want to manage collectively.
- Every Stack contains one or more Layers and Layers automate the deployment of packages.
- Stacks can be cloned – but only within the same region.
- Layers represent different components of the application delivery hierarchy.
- EC2 instances, RDS instances, and ELBS are examples of Layers.

OpsWorks is a global service. But when you create a stack, you must specify a region and that stack can only control resources in that region.

There are three offerings: OpsWorks for Chef Automate, OpsWorks for Puppet Enterprise, and OpsWorks Stacks.

AWS OPSWORKS FOR CHEF AUTOMATE

- A fully managed configuration management service that hosts Chef Automate, a suite of automation tools from Chef for configuration management, compliance and security, and continuous deployment.
- Completely compatible with tooling and cookbooks from the Chef community and automatically registers new nodes with your Chef server.
- Chef server stores recipes and configuration data.
- Chef client (node) is installed on each server.

AWS OPSWORKS FOR PUPPET ENTERPRISE

- A fully managed configuration management service that hosts Puppet Enterprise, a set of automation tools from Puppet for **infrastructure and application management.**

AWS OPSWORKS STACKS

- An application and server management service that allows you to model your application as a stack containing different layers, such as load balancing, database, and application server.
- OpsWorks Stacks is an AWS creation and uses and embedded Chef Solo client installed on EC2 instances to run Chef recipes.

OpsWorks Stacks supports EC2 instances and on-premises servers as well as an agent.

AWS CLOUDFORMATION

AWS CLOUDFORMATION FEATURES

AWS CloudFormation is a service that allows you to manage, configure and provision your AWS infrastructure as code.

AWS CloudFormation provides a common language for you to describe and provision all the infrastructure resources in your cloud environment.

Resources are defined using a CloudFormation template.

CloudFormation interprets the template and makes the appropriate API calls to create the resources you have defined.

Supports YAML or JSON.

CloudFormation can be used to provision a broad range of AWS resources.

Think of CloudFormation as deploying infrastructure as code.

CloudFormation has some similarities with AWS Elastic Beanstalk though they are also quite different as detailed in the table below:

CloudFormation	Elastic Beanstalk
"Template-driven provisioning"	"Web apps made easy"
Deploys infrastructure using code	Deploys applications on EC2 (PaaS)
Can be used to deploy almost any AWS service	Deploys web applications based on Java, .NET, PHP, Node.js, Python, Ruby, Go, and Docker
Uses JSON or YAML template files	Uses ZIP or WAR files
Similar to Terraform	Similar to Google App Engine

KEY BENEFITS

Infrastructure is provisioned consistently, with fewer mistakes (human error).

Less time and effort than configuring resources manually.

You can use version control and peer review for your CloudFormation templates.

Free to use (you're only charged for the resources provisioned).

It can be used to manage updates and dependencies.

It can be used to rollback and delete the entire stack as well.

KEY CONCEPTS

The following table describes the key concepts associated with AWS CloudFormation:

Component	Description
Templates	The JSON or YAML text file that contains the instructions for building out the AWS environment
Stacks	The entire environment described by the template and created, updated, and deleted as a single unit
StackSets	AWS CloudFormation StackSets extends the functionality of stacks by enabling you to create, update, or delete stacks across multiple accounts and regions with a single operation
Change Sets	A summary of proposed changes to your stack that will allow you to see how those changes might impact your existing resources before implementing them
Templates	The JSON or YAML text file that contains the instructions for building out the AWS environment

TEMPLATES

A template is a YAML or JSON template used to describe the end-state of the infrastructure you are either provisioning or changing.

After creating the template, you upload it to CloudFormation directly or using Amazon S3.

CloudFormation reads the template and makes the API calls on your behalf.

The resulting resources are called a "Stack".

Logical IDs are used to reference resources within the template.

Physical IDs identify resources outside of AWS CloudFormation templates, but only after the resources have been created.

Template elements

Mandatory:

- List of resources and associated configuration values.

Not mandatory:

- Template parameters (limited to 60).
- Output values (limited to 60).
- List of data tables.

Template components

Resources – the *required* Resources section declares the AWS resources that you want to include in the stack, such as an Amazon EC2 instance or an Amazon S3 bucket.

- Mandatory.
- Represent AWS components that will be created.
- Resources are declared and can reference each other.

The following example YAML code declares an EC2 instance as a resource:

```
Resources:
 MyEC2Instance:
  Type: "AWS::EC2::Instance"
  Properties:
   ImageId: "ami-0ff8a91507f77f867"
```

Parameters

Use the *optional* Parameters section to customize your templates. Parameters enable you to input custom values to your template each time you create or update a stack.

- Provide inputs to your CloudFormation template.
- Useful for template reuse.

The following example declares a parameter named InstanceTypeParameter. This parameter lets you specify the Amazon EC2 instance type for the stack to use when you create or update the stack.

Note: *the InstanceTypeParameter has a default value of t2.micro. This is the value that AWS CloudFormation uses to provision the stack unless another value is provided.*

```
Parameters:
 InstanceTypeParameter:
  Type: String
  Default: t2.micro
  AllowedValues:
   - t2.micro
   - m1.small
   - m1.large
  Description: Enter t2.micro, m1.small, or m1.large. Default is t2.micro.
```

Pseudo Parameters

Pseudo parameters are parameters that are predefined by AWS CloudFormation. You do not declare them in your template. Use them the same way as you would a parameter, as the argument for the Ref function.

Examples include:

- AWS::AccountId – Returns the AWS account ID of the account in which the stack is being created.
- AWS::NotificationARNs – Returns the list of notification Amazon Resource Names (ARNs) for the current stack.
- AWS::Region – Returns a string representing the AWS Region in which the encompassing resource is being created.
- AWS::StackId – Returns the ID of the stack as specified with the aws cloudformation create-stack command.

Mappings

The *optional* Mappings section matches a key to a corresponding set of named values.

- Fixed variables.
- Good for differentiating between regions, environments, AMIs etc.
- Need to know the values in advance.
- For user-specific values use parameters instead.

The following example has region keys that are mapped to two sets of values: one named HVM64 and the other HVMG2.

```
RegionMap:
 us-east-1:
  HVM64: ami-0ff8a91507f77f867
  HVMG2: ami-0a584ac55a7631c0c
```

```
    us-west-1:
     HVM64: ami-0bdb828fd58c52235
     HVMG2: ami-066ee5fd4a9ef77f1
```

Exam tip: with mappings you can, for example, set values based on a region. You can create a mapping that uses the region name as a key and contains the values you want to specify for each specific region.

Outputs

The *optional* Outputs section declares output values that you can import into other stacks (to create cross-stack references), return in response (to describe stack calls), or view on the AWS CloudFormation console.

- Outputs can be imported into other stacks.
- Can view the outputs in the console or using the AWS CLI.
- Cannot delete a Stack if its outputs are being referenced by another CloudFormation Stack.

In the following example YAML code, the output named StackVPC returns the ID of a VPC, and then exports the value for cross-stack referencing with the name VPCID appended to the stack's name

```
    Outputs:
     StackVPC:
      Description: The ID of the VPC
      Value: !Ref MyVPC
      Export:
       Name: !Sub "${AWS::StackName}-VPCID"
```

Conditions

The *optional* Conditions section contains statements that define the circumstances under which entities are created or configured.

- Control the creation of resources based on a condition.
- Applied to resources and outputs.

In the sample YAML code below, resources are created only if the EnvType parameter is equal to prod:

```
    Conditions:
     CreateProdResources: !Equals [ !Ref EnvType, prod ]
```

Transform

The optional Transform section specifies one or more macros that AWS CloudFormation uses to process your template.

The transform section can be used to reference additional code stored in S3, such as Lambda code or reusable snippets of CloudFormation code.

The AWS::Serverless transform, which is a macro hosted by AWS CloudFormation, takes an entire template written in the AWS Serverless Application Model (AWS SAM) syntax and transforms and

© 2023 Digital Cloud Training

expands it into a compliant AWS CloudFormation template.

In the following example, the template uses AWS SAM syntax to simplify the declaration of a Lambda function and its execution role:

```
Transform: AWS::Serverless-2016-10-31
Resources:
 MyServerlessFunctionLogicalID:
   Type: AWS::Serverless::Function
   Properties:
     Handler: index.handler
     Runtime: nodejs8.10
     CodeUri: 's3://testBucket/mySourceCode.zip'
```

Intrinsic Functions

AWS CloudFormation provides several built-in functions that help you manage your stacks. Use intrinsic functions in your templates to assign values to properties that are not available until runtime.

EXAM TIP: *At a minimum, know the intrinsic functions listed below for the exam. The full list can be found at: https://docs.aws.amazon.com/AWSCloudFormation/latest/UserGuide/intrinsic-function-reference.html*

Ref

- Fn::Ref (or !Ref in YAML),
- The intrinsic function Ref returns the value of the specified parameter or resource.
- When you specify a parameter's logical name, it returns the value of the parameter.
- When you specify a resource's logical name, it returns a value that you can typically use to refer to that resource, such as a physical ID.

The following resource declaration for an Elastic IP address needs the instance ID of an EC2 instance and uses the Ref function to specify the instance ID of the MyEC2Instance resource:

```
MyEIP:
 Type: "AWS::EC2::EIP"
 Properties:
   InstanceId: !Ref MyEC2Instance
```

Fn::GetAtt

- The Fn::GetAtt intrinsic function returns the value of an attribute from a resource in the template.
- Full syntax (YAML): Fn::GetAtt: [logicalNameOfResource, attributeName]
- Short form (YAML): !GetAtt logicalNameOfResource.attributeName

The following example template returns the SourceSecurityGroup.OwnerAlias and SourceSecurityGroup.GroupName of the load balancer with the logical name myELB.

```
AWSTemplateFormatVersion: 2010-09-09
```

```
Resources:
 myELB:
  Type: AWS::ElasticLoadBalancing::LoadBalancer
  Properties:
   AvailabilityZones:
   - eu-west-1a
   Listeners:
   - LoadBalancerPort: '80'
    InstancePort: '80'
    Protocol: HTTP
 myELBIngressGroup:
  Type: AWS::EC2::SecurityGroup
  Properties:
   GroupDescription: ELB ingress group
   SecurityGroupIngress:
   - IpProtocol: tcp
    FromPort: '80'
    ToPort: '80'
    SourceSecurityGroupOwnerId: !GetAtt myELB.SourceSecurityGroup.OwnerAlias
    SourceSecurityGroupName: !GetAtt myELB.SourceSecurityGroup.GroupName
```

Fn::FindInMap

- The intrinsic function Fn::FindInMap returns the value corresponding to keys in a two-level map that is declared in the Mappings section.
- Full syntax (YAML): Fn::FindInMap: [MapName, TopLevelKey, SecondLevelKey]
- Short form (YAML): !FindInMap [MapName, TopLevelKey, SecondLevelKey]

The following example shows how to use Fn::FindInMap for a template with a Mappings section that contains a single map, RegionMap, that associates AMIs with AWS regions:

```
Mappings:
 RegionMap:
  us-east-1:
   HVM64: "ami-0ff8a91507f77f867"
   HVMG2: "ami-0a584ac55a7631c0c"
  us-west-1:
   HVM64: "ami-0bdb828fd58c52235"
   HVMG2: "ami-066ee5fd4a9ef77f1"
Resources:
 myEC2Instance:
  Type: "AWS::EC2::Instance"
  Properties:
   ImageId: !FindInMap
   - RegionMap
   - !Ref 'AWS::Region'
   - HVM64
```

InstanceType: m1.small

Fn::ImportValue

- The intrinsic function Fn::ImportValue returns the value of an output exported by another stack.
- You typically use this function to create cross-stack references.

Fn::ImportValue:
!Sub "${NetworkStackName}-SecurityGroupID"

Fn::Join

- Full syntax (YAML): Fn::Join: [delimiter, [comma-delimited list of values]]
- Short form (YAML): !Join [delimiter, [comma-delimited list of values]]

The following example uses Fn::Join to construct a string value. It uses the Ref function with the Partition parameter and the AWS::AccountId pseudo parameter.

!Join
- ''
- - 'arn:'
* - !Ref Partition*
* - ':s3:::elasticbeanstalk-*-'*
* - !Ref 'AWS::AccountId'*

Fn::Sub

- The intrinsic function Fn::Sub substitutes variables in an input string with values that you specify.
- In your templates, you can use this function to construct commands or outputs that include values that aren't available until you create or update a stack.

The following example uses a mapping to substitute the ${Domain} variable with the resulting value from the Ref function:

Name: !Sub
- www.${Domain}
- { Domain: !Ref RootDomainName }

STACKS AND STACK SETS

Stacks

Deployed resources based on templates.

Create, update, and delete stacks using templates.

Deployed through the Management Console, CLI or APIs.

Stack creation errors:

- Automatic rollback on error is enabled by default.
- You will be charged for resources provisioned even if there is an error.

Updating stacks:

- AWS CloudFormation provides two methods for updating stacks: direct update or creating and executing change sets.
- When you directly update a stack, you submit changes and AWS CloudFormation immediately deploys them.
- Use direct updates when you want to quickly deploy your updates.
- With change sets, you can preview the changes AWS CloudFormation will make to your stack, and then decide whether to apply those changes.

Stack Sets

AWS CloudFormation StackSets extends the functionality of stacks by enabling you to create, update, or delete stacks across multiple accounts and regions with a single operation.

Using an administrator account, you define and manage an AWS CloudFormation template, and use the template as the basis for provisioning stacks into selected target accounts across specified regions.

An administrator account is the AWS account in which you create stack sets.

A stack set is managed by signing in to the AWS administrator account in which it was created.

A target account is the account into which you create, update, or delete one or more stacks in your stack set.

Before you can use a stack set to create stacks in a target account, you must set up a trust relationship between the administrator and target accounts.

Nested Stacks

Nested stacks allow re-use of CloudFormation code for common use cases.

For example standard configuration for a load balancer, web server, application server etc.

Instead of copying out the code each time, create a standard template for each common use case and reference from within your CloudFormation template.

BEST PRACTICES

AWS provides Python "helper scripts" which can help you install software and start services on your EC2 instances.

- Use CloudFormation to make changes to your landscape rather than going directly into the resources.
- Make use of Change Sets to identify potential trouble spots in your updates.
- Use Stack Policies to explicitly protect sensitive portions of your stack.
- Use a version control system such as CodeCommit or GitHub to track changes to templates.

USER DATA WITH EC2

User data can be included in CloudFormation.

The script is passed into Fn::Base64

The user data script logs are stored in /var/log/cloud-init-output.log

Binary is available on Amazon EC2 at /opt/aws/bin/cfn-init

CLOUDFORMATION HELPER SCRIPTS

cfn-init:

- The cfn-init helper script reads template metadata from the AWS::CloudFormation::Init key and acts accordingly to:
- Fetch and parse metadata from AWS CloudFormation
- Install packages
- Write files to disk
- Enable/disable and start/stop services
- cfn-init does not require credentials, so you do not need to use the –access-key, –secret-key, –role, or –credential-file options.
- Logs go to /var/log/cfn-init.log

cfn-signal:

- The cfn-signal helper script signals AWS CloudFormation to indicate whether Amazon EC2 instances have been successfully created or updated.
- If you install and configure software applications on instances, you can signal AWS CloudFormation when those software applications are ready.
- You use the cfn-signal script in conjunction with a CreationPolicy or an Auto Scaling group with a WaitOnResourceSignals update policy.
- When AWS CloudFormation creates or updates resources with those policies, it suspends work on the stack until the resource receives the requisite number of signals or until the timeout period is exceeded.
- You can signal a creation policy (CreationPolicy) or a wait condition handle (WaitOnResourceSignals).

Troubleshooting errors:

- Make sure the AMI has the CloudFormation helper scripts included.
- Check that the cfn-init and cfn-signal commands have run successfully.
- Verify internet connectivity.

CREATION POLICIES AND WAIT CONDITIONS

- CreationPolicy attribute:
- Use the CreationPolicy attribute when you want to wait on resource configuration actions before stack creation proceeds.
- You can associate the CreationPolicy attribute with a resource to prevent its status from reaching create complete until AWS CloudFormation receives a specified number of success signals, or the timeout period is exceeded.
- To signal a resource, you can use the cfn-signal helper script or SignalResource API.
- AWS CloudFormation publishes valid signals to the stack events so that you track the number of signals sent.

The following CloudFormation resources support creation policies:

- AWS::AutoScaling::AutoScalingGroup
- AWS::EC2::Instance
- AWS::CloudFormation::WaitCondition

DeletionPolicy attribute:

- With the DeletionPolicy attribute you can preserve or (in some cases) backup a resource when its stack is deleted.
- You specify a DeletionPolicy attribute for each resource that you want to control.
- If a resource has no DeletionPolicy attribute, AWS CloudFormation deletes the resource by default.

DependsOn attribute:

- With the DependsOn attribute you can specify that the creation of a specific resource follows another.
- When you add a DependsOn attribute to a resource, that resource is created only after the creation of the resource specified in the DependsOn attribute.

WaitCondition:

- Note: For Amazon EC2 and Auto Scaling resources, AWS recommends that you use a CreationPolicy attribute instead of wait conditions.
- You can use a wait condition for situations like the following:
- To coordinate stack resource creation with configuration actions that are external to the stack creation.
- To track the status of a configuration process.

UpdatePolicy Attribute (WaitOnResourceSignals)

Use the UpdatePolicy attribute to specify how AWS CloudFormation handles updates to the following resources:

- AWS::AutoScaling::AutoScalingGroup,
- AWS::ElastiCache::ReplicationGroup
- AWS::Elasticsearch::Domain
- AWS::Lambda::Alias

UpdateReplacePolicy attribute:

- Use the UpdateReplacePolicy attribute to retain or (in some cases) backup the existing physical instance of a resource when it is replaced during a stack update operation.

ROLLBACKS AND CREATION FAILURES

Stack creation failures:

- By default everything will be deleted.
- You can optionally disable rollback (good for troubleshooting failures).

Stack update failures:

- The stack will automatically roll back to the previous known working state.

- The logs can assist with understanding what issue occurred.

MONITORING AND REPORTING

You can monitor the progress of a stack update by viewing the stack's events. The console's **Events** tab displays each major step in the creation and update of the stack sorted by the time of each event with latest events on top.

For resources created by CloudFormation, use AWS monitoring and reporting tools applicable to the service.

AUTHORIZATION AND ACCESS CONTROL

You can use IAM with AWS CloudFormation to control what users can do with AWS CloudFormation, such as whether they can view stack templates, create stacks, or delete stacks.

In addition to AWS CloudFormation actions, you can manage what AWS services and resources are available to each user.

That way, you can control which resources users can access when they use AWS CloudFormation.

For example, you can specify which users can create Amazon EC2 instances, terminate database instances, or update VPCs. Those same permissions are applied anytime they use AWS CloudFormation to do those actions.

CHARGES

There is no additional charge for AWS CloudFormation.

You pay for AWS resources (such as Amazon EC2 instances, Elastic Load Balancing load balancers, etc.) created using AWS CloudFormation in the same manner as if you created them manually.

You only pay for what you use, as you use it; there are no minimum fees and no required upfront commitments.

AWS CONFIG

AWS CONFIG FEATURES

AWS Config is a fully managed service that provides you with an AWS resource inventory, configuration history, and configuration change notifications to enable security and governance.

With AWS Config you can discover existing AWS resources, export a complete inventory of your AWS resources with all configuration details, and determine how a resource was configured at any point in time.

These capabilities enable compliance auditing, security analysis, resource change tracking, and troubleshooting.

Allow you to assess, audit and evaluate configurations of your AWS resources.

Very useful for Configuration Management as part of an ITIL program.

Creates a baseline of various configuration settings and files and can then track variations against that baseline.

AWS CONFIG VS CLOUDTRAIL

AWS CloudTrail records user API activity on your account and allows you to access information about this activity.

AWS Config records point-in-time configuration details for your AWS resources as Configuration Items (CIs).

You can use an AWS Config CI to answer, "What did my AWS resource look like?" at a point in time.

You can use AWS CloudTrail to answer, "Who made an API call to modify this resource?".

AWS CONFIG RULES

A Config Rule represents desired configurations for a resource and is evaluated against configuration changes on the relevant resources, as recorded by AWS Config.

AWS Config Rules can check resources for certain desired conditions and if violations are found the resources are flagged as "noncompliant".

Examples of Config Rules:

- Is backup enabled on Amazon RDS?
- Is CloudTrail enabled on the AWS account?
- Are Amazon EBS volumes encrypted.

CONFIGURATION ITEMS

A Configuration Item (CI) is the configuration of a resource at a given point-in-time. A CI consists of 5 sections:

1. Basic information about the resource that is common across different resource types (e.g., Amazon Resource Names, tags).
2. Configuration data specific to the resource (e.g., Amazon EC2 instance type).
3. Map of relationships with other resources (e.g., EC2::Volume vol-3434df43 is "attached to instance" EC2 Instance i-3432ee3a).
4. AWS CloudTrail event IDs that are related to this state.
5. Metadata that helps you identify information about the CI, such as the version of this CI, and when this CI was captured.

CHARGES

With AWS Config, you are charged based on the number configuration items (CIs) recorded for supported resources in your AWS account.

AWS Config creates a configuration item whenever it detects a change to a resource type that it is recording.

AWS SYSTEMS MANAGER

AWS SYSTEMS MANAGER FEATURES

AWS Systems Manager is an AWS service that provides visibility and control of infrastructure on AWS.

© 2023 Digital Cloud Training

AWS Systems Manager provides a unified interface through which you can view operational data from multiple AWS services.

AWS Systems Manager allows you to automate operational tasks across your AWS resources.

With Systems Manager, you can group resources, like Amazon EC2 instances, Amazon S3 buckets, or Amazon RDS instances, by application, view operational data for monitoring and troubleshooting, and take action on your groups of resources.

You can create logical groups of resources such as applications, different layers of an application stack, or production versus development environments.

With Systems Manager, you can select a resource group and view its recent API activity, resource configuration changes, related notifications, operational alerts, software inventory, and patch compliance status.

You can also take action on each resource group depending on your operational needs.

Systems Manager simplifies resource and application management, shortens the time to detect and resolve operational problems, and makes it easy to operate and manage your infrastructure securely at scale.

SYSTEMS MANAGER COMPONENTS

Systems Manager Inventory

AWS Systems Manager collects information about your instances and the software installed on them, helping you to understand your system configurations and installed applications.

You can collect data about applications, files, network configurations, Windows services, registries, server roles, updates, and any other system properties.

The gathered data enables you to manage application assets, track licenses, monitor file integrity, discover applications not installed by a traditional installer, and more.

Configuration Compliance

AWS Systems Manager lets you scan your managed instances for patch compliance and configuration inconsistencies.

You can collect and aggregate data from multiple AWS accounts and Regions, and then drill down into specific resources that aren't compliant.

By default, AWS Systems Manager displays data about patching and associations. You can also customize the service and create your own compliance types based on your requirements.

Systems Manager Automation

AWS Systems Manager allows you to safely automate common and repetitive IT operations and management tasks across AWS resources.

With Systems Manager, you can create JSON/YAML documents that specify a specific list of tasks or use community published documents.

These documents can be executed directly through the AWS Management Console, CLIs, and SDKs, scheduled in a maintenance window, or triggered based on changes to AWS resources through Amazon CloudWatch Events.

You can track the execution of each step in the documents as well as require approvals for each step.

You can also incrementally roll out changes and automatically halt when errors occur.

Systems Manager Run Command

Use Systems Manager Run Command to remotely and securely manage the configuration of your managed instances at scale. Use Run Command to perform on-demand changes like updating applications or running Linux shell scripts and Windows PowerShell commands on a target set of dozens or hundreds of instances.

Run command requires the SSM agent to be installed on all managed instances.

Example tasks include: stopping, restarting, terminating, and resizing instances. Attaching and detaching EBS volumes, creating snapshots etc.

Often used to apply patches and updates.

Commands can be applied to a group of systems based on AWS instance tags or manual selection.

The commands and parameters are defined in a Systems Manager document.

Commands can be issued using the AWS Console, AWS CLI, AWS Tools for Windows PowerShell, the Systems Manager API, or Amazon SDKs.

Systems Manager Session Manager

AWS Systems Manager provides you safe, secure remote management of your instances at scale without logging into your servers, replacing the need for bastion hosts, SSH, or remote PowerShell.

It provides a simple way of automating common administrative tasks across groups of instances such as registry edits, user management, and software and patch installations.

Provides a command terminal for Linux instances and Windows PowerShell terminal for Windows instances.

Through integration with AWS Identity and Access Management (IAM), you can apply granular permissions to control the actions users can perform on instances.

All actions taken with Systems Manager are recorded by AWS CloudTrail, allowing you to audit changes throughout your environment.

Requires IAM permissions for EC2 instance to access SSM, S3, and CloudWatch Logs.

CloudTrail can intercept StartSession events using Session Manager.

Compared to SSH:

- Do not need to open port 22.
- Do not need bastion hosts for management.

© 2023 Digital Cloud Training

- All commands are logged to S3 / CloudWatch.
- Secure shell access is authenticated using IAM user accounts, not key pairs.

Systems Manager Patch Manager

AWS Systems Manager helps you select and deploy operating system and software patches automatically across large groups of Amazon EC2 or on-premises instances.

Through patch baselines, you can set rules to auto-approve select categories of patches to be installed, such as operating system or high severity patches, and you can specify a list of patches that override these rules and are automatically approved or rejected.

You can also schedule maintenance windows for your patches so that they are only applied during preset times.

Systems Manager helps ensure that your software is up-to-date and meets your compliance policies.

Systems Manager Parameter Store

AWS Systems Manager provides a centralized store to manage your configuration data, whether plain-text data such as database strings or secrets such as passwords.

This allows you to separate your secrets and configuration data from your code. Parameters can be tagged and organized into hierarchies, helping you manage parameters more easily.

For example, you can use the same parameter name, "db-string", with a different hierarchical path, "dev/db-string" or "prod/db-string", to store different values.

Systems Manager is integrated with AWS Key Management Service (KMS), allowing you to automatically encrypt the data you store.

You can also control user and resource access to parameters using AWS Identity and Access Management (IAM). Parameters can be referenced through other AWS services, such as Amazon Elastic Container Service, AWS Lambda, and AWS CloudFormation.

Distributor

Distributor is an AWS Systems Manager feature that enables you to securely store and distribute software packages in your organization.

You can use Distributor with existing Systems Manager features like Run Command and State Manager to control the lifecycle of the packages running on your instances.

State Manager

AWS Systems Manager provides configuration management, which helps you maintain consistent configuration of your Amazon EC2 or on-premises instances.

With Systems Manager, you can control configuration details such as server configurations, anti-virus definitions, firewall settings, and more.

You can define configuration policies for your servers through the AWS Management Console or use existing scripts, PowerShell modules, or Ansible playbooks directly from GitHub or Amazon S3 buckets.

Systems Manager automatically applies your configurations across your instances at a time and frequency that you define.

You can query Systems Manager at any time to view the status of your instance configurations, giving you on-demand visibility into your compliance status.

MAINTENANCE WINDOWS

AWS Systems Manager lets you schedule windows of time to run administrative and maintenance tasks across your instances.

This ensures that you can select a convenient and safe time to install patches and updates or make other configuration changes, improving the availability and reliability of your services and applications.

DEPLOYMENT AND PROVISIONING

Resource Groups

You can use *resource groups* to organize your AWS resources. Resource groups make it easier to manage, monitor, and automate tasks on large numbers of resources at one time.

AWS Resource Groups provides two general methods for defining a resource group. Both methods involve using a query to identify the members for a group.

The first method relies on tags applied to AWS resources to add resources to a group. Using this method, you apply the same key/value pair tags to resources of various types in your account and then use the AWS Resource Groups service to create a group based on that tag pair.

The second method is based on resources available in an individual AWS CloudFormation stack. Using this method, you choose an AWS CloudFormation stack, and then choose resource types in the stack that you want to be in the group.

Allows the creation of logical groups of resources that you can perform actions on (such as patching).

Resource groups are regional in scope.

Systems Manager Document

An AWS Systems Manager document (SSM document) defines the actions that Systems Manager performs on your managed instances.

Systems Manager includes more than a dozen pre-configured documents that you can use by specifying parameters at runtime.

Documents use JavaScript Object Notation (JSON) or YAML, and they include steps and parameters that you specify.

MONITORING AND REPORTING

Insights Dashboard

AWS Systems Manager automatically aggregates and displays operational data for each resource group through a dashboard.

Systems Manager eliminates the need for you to navigate across multiple AWS consoles to view your operational data.

With Systems Manager you can view API call logs from AWS CloudTrail, resource configuration changes from AWS Config, software inventory, and patch compliance status by resource group.

You can also easily integrate your AWS CloudWatch Dashboards, AWS Trusted Advisor notifications, and AWS Personal Health Dashboard performance and availability alerts into your Systems Manager dashboard.

Systems Manager centralizes all relevant operational data, so you can have a clear view of your infrastructure compliance and performance.

Amazon CloudWatch

You can configure and use the Amazon CloudWatch agent to collect metrics and logs from your instances instead of using SSM Agent for these tasks. The CloudWatch agent enables you to gather more metrics on EC2 instances than are available using SSM Agent. In addition, you can gather metrics from on-premises servers using the CloudWatch agent.

LOGGING AND AUDITING

Systems Manager is integrated with AWS CloudTrail, a service that provides a record of actions taken by a user, role, or an AWS service in Systems Manager. CloudTrail captures all API calls for Systems Manager as events, including calls from the Systems Manager console and from code calls to the Systems Manager APIs.

SSM Agent writes information about executions, commands, scheduled actions, errors, and health statuses to log files on each instance. You can view log files by manually connecting to an instance, or you can automatically send logs to Amazon CloudWatch Logs.

AUTHORIZATION AND ACCESS CONTROL

AWS Systems Manager supports identity-based policies.

AWS Systems Manager does not support resource-based policies.

You can attach tags to Systems Manager resources or pass tags in a request to Systems Manager.

To control access based on tags, you provide tag information in the condition element of a policy using the ssm:resourceTag/key-name, aws:ResourceTag/key-name, aws:RequestTag/key-name, or aws:TagKeys condition keys.

AWS SERVICE CATALOG

AWS SERVICE CATALOG FEATURES

AWS Service Catalog enables organizations to create and manage catalogs of IT services that are approved for AWS.

These IT services can include everything from virtual machine images, servers, software, and databases to complete multi-tier application architectures.

AWS Service Catalog allows organizations to centrally manage commonly deployed IT services, and helps organizations achieve consistent governance and meet compliance requirements.

End users can quickly deploy only the approved IT services they need, following the constraints set by your organization.

AWS Service Catalog supports the following types of users:

- **Catalog administrators (administrators)** – Manage a catalog of products (applications and services), organizing them into portfolios and granting access to end users. Catalog administrators prepare AWS CloudFormation templates, configure constraints, and manage IAM roles that are assigned to products to provide for advanced resource management.
- **End users** – Receive AWS credentials from their IT department or manager and use the AWS Management Console to launch products to which they have been granted access.

Products:

- A *product* is an IT service that you want to make available for deployment on AWS.
- A product consists of one or more AWS resources, such as EC2 instances, storage volumes, databases, monitoring configurations, and networking components, or packaged AWS Marketplace products.
- AWS CloudFormation templates define the AWS resources required for the product, the relationships between resources, and the parameters that end users can plug in when they launch the product to configure security groups, create key pairs, and perform other customizations.

Portfolios:

- A *portfolio* is a collection of *products*, together with configuration information.
- Portfolios help manage who can use specific products and how they can use them.
- With AWS Service Catalog, you can create a customized portfolio for each type of user in your organization and selectively grant access to the appropriate portfolio.
- When you add a new *version* of a product to a portfolio, that version is automatically available to all current users.
- You also can share your portfolios with other AWS accounts and allow the administrator of those accounts to distribute your portfolios with additional *constraints*, such as limiting which EC2 instances a user can create.
- Through the use of portfolios, permissions, sharing, and constraints, you can ensure that users are launching products that are configured properly for the organization's needs and standards.

Versioning:

- AWS Service Catalog allows you to manage multiple versions of the products in your catalog.
- This allows you to add new versions of templates and associated resources based on software updates or configuration changes.
- When you create a new version of a product, the update is automatically distributed to all users who have access to the product, allowing the user to select which version of the product to use.

Permissions:

- Granting a user access to a portfolio enables that user to browse the portfolio and launch the products in it.
- You apply AWS Identity and Access Management (IAM) permissions to control who can view and modify your catalog. IAM permissions can be assigned to IAM users, groups, and roles.
- When a user launches a product that has an IAM role assigned to it, AWS Service Catalog uses the role to launch the product's cloud resources using AWS CloudFormation.
- By assigning an IAM role to each product, you can avoid giving users permissions to perform unapproved operations and enable them to provision resources using the catalog.

Constraints:

- *Constraints* control the ways that specific AWS resources can be deployed for a product.
- You can use them to apply limits to products for governance or cost control.
- There are different types of AWS Service Catalog constraints: *launch constraints*, *notification constraints*, and *template constraints*.
- With **launch constraints**, you specify a role for a product in a portfolio. This role is used to provision the resources at launch, so you can restrict user permissions without impacting users' ability to provision products from the catalog.
- **Notification constraints** enable you to get notifications about stack events using an Amazon SNS topic.
- **Template constraints** restrict the configuration parameters that are available for the user when launching the product (for example, EC2 instance types or IP address ranges). With template constraints, you reuse generic AWS CloudFormation templates for products and apply restrictions to the templates on a per-product or per-portfolio basis.

SHARING AND IMPORTING PORTFOLIOS

To make your AWS Service Catalog products available to users who are not in your AWS account, such as users who belong to other organizations or to other AWS accounts in your organization, you share your portfolios with them.

You can share in several ways, including account-to-account sharing, organizational sharing, and deploying catalogs using stack sets.

Before you share your products and portfolios to other accounts, you must decide whether you want to share a reference of the catalog or to deploy a copy of the catalog into each recipient account.

Note that if you deploy a copy, you must redeploy if there are updates you want to propagate to the recipient accounts.

You can use stack sets to deploy your catalog to many accounts at the same time. If you want to share a reference (an imported version of your portfolio that stays in sync with the original), you can use account-to-account sharing or you can share using AWS Organizations.

When you share a portfolio using account-to-account sharing or AWS Organizations, you allow an AWS Service Catalog administrator of another AWS account to import your portfolio into his or her account and distribute the products to end users in that account.

This *imported portfolio* isn't an independent copy. The products and constraints in the imported portfolio stay in sync with changes that you make to the *shared portfolio*, the original portfolio that you shared.

The *recipient administrator*, the administrator with whom you share a portfolio, cannot change the products or constraints, but can add AWS Identity and Access Management (IAM) access for end users.

The recipient administrator can distribute the products to end users who belong to his or her AWS account in the following ways:

- By adding IAM users, groups, and roles to the imported portfolio.
- By adding products from the imported portfolio to a *local portfolio*, a separate portfolio that the recipient administrator creates and that belongs to his or her AWS account. The recipient administrator then adds IAM users, groups, and roles to the local portfolio. The constraints that you applied to the products in the shared portfolio are also present in the local portfolio. The recipient administrator can add additional constraints to the local portfolio but cannot remove the imported constraints.

AWS COST MANAGEMENT SERVICES

AWS COST EXPLORER

The AWS Cost Explorer is a free tool that allows you to view charts of your costs.

You can view cost data for the past 13 months and forecast how much you are likely to spend over the next three months.

Cost Explorer can be used to discover patterns in how much you spend on AWS resources over time and to identify cost problem areas.

Cost Explorer can help you to identify service usage statistics such as:

- Which services you use the most.
- View metrics for which AZ has the most traffic.
- Which linked account is used the most.

AWS COST & USAGE REPORT

Publish AWS billing reports to an Amazon S3 bucket.

Reports break down costs by:

- Hour, day, month, product, product resource, tags.

Can update the report up to three times a day.

Create, retrieve, and delete your reports using the AWS CUR API Reference.

AWS PRICE LIST API

Query the prices of AWS services.

Price List Service API (AKA the Query API) – query with JSON.

AWS Price List API (AKA the Bulk API) – query with HTML.

Alerts via Amazon SNS when prices change.

AWS BUDGETS

Used to track cost, usage, or coverage and utilization for your Reserved Instances and Savings Plans, across multiple dimensions, such as service, or Cost Categories.

Alerting through event-driven alert notifications for when actual or forecasted cost or usage exceeds your budget limit, or when your RI and Savings Plans' coverage or utilization drops below your threshold.

Create annual, quarterly, monthly, or even daily budgets depending on your business needs.

AWS BACKUP

AWS BACKUP FEATURES

AWS Backup provides centralized and automated data protection.

Works across AWS services and hybrid workloads.

Helps to support regulatory compliance and business policies for data protection.

Integrates with AWS Organizations for central deployment of data protection policies.

Configure, manage, and govern backup activities across AWS accounts and resources.

AWS Backup can protect many AWS resources including:

- Amazon EC2 instances.
- Amazon EBS volumes.
- Amazon RDS databases.
- Amazon DynamoDB tables.
- Amazon Neptune databases.
- Amazon DocumentDB databases.
- Amazon EFS file systems.
- Amazon FSx for Lustre and Windows File Server file systems.
- AWS Storage Gateway volumes.
- VMware workloads on-premises and in VMware Cloud on AWS.
- Amazon S3 buckets.

AWS Backup can be used to copy backups across multiple AWS services to different Regions.

Cross-Region backup copies can be deployed manually or automatically using scheduling.

Cross-account backup can also be configured for accounts within an AWS Organization.

POLICY-BASED BACKUP

With AWS Backup, you can create backup policies called backup plans.

Backup plans are used to define backup requirements.

Backup plans are then applied to the AWS resources you want to back up.

You can create separate backup plans that meet specific business and regulatory compliance requirements.

Backup plans make it easy to implement your backup strategy across your organization and across your applications.

TAG-BASED BACKUP POLICIES

AWS Backup allows you to apply backup plans to your AWS resources by simply tagging them.

Ensure that all your AWS resources are backed up and protected according to your strategy.

AWS tags are a great way to organize and classify your AWS resources.

Integration with AWS tags enables you to quickly apply a backup plan to a group of AWS resources so that they are backed up in a consistent and compliant manner.

AUTOMATED BACKUP SCHEDULING

AWS Backup allows you to create backup schedules that you can customize to meet your business and regulatory backup requirements.

You can also choose from predefined backup schedules based on common best practices.

AWS Backup will automatically back up your AWS resources according to the policies and schedules you define.

A backup schedule includes the backup start time, backup frequency, and backup window.

AUTOMATED RETENTION MANAGEMENT

You can configure backup retention policies that automatically retain and expire backups according to business and regulatory compliance requirements.

Automated backup retention management minimizes backup storage costs by retaining backups only if they are needed.

AWS BACKUP VAULT LOCK

AWS Backup Vault Lock allows you to protect your backups from deletion or changes to their lifecycle by inadvertent or malicious changes.

You can use the AWS CLI, AWS Backup API, or AWS Backup SDK to apply the AWS Backup Vault Lock protection to an existing vault or a new one.

ANALYTICS

AMAZON OPENSEARCH

AMAZON OPENSEARCH FEATURES

The Amazon OpenSearch Service is the successor to the Amazon Elasticsearch Service.

Amazon OpenSearch Service is an open source, distributed search and analytics suite based on Elasticsearch.

Elasticsearch is a distributed search and analytics engine built on Apache Lucene.

Elasticsearch is a popular search engine commonly used for log analytics, full-text search, security intelligence, business analytics, and operational intelligence use cases.

With OpenSearch you can perform log analytics interactively, perform real-time application monitoring, website search, performance metric analysis and more.

You can choose from a variety of open-source engine options for your OpenSearch cluster.

Options include the latest version of OpenSearch and many versions of ALv2 Elasticsearch.

DEPLOYMENT AND MONITORING

An OpenSearch cluster can be created using the AWS Management Console, API, or AWS CLI.

Specify the number of instances, instance types, and storage options.

In-place upgrades can be performed without downtime.

Provides built-in monitoring and alerting with automatic notifications.

You can configure alerts using the Kibana or OpenSearch Dashboards and the REST API.

Notifications can be sent via custom webhooks, Slack, Amazon SNS, and Amazon Chime.

OpenSearch Service supports multiple query languages such as:

- Domain-Specific Language (DSL).
- SQL queries with OpenSearch SQL.
- OpenSearch Piped Processing Language (PPL).

OpenSearch integrates with open-source tools including:

- Logstash.
- OpenTelemetry.
- ElasticSearch APIs.

OPENSEARCH IN AN AMAZON VPC

OpenSearch Services domains can be launched into an Amazon VPC.

Using a VPC enables secure communication between the OpenSearch Service and other services within the VPC.

The following are some of the ways VPC domains differ from public domains. Each difference is described later in more detail.

- Because of their logical isolation, domains that reside within a VPC have an extra layer of security compared to domains that use public endpoints.
- While public domains are accessible from any internet-connected device, VPC domains require some form of VPN or proxy.
- Compared to public domains, VPC domains display less information in the console. Specifically, the **Cluster health** tab does not include shard information, and the **Indices** tab isn't present.
- The domain endpoints take different forms (https://**search**-domain-name vs. https://**vpc**-domain-name).
- You can't apply IP-based access policies to domains that reside within a VPC because security groups already enforce IP-based access policies.

Note the following limitations:

- If you launch a new domain within a VPC, you can't later switch it to use a public endpoint. The reverse is also true.
- You can either launch your domain within a VPC or use a public endpoint, but you can't do both.
- You can't launch your domain within a VPC that uses dedicated tenancy. You must use a VPC with tenancy set to **Default**.
- After you place a domain within a VPC, you can't move it to a different VPC, but you can change the subnets and security group settings.
- To access the default installation of OpenSearch Dashboards for a domain that resides within a VPC, users must have access to the VPC.

THE ELK STACK

ELK is an acronym that describes a popular combination of projects: Elasticsearch, Logstash, and Kibana.

The ELK stack gives you the ability to aggregate logs from all your systems and applications, analyze these logs, and create visualizations.

ELK is useful for visualizing application and infrastructure monitoring data, troubleshooting, security analytics and more.

SECURITY

OpenSearch Service domains offer encryption of data at rest.

Uses AWS KMS for storage and management of encryption keys.

Encryption uses AES-256.

Encryption also encrypts node-to-node communications using TLS 1.2.

Node-to-node encryption is optional and can be enabled through the console, CLI, or API.

Once node-to-node encryption is enabled it cannot be disabled. Instead you must create a new domain from a snapshot without this setting enabled.

Amazon OpenSearch Service supports three types of access policies:

- Resource-based policies
- Identity-based policies
- IP-based policies

Fine-grained access control offers additional capabilities within Amazon OpenSearch Service.

Fine-grained access control offers the following benefits:

- Role-based access control.
- Security at the index, document, and field level.
- OpenSearch Dashboards multi-tenancy.
- HTTP basic authentication for OpenSearch and OpenSearch Dashboards.

OpenSearch Service supports authentication through SAML and Amazon Cognito.

APPLICATION INTEGRATION

AWS APPLICATION INTEGRATION SERVICES

AWS APPLICATION INTEGRATION SERVICES

The AWS application integration services are a family of services that enable decoupled communication between applications.

These services provide decoupling for microservices, distributed systems, and serverless applications.

AWS application integration services allow you to connect apps, without needing to write custom code to enable interoperability.

Decoupled applications can interoperate whilst being resilient to the failure or overload of any individual component.

The following services are involved with application integration:

Service	What it does	Example use cases
Simple Queue Service (SQS)	Messaging queue; store and forward patterns	Building distributed / decoupled applications
Simple Notification Service (SNS)	Set up, operate, and send notifications from the cloud	Send email notification when CloudWatch alarm is triggered
Step Functions	Out-of-the-box coordination of AWS service components with visual workflow	Order processing workflow
Simple Workflow Service (SWF)	Need to support external processes or specialized execution logic	Human-enabled workflows like an order fulfilment system or for procedural requests **Note**: *AWS recommends that for new applications customers consider Step Functions instead of SWF*
Amazon MQ	Message broker service for Apache Active MQ and RabbitMQ	Need a message queue that supports industry standard APIs and protocols; migrate queues to AWS
Amazon Kinesis	Collect, process, and analyze streaming data.	Collect data from IoT devices for later processing

AMAZON SNS

Amazon Simple Notification Service (Amazon SNS) is a fully managed messaging service for both application-to-application (A2A) and application-to-person (A2P) communication.

© 2023 Digital Cloud Training

The pub/sub functionality provides messaging for high-throughput, push-based, many-to-many use cases.

Amazon SNS is used for sending notifications between distributed systems, microservices, and event-driven serverless applications.

Push notifications can go to Apple, Google, Fire OS, and Windows devices as well as Android devices in China with Baidu Cloud Push.

Amazon SNS can also send notifications via SMS text message, email, SQS queues or to any HTTP endpoint.

Amazon SNS notifications can also trigger Lambda functions.

Amazon SNS is inexpensive and based on a pay-as-you-go model with no upfront costs.

SNS uses a pub-sub model whereby users or applications subscribe to SNS topics.

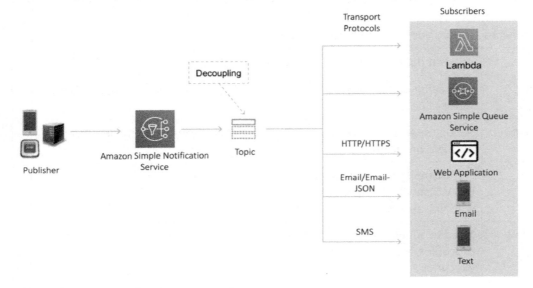

Amazon SNS provides decoupling of your applications so messages can be processed asynchronously.

SNS Topics

Multiple recipients can be grouped using Topics.

A topic is an "access point" for allowing recipients to dynamically subscribe for identical copies of the same notification.

One topic can support deliveries to multiple endpoint types.

All messages are stored redundantly across multiple availability zones.

Provides instantaneous, push-based delivery.

Flexible message delivery is provided over multiple transport protocols.

SNS Subscribers and Endpoints

When subscribing to an SNS topic the following endpoint types are supported:

- HTTP/HTTPS.
- Email/Email-JSON.
- Amazon Kinesis Data Firehose.
- Amazon SQS.
- AWS Lambda.
- Platform application endpoint (mobile push).
- SMS.

SNS Fanout

Your publisher systems can fanout messages to many subscriber systems including Amazon SQS queues, AWS Lambda functions and HTTPS endpoints, for parallel processing, and Amazon Kinesis Data Firehose.

You can subscribe one or more Amazon SQS queues to an Amazon SNS topic from a list of topics available for the selected queue.

Amazon SQS manages the subscription and any necessary permissions.

When you publish a message to a topic, Amazon SNS sends the message to every subscribed queue.

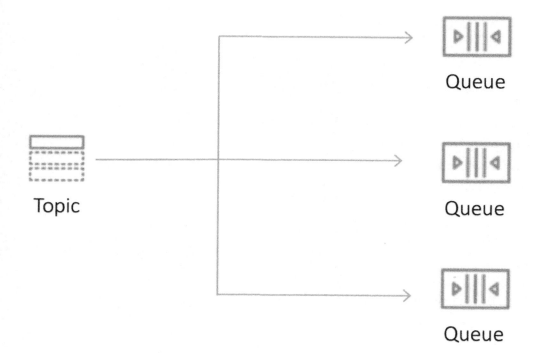

Fanout is supported for application-to-application (A2A) messaging:

© 2023 Digital Cloud Training

- Fanout to Kinesis Data Firehose delivery streams.
- Fanout to Lambda functions.
- Fanout to Amazon SQS queues.
- Fanout to HTTP/S endpoints.
- Fanout to AWS Event Fork Pipelines.

AMAZON SQS

Amazon Simple Queue Service (SQS) is a distributed queue system that enables web service applications to quickly and reliably queue messages that one component in the application generates to be consumed by another component.

Amazon SQS enables you to send, store, and receive messages between software components.

An Amazon SQS queue is a temporary repository for messages that are awaiting processing.

The SQS queue acts as a buffer between the component producing and saving data, and the component receiving the data for processing.

The SQS queue resolves issues that arise if the producer is producing work faster than the consumer can process it, or if the producer or consumer are only intermittently connected to the network.

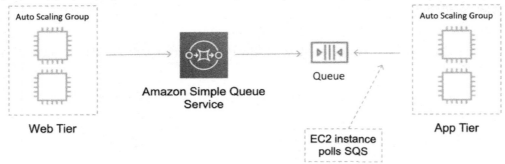

This is known as decoupling / loose coupling and helps to enable elasticity for your application.

Amazon SQS is pull-based, not push-based (like Amazon SNS).

Messages are up to 256KB in size.

Messages can be kept in the queue from 1 minute to 14 days.

The default retention period is 4 days.

SQS guarantees that your messages will be processed at least once.

SQS Queues

Queue names must be unique within a region.

There are two types of queue – standard queues and FIFO queues.

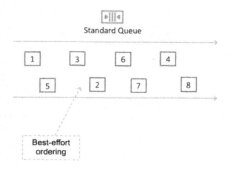

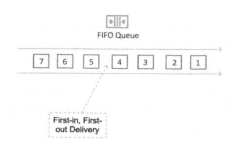

Standard

Default queue type.

Nearly unlimited transactions per second.

Guarantee that a message is delivered at least once.

Occasionally more than one copy of a message might be delivered out of order.

Provides best-effort ordering which ensures that messages are generally delivered in the same order as they are sent.

First in First Out (FIFO)

Delivers exactly-once processing.

The order in which messages are sent and received is strictly preserved and a message is delivered once and remains available until a consumer processes and deletes it.

Duplicates are not introduced into the queue.

FIFO queues also support message groups that allow multiple ordered message groups within a single queue.

Limited to 300 transactions per second (TPS) but have all the capabilities of standard queues.

Deduplication with FIFO queues:

- Provide a MessageDeduplicationId with the message.
- The de-duplication interval is 5 minutes.
- Content based duplication – the MessageDeduplicationId is generated as the SHA-256 with the message body.

Sequencing with FIFO queues:

- To ensure strict ordering between messages, specify a MessageGroupId.
- Messages with a different Group ID may be received out of order.
- Messages with the same Group ID are delivered to one consumer at a time.

FIFO queues require the Message Group ID and Message Deduplication ID parameters to be added to messages.

Message Group ID:

- The tag that specifies that a message belongs to a specific message group. Messages that belong to the same message group are guaranteed to be processed in a FIFO manner.

Message Deduplication ID:

- The token used for deduplication of messages within the deduplication interval.

The following table provides a side-by-side comparison of standard and FIFO queues:

Standard Queue	FIFO Queue
Unlimited Throughput: Standard queues support a nearly unlimited number of transactions per second (TPS) per API action.	High Throughput: FIFO queues support up to 300 messages per second (300 send, receive, or delete operations per second). When you batch 10 messages per operation (maximum), FIFO queues can support up to 3,000 messages per second
Best-Effort Ordering: Occasionally, messages might be delivered in an order different from which they were sent	First-In-First-out Delivery: The order in which messages are sent and received is strictly preserved
At-Least-Once Delivery: A message is delivered at least once, but occasionally more than one copy of a message is delivered	Exactly-Once Processing: A message is delivered once and remains available until a consumer processes and deletes it. Duplicates are not introduced into the queue

Scalability and Durability

You can have multiple queues with different priorities.

Scaling is performed by creating more queues.

SQS stores all message queues and messages within a single, highly available AWS region with multiple redundant AZs.

Monitoring

CloudWatch is integrated with SQS and you can view and monitor queue metrics.

CloudWatch metrics are automatically collected every 5 minutes.

CloudWatch considers a queue to be active for up to 6 hours if it contains any messages or if any API action accesses it.

No charge for CloudWatch (no detailed monitoring).

CloudTrail captures API calls from SQS and logs to a specified S3 bucket.

Security

You can use IAM policies to control who can read/write messages.

Authentication can be used to secure messages within queues (who can send and receive).

SQS is PCI DSS level 1 compliant and HIPAA eligible.

In-flight security is provided using HTTPS.

Can enable server-side encryption (SSE) using KMS.

- Can set the CMK you want to use.
- Can set the data key reuse period.
- SSE only encrypts the message body not the message attributes.

IAM policy must allow usage of SQS.

You can also specify permissions in an SQS queue access policy:

- Providers finer grained control.
- Control over the requests that come in.

AWS STEP FUNCTIONS

AWS Step Functions can be used to coordinate the components of distributed applications as a series of steps in a visual workflow.

You can quickly build and run state machines to execute the steps of your application in a reliable and scalable fashion.

How it works:

1. Define the steps of your workflow in the JSON-based Amazon States Language. The visual console automatically graphs each step in the order of execution.
2. Start an execution to visualize and verify the steps of your application are operating as intended. The console highlights the real-time status of each step and provides a detailed history of every execution.
3. AWS Step Functions operates and scales the steps of your application and underlying compute for you to help ensure your application executes reliably under increasing demand.

It is a managed workflow and orchestration platform.

It is scalable and highly available.

You define your app as a state machine.

Create tasks, sequential steps, parallel steps, branching paths or timers.

Uses Amazon State Language declarative JSON.

Apps can interact and update the stream via Step Function API.

Provides a visual interface which describes flow and real-time status.

Provides detailed logs of each step execution.

AWS Step Functions features:

- **Built-in error handling** – AWS Step Functions tracks the state of each step, so you can automatically retry failed or timed-out tasks, catch specific errors, and recover gracefully, whether the task takes seconds or months to complete.
- **Automatic Scaling** – AWS Step Functions automatically scales the operations and underlying compute to run the steps of your application for you in response to changing workloads. Step

Functions scales automatically to help ensure the performance of your application workflow remains consistently high as the frequency of requests increases.

- **Pay per use** – With AWS Step Functions, you pay only for the transition from one step of your application workflow to the next, called a state transition. Billing is metered by state transition, regardless of how long each state persists (up to one year).
- **Execution event history** – AWS Step Functions creates a detailed event log for every execution, so when things do go wrong, you can quickly identify not only where, but why. All of the execution history is available visually and programmatically to quickly troubleshoot and remediate failures.
- **High availability** – AWS Step Functions has built-in fault tolerance. Step Functions maintains service capacity across multiple Availability Zones in each region to help protect application workflows against individual machine or data center facility failures. There are no maintenance windows or scheduled downtimes.
- **Administrative security** – AWS Step Functions is integrated with AWS Identity and Access Management (IAM). IAM policies can be used to control access to the Step Functions APIs.

SECURITY, IDENTITY & COMPLIANCE

AWS IAM

AWS IAM FEATURES

IAM is the AWS Identity and Access Management Service.

IAM is used to securely control individual and group access to AWS resources.

IAM makes it easy to provide multiple users secure access to AWS resources.

IAM can be used to manage:

- Users.
- Groups.
- Access policies.
- Roles.
- User credentials.
- User password policies.
- Multi-factor authentication (MFA).
- API keys for programmatic access (CLI).

Provides centralized control of your AWS account.

Enables shared access to your AWS account.

By default new users are created with NO access to any AWS services – they can only login to the AWS console.

Permission must be explicitly granted to allow a user to access an AWS service.

IAM users are individuals who have been granted access to an AWS account.

Each IAM user has three main components:

- A username.
- A password.
- Permissions to access various resources.

You can apply granular permissions with IAM.

You can assign users individual security credentials such as access keys, passwords, and multi-factor authentication devices.

IAM is not used for application-level authentication.

Identity Federation (including AD, Facebook etc). can be configured allowing secure access to resources in an AWS account without creating an IAM user account.

Multi-factor authentication (MFA) can be enabled/enforced for the AWS account and for individual users under the account.

MFA uses an authentication device that continually generates random, six-digit, single-use authentication codes.

You can authenticate using an MFA device in the following three ways:

© 2023 Digital Cloud Training

- Through the **AWS Management Console** – the user is prompted for a user name, password, and authentication code.
- Using the **AWS API** – restrictions are added to IAM policies and developers can request temporary security credentials and pass MFA parameters in their AWS STS API requests.
- Using the **AWS CLI** by obtaining temporary security credentials from STS (aws sts get-session-token).

Want to see how to setup MFA? In the brief AWS Hands-on Labs video tutorial below, you'll learn how to activate a virtual Multi-factor Authentication (MFA) for your AWS Root Account. In under 5 minutes, we cover: Deleting the Root Account Access Key and Activating Multi-Factor Authentication.

It is a best practice to use MFA for all users and to use U2F or hardware MFA devices for all privileged users.

IAM is universal (global) and does not apply to regions.

IAM is eventually consistent.

IAM replicates data across multiple data centers around the world.

The "root account" is the account created when you setup the AWS account. It has complete Admin access and is the only account that has this access by default.

It is a best practice to not use the root account for anything other than billing.

Power user access allows all permissions except the management of groups and users in IAM.

Temporary security credentials consist of the AWS access key ID, secret access key, and security token.

IAM can assign temporary security credentials to provide users with temporary access to services/resources.

To sign-in you must provide your account ID or account alias in addition to a user name and password.

The sign-in URL includes the account ID or account alias, e.g.:

https://**My_AWS_Account_ID**.signin.aws.amazon.com/console/.

Alternatively you can sign-in at the following URL and enter your account ID or alias manually:

https://console.aws.amazon.com/.

IAM integrates with many different AWS services.

IAM supports PCI DSS compliance.

AWS recommend that you use the AWS SDKs to make programmatic API calls to IAM.

However, you can also use the IAM Query API to make direct calls to the IAM web service.

IAM ELEMENTS

Principals:

- An entity that can take an action on an AWS resource.
- Your administrative IAM user is your first principal.
- You can allow users and services to assume a role.
- IAM supports federated users.
- IAM supports programmatic access to allow an application to access your AWS account.
- IAM users, roles, federated users, and applications are all AWS principals.

Requests:

- Principals send requests via the Console, CLI, SDKs, or APIs.
- Requests are:
  - Actions (or operations) that the principal wants to perform.
  - Resources upon which the actions are performed.
  - Principal information including the environment from which the request was made.
- Request context – AWS gathers the request information:
  - Principal (requester).
  - Aggregate permissions associated with the principal.
  - Environment data, such as IP address, user agent, SSL status etc.
  - Resource data, or data that is related to the resource being requested.

Authentication:

- A principal sending a request must be authenticated to send a request to AWS.
- To authenticate from the console, you must sign in with your user name and password.
- To authenticate from the API or CLI, you must provide your access key and secret key.

Authorization:

- IAM uses values from the request context to check for matching policies and determines whether to allow or deny the request.
- IAM policies are stored in IAM as JSON documents and specify the permissions that are allowed or denied.
- IAM policies can be:
  - User (identity) based policies.
  - Resource-based policies.
- IAM checks each policy that matches the context of your request.
- If a single policy has a deny action IAM denies the request and stops evaluating (explicit deny).
- Evaluation logic:
  - By default all requests are denied (implicit deny).
  - An explicit allow overrides the implicit deny.
  - An explicit deny overrides any explicit allows.
- Only the root user has access to all resources in the account by default.

Actions:

- Actions are defined by a service.
- Actions are the things you can do to a resource such as viewing, creating, editing, deleting.
- Any actions on resources that are not explicitly allowed are denied.
- To allow a principal to perform an action you must include the necessary actions in a policy that applies to the principal or the affected resource.

Resources:

- A resource is an entity that exists within a service.
- E.g. EC2 instances, S3 buckets, IAM users, and DynamoDB tables.

- Each AWS service defines a set of actions that can be performed on the resource.
- After AWS approves the actions in your request, those actions can be performed on the related resources within your account.

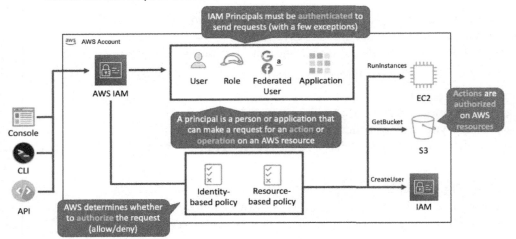

AUTHENTICATION METHODS

Console password:

- A password that the user can enter to sign into interactive sessions such as the AWS Management Console.
- You can allow users to change their own passwords.
- You can allow selected IAM users to change their passwords by disabling the option for all users and using an IAM policy to grant permissions for the selected users.

Access Keys:

- A combination of an access key ID and a secret access key.
- You can assign two active access keys to a user at a time.
- These can be used to make programmatic calls to AWS when using the API in program code or at a command prompt when using the AWS CLI or the AWS PowerShell tools.
- You can create, modify, view, or rotate access keys.
- When created IAM returns the access key ID and secret access key.
- The secret access is returned only at creation time and if lost a new key must be created.
- Ensure access keys and secret access keys are stored securely.
- Users can be given access to change their own keys through IAM policy (not from the console).
- You can disable a user's access key which prevents it from being used for API calls.

Server certificates:

- SSL/TLS certificates that you can use to authenticate with some AWS services.
- AWS recommends that you use the AWS Certificate Manager (ACM) to provision, manage and deploy your server certificates.
- Use IAM only when you must support HTTPS connections in a region that is not supported by ACM.

The following diagram shows the different methods of authentication available with IAM:

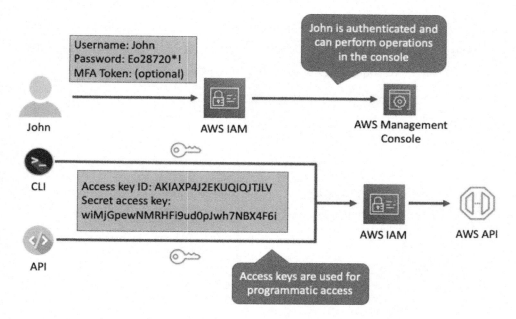

IAM USERS

An IAM user is an entity that represents a person or service.

Can be assigned:

- An access key ID and secret access key for programmatic access to the AWS API, CLI, SDK, and other development tools.
- A password for access to the management console.

By default users cannot access anything in your account.

The account root user credentials are the email address used to create the account and a password.

The root account has full administrative permissions, and these cannot be restricted.

Best practice for root accounts:

- Don't use the root user credentials.
- Don't share the root user credentials.
- Create an IAM user and assign administrative permissions as required.
- Enable MFA.

IAM users can be created to represent applications, and these are known as "service accounts".

You can have up to 5000 users per AWS account.

Each user account has a friendly name and an ARN which uniquely identifies the user across AWS.

A unique ID is also created which is returned only when you create the user using the API, Tools for Windows PowerShell, or the AWS CLI.

You should create individual IAM accounts for users (best practice not to share accounts).

The Access Key ID and Secret Access Key are not the same as a password and cannot be used to login to the AWS console.

The Access Key ID and Secret Access Key can only be generated once and must be regenerated if lost.

A password policy can be defined for enforcing password length, complexity etc. (applies to all users).

You can allow or disallow the ability to change passwords using an IAM policy.

Access keys and passwords should be changed regularly.

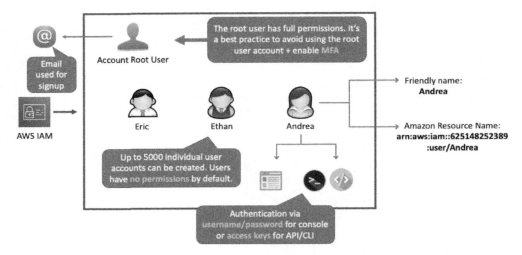

GROUPS

Groups are collections of users and have policies attached to them.

A group is not an identity and cannot be identified as a principal in an IAM policy.

Use groups to assign permissions to users.

Use the principal of least privilege when assigning permissions.

You cannot nest groups (groups within groups).

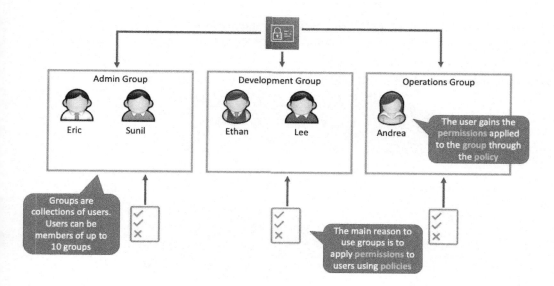

ROLES

Roles are created and then "assumed" by trusted entities and define a set of permissions for making AWS service requests.

With IAM Roles you can delegate permissions to resources for users and services without using permanent credentials (e.g. user name and password).

IAM users or AWS services can assume a role to obtain temporary security credentials that can be used to make AWS API calls.

You can delegate using roles.

There are no credentials associated with a role (password or access keys).

IAM users can temporarily assume a role to take on permissions for a specific task.

A role can be assigned to a federated user who signs in using an external identity provider.

Temporary credentials are primarily used with IAM roles and automatically expire.

Roles can be assumed temporarily through the console or programmatically with the **AWS CLI, Tools for Windows PowerShell,** or **API.**

IAM roles with EC2 instances:

- IAM roles can be used for granting applications running on EC2 instances permissions to AWS API requests using instance profiles.
- Only one role can be assigned to an EC2 instance at a time.
- A role can be assigned at the **EC2 instance creation time or at any time afterwards.**
- When using the AWS CLI or API instance profiles must be created manually (it's automatic and transparent through the console).
- Applications retrieve temporary security credentials from the instance metadata.

Role Delegation:

- Create an IAM role with two policies:

- o   Permissions policy – grants the user of the role the required permissions on a resource.
- o   Trust policy – specifies the trusted accounts that are allowed to assume the role.
- Wildcards (*) cannot be specified as a principal.
- A permissions policy must also be attached to the user in the trusted account.

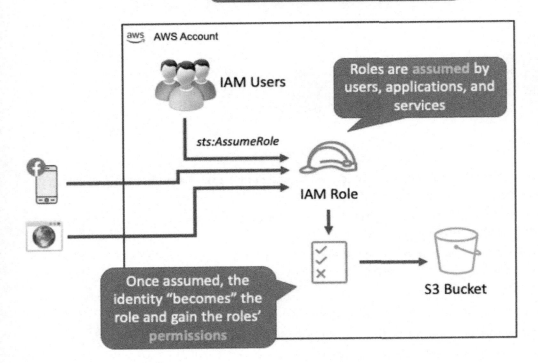

POLICIES

Policies are documents that define permissions and can be applied to users, groups, and roles.

Policy documents are written in JSON (key value pair that consists of an attribute and a value).

All permissions are implicitly denied by default.

The most restrictive policy is applied.

The IAM policy simulator is a tool to help you understand, test, and validate the effects of access control policies.

The Condition element can be used to apply further conditional logic.

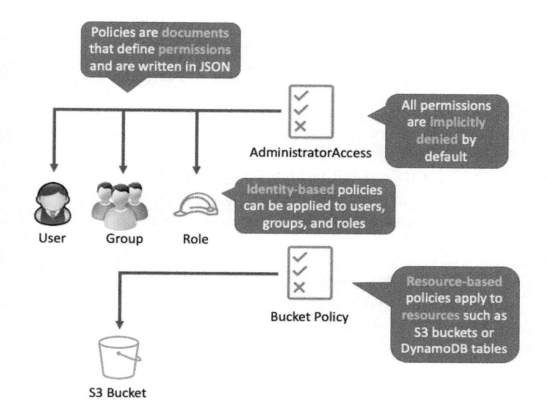

Policies are documents that define permissions and are written in JSON

AdministratorAccess

All permissions are implicitly denied by default

User   Group   Role

Identity-based policies can be applied to users, groups, and roles

Bucket Policy

Resource-based policies apply to resources such as S3 buckets or DynamoDB tables

S3 Bucket

INLINE POLICIES VS MANAGED POLICIES

There are 3 types of policies:

- Managed policies.
- Customer managed policies.
- Inline policies.

Managed Policy:

- Created and administered by AWS.
- Used for common use cases based on job function.
- Save you having to create policies yourself.
- Can be attached to multiple users, groups, or roles within and across AWS accounts.
- Cannot change the permissions assigned.

Customer Managed Policy:

- Standalone policy that you create and administer in your own AWS account.
- Can be attached to multiple users, groups, and roles – but only within your own account.
- Can be created by copying an existing managed policy and then customizing it.
- Recommended for use cases where the existing AWS Managed Policies don't meet the needs of your environment.

Inline Policy:

- Inline policies are embedded within the user, group, or role to which it is applied.
- Strict 1:1 relationship between the entity and the policy.
- When you delete the user, group, or role in which the inline policy is embedded, the policy will also be deleted.
- In most cases, AWS recommends using Managed Policies instead of inline policies.
- Inline policies are useful when you want to be sure that the permissions in a policy are not inadvertently assigned to any other user, group, or role.

AWS MANAGED AND CUSTOMER MANAGED POLICIES

An AWS managed policy is a standalone policy that is created and administered by AWS.

Standalone policy means that the policy has its own Amazon Resource Name (ARN) that includes the policy name.

AWS managed policies are designed to provide permissions for many common use cases.

You cannot change the permissions defined in AWS managed policies.

Some AWS managed policies are designed for specific job functions.

The job-specific AWS managed policies include:

- Administrator.
- Billing.
- Database Administrator.
- Data Scientist.
- Developer Power User.
- Network Administrator.
- Security Auditor.
- Support User.
- System Administrator.
- View-Only User.

You can create standalone policies that you administer in your own AWS account, which we refer to as customer managed policies.

You can then attach the policies to multiple principal entities in your AWS account.

When you attach a policy to a principal entity, you give the entity the permissions that are defined in the policy.

IAM POLICY EVALUATION LOGIC

By default, all requests are implicitly denied. (Alternatively, by default, the AWS account root user has full access).

An explicit allow in an identity-based or resource-based policy overrides this default.

If a permissions boundary, Organizations SCP, or session policy is present, it might override the allow with an implicit deny.

An explicit deny in any policy overrides any allows.

A few concepts should be known to understand the logic:

- **Identity-based policies** – Identity-based policies are attached to an IAM identity (user, group of users, or role) and grant permissions to IAM entities (users and roles).
- **Resource-based policies** – Resource-based policies grant permissions to the principal (account, user, role, or federated user) specified as the principal.
- **IAM permissions boundaries** – Permissions boundaries are an advanced feature that sets the maximum permissions that an identity-based policy can grant to an IAM entity (user or role).
- **AWS Organizations service control policies (SCPs)** – Organizations SCPs specify the maximum permissions for an organization or organizational unit (OU). Session policies – Session policies are advanced policies that you pass as parameters when you programmatically create a temporary session for a role or federated user.

The following flowchart details the IAM policy evaluation logic:

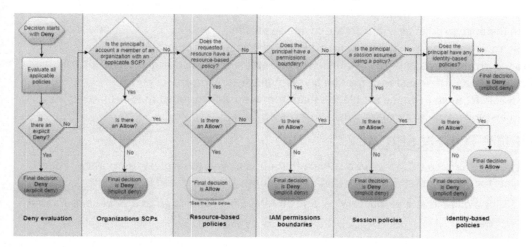

IAM INSTANCE PROFILES

An instance profile is a container for an IAM role that you can use to pass role information to an EC2 instance when the instance starts.

An instance profile can contain only one IAM role, although a role can be included in multiple instance profiles.

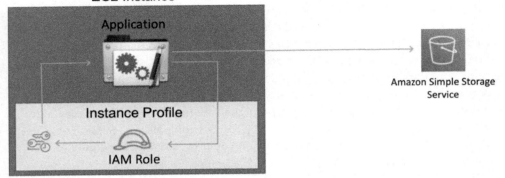

You can use the following AWS CLI commands to work with instance profiles in an AWS account:

- Create an instance profile: aws iam create-instance-profile
- Add a role to an instance profile: aws iam add-role-to-instance-profile
- List instance profiles: aws iam list-instance-profiles, aws iam list-instance-profiles-for-role
- Get information about an instance profile: aws iam get-instance-profile
- Remove a role from an instance profile: aws iam remove-role-from-instance-profile
- Delete an instance profile: aws iam delete-instance-profile

AWS SECURITY TOKEN SERVICE

The AWS Security Token Service (STS) is a web service that enables you to request temporary, limited-privilege credentials for IAM users or for users that you authenticate (federated users).

By default, AWS STS is available as a global service, and all AWS STS requests go to a single endpoint at https://sts.amazonaws.com

You can optionally send your AWS STS requests to endpoints in any region (can reduce latency).

Credentials will always work globally.

STS supports AWS CloudTrail, which records AWS calls for your AWS account and delivers log files to an S3 bucket.

Temporary security credentials work almost identically to long-term access key credentials that IAM users can use, with the following differences:

- Temporary security credentials are short-term.
- They can be configured to last anywhere from a few minutes to several hours.
- After the credentials expire, AWS no longer recognizes them or allows any kind of access to API requests made with them.
- Temporary security credentials are not stored with the user but are generated dynamically and provided to the user when requested.
- When (or even before) the temporary security credentials expire, the user can request new credentials, if the user requesting them still has permission to do so.

Advantages of STS are:

- You do not have to distribute or embed long-term AWS security credentials with an application.

- You can provide access to your AWS resources to users without having to define an AWS identity for them (temporary security credentials are the basis for IAM Roles and ID Federation).
- The temporary security credentials have a limited lifetime, so you do not have to rotate them or explicitly revoke them when they're no longer needed.
- After temporary security credentials expire, they cannot be reused (you can specify how long the credentials are valid for, up to a maximum limit).

The AWS STS API action returns temporary security credentials that consist of:

- An access key which consists of an access key ID and a secret ID.
- A session token.
- Expiration or duration of validity.
- Users (or an application that the user runs) can use these credentials to access your resources.

With STS you can request a session token using one of the following APIs:

- AssumeRole – can only be used by IAM users (can be used for MFA).
- AssumeRoleWithSAML – can be used by any user who passes a SAML authentication response that indicates authentication from a known (trusted) identity provider.
- AssumeRoleWithWebIdentity – can be used by an user who passes a web identity token that indicates authentication from a known (trusted) identity provider.
- GetSessionToken – can be used by an IAM user or AWS account root user (can be used for MFA).
- GetFederationToken – can be used by an IAM user or AWS account root user.

AWS recommends using Cognito for identity federation with Internet identity providers.

Users can come from three sources.

Federation (typically AD):

- Uses SAML 2.0.
- Grants temporary access based on the users AD credentials.
- Does not need to be a user in IAM.
- Single sign-on allows users to login to the AWS console without assigning IAM credentials.

Federation with Mobile Apps:

- Use Facebook/Amazon/Google or other OpenID providers to login.

Cross Account Access:

- Lets users from one AWS account access resources in another.
- To make a request in a different account the resource in that account must have an attached resource-based policy with the permissions you need.
- Or you must assume a role (identity-based policy) within that account with the permissions you need.

There are a couple of ways STS can be used.

Scenario 1:

1. Develop an Identity Broker to communicate with LDAP and AWS STS.
2. Identity Broker always authenticates with LDAP first, then with AWS STS.
3. Application then gets temporary access to AWS resources.

Scenario 2:

1. Develop an Identity Broker to communicate with LDAP and AWS STS.
2. Identity Broker authenticates with LDAP first, then gets an IAM role associated with the user.
3. Application then authenticates with STS and assumes that IAM role.
4. Application uses that IAM role to interact with the service.

CROSS ACCOUNT ACCESS

Useful for situations where an AWS customer has separate AWS account – for example for development and production resources.

Cross Account Access makes is easier to work productively within a multi-account (or multi-role) AWS environment by making is easy to switch roles within the AWS Management Console.

Can sign-in to the console using your IAM user name and then switch the console to manage another account without having to enter another user name and password.

Lets users from one AWS account access resources in another.

To make a request in a different account the resource in that account must have an attached resource-based policy with the permissions you need.

Or you must assume a role (identity-based policy) within that account with the permissions you need.

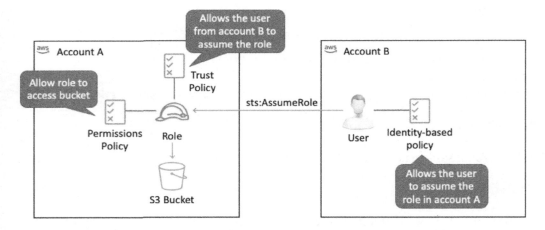

IAM BEST PRACTICES

To secure AWS resources it is recommended that you follow these best practices:

- Lock away your AWS account root user access keys.
- Use roles to delegate permissions.
- Grant least privilege.
- Get started using permissions with AWS managed policies.

- Validate your policies.
- Use customer managed policies instead of inline policies.
- Use access levels to review IAM permissions.
- Configure a strong password policy for your users.
- Enable MFA.
- Use roles for applications that run on Amazon EC2 instances.
- Do not share access keys.
- Rotate credentials regularly.
- Remove unnecessary credentials.
- Use policy conditions for extra security.
- Monitor activity in your AWS account.

AWS DIRECTORY SERVICE

AWS DIRECTORY SERVICE FEATURES

AWS provide several directory types.

The following three types currently feature on the exam and will be covered on this page:

- Active Directory Service for Microsoft Active Directory.
- Simple AD.
- AD Connector.

As an alternative to the AWS Directory service you can build your own Microsoft AD DCs in the AWS cloud (on EC2).

- When you build your own you can join an existing on-premises Active Directory domain (replication mode).
- You must establish a VPN (on top of Direct Connect if you have it).
- Replication mode is less secure than establishing trust relationships.

The table below summarizes the directory services covered on this page as well as a couple of others, and provides some typical use cases:

Directory Service Option	Description	Use Case
AWS Cloud Directory	Cloud-native directory to share and control access to hierarchical data between applications	Cloud applications that need hierarchical data with complex relationships
Amazon Cognito	Sign-up and sign-in functionality that scales to millions of users and federated to public social media services	Develop consumer apps or SaaS
AWS Directory Service for Microsoft Active Directory	AWS-managed full Microsoft AD running on Windows Server 2012 R2	Enterprises that want hosted Microsoft AD or you need LDAP for Linux apps

AD Connector	Allows on-premises users to log into AWS services with their existing AD credentials. Also allows EC2 instances to join AD domain	Single sign-on for on-premises employees and for adding EC2 instances to the domain
Simple AD	Low scale, low cost, AD implementation based on Samba	Simple user directory, or you need LDAP compatibility

ACTIVE DIRECTORY SERVICE FOR MICROSOFT ACTIVE DIRECTORY

Fully managed AWS services on AWS infrastructure.

Best choice if you have more than 5000 users and/or need a trust relationship set up.

Includes software patching, replication, automated backups, replacing failed DCs and monitoring.

Runs on a Windows Server.

Can perform schema extensions.

Works with SharePoint, Microsoft SQL Server and .Net apps.

You can setup trust relationships to extend authentication from on-premises Active Directories into the AWS cloud.

On-premises users and groups can access resources in either domain using SSO.

Requires a VPN or Direct Connect connection.

Can be used as a standalone AD in the AWS cloud.

When used standalone users can access 3rd party applications such as Microsoft O365 through federation.

You can also use Active Directory credentials to authenticate to the AWS management console without having to set up SAML authentication.

AWS Microsoft AD supports AWS applications including Workspaces, WorkDocs, QuickSight, Chime, Amazon Connect, and RDS for Microsoft SQL Server.

The following diagram shows some of the use cases for your AWS Microsoft AD directory, including the ability to grant your users access to external cloud applications and allow your on-premises AD users to manage and have access to resources in the AWS Cloud.

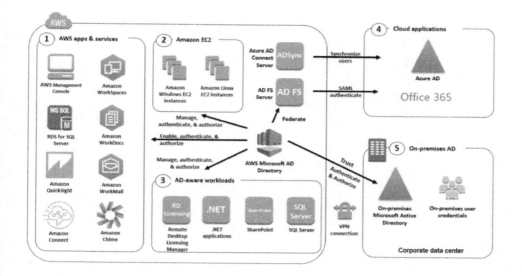

Includes security features such as:

- Fine-grained password policy management.
- LDAP encryption through SSL/TLS.
- HIPAA and PCI DSS approved.
- Multi-factor authentication through integration with existing RADIUS-based MFA infrastructure.

Monitoring provided through CloudTrail, notifications through SNS, daily automated snapshots.

Scalable service that scales by adding Domain Controllers.

Deployed in a HA configuration across two AZs in the same region.

AWS Microsoft AD does not support replication mode where replication to an on-premises AD takes place.

Two editions:

- Standard Edition is optimized to be a primary directory for small and midsize businesses with up to 5,000 employees. It provides you enough storage capacity to support up to 30,000 directory objects, such as users, groups, and computers.
- Enterprise Edition is designed to support enterprise organizations with up to 500,000 directory objects.

Directory Sharing:

- AWS Directory Service for Microsoft Active Directory allows you to use a directory in one account and share it with multiple accounts and VPCs.
- There is an hourly sharing charge for each additional account to which you share a directory.
- There is no sharing charge for additional VPCs to which you share a directory, or for the account in which you install the directory.

SIMPLE AD

An inexpensive Active Directory-compatible service with common directory features.

Standalone, fully managed, directory on the AWS cloud.

Simple AD is generally the least expensive option.

Best choice for less than 5000 users and don't need advanced AD features.

Powered by SAMBA 4 Active Directory compatible server.

Can create users and control access to applications on AWS.

Provides a subset of the features provided by AWS MS AD.

Features include:

- Manage user accounts.
- Manage groups.
- Apply group policies.
- Securely connect to EC2 instances.
- Kerberos-based SSO.
- Supports joining Linux or Windows based EC2 instances.

AWS provides monitoring, daily snapshots, and recovery services.

Manual snapshots possible.

Simple AD is compatible with WorkSpaces, WorkDocs, Workmail and QuickSight.

You can also sign on to the AWS management console with Simple AD user accounts to manage AWS resources.

Available in two editions:

- Small – supports up to 500 users (approximately 2000 objects).
- Large – supports up to 5000 users (approximately 20,000 objects).

AWS creates two directory servers and DNS servers on two different subnets within an AZ.

Simple AD does not support:

- DNS dynamic updates.
- Schema extensions.
- Multi-factor authentication.
- Communication over LDAPS.
- PowerShell AD cmdlets.
- FSMO role transfer.

Not compatible with RDS SQL server.

Does not support trust relationships with other domains (use AWS MS AD).

AD CONNECTOR

AD Connector is a directory gateway for redirecting directory requests to your on-premises Active Directory.

AD Connector eliminates the need for directory synchronization and the cost and complexity of hosting a federation infrastructure.

Connects your existing on-premises AD to AWS.

Best choice when you want to use an existing Active Directory with AWS services.

AD Connector comes in two sizes:

- Small – designed for organizations up to 500 users.
- Large – designed for organizations up to 5000 users.

The VPC must be connected to your on-premises network via VPN or Direct Connect.

When users log in to AWS applications AD connector forwards sign-in requests to your on-premises AD DCs.

You can also join EC2 instances to your on-premises AD through AD Connector.

You can also login to the AWS Management Console using your on-premises AD DCs for authentication.

Not compatible with RDS SQL.

You can use AD Connector for multi-factor authentication using RADIUS-based MFA infrastructure.

AD CONNECTOR VS SIMPLE AD

The table below describes some of the key differences to consider when choosing AD Connector or Simple AD:

AD Connector	Simple AD
Must have an existing AD	Standalone AD based on Samba
Existing AD users can access AWS assets via IAM roles	Supports user accounts, groups, group policies, and domains
Supports MFA via existing RADIUS-based MFA infrastructure	Kerberos-based SSO
	MFA not supported
	Trust relationships not supported

AMAZON INSPECTOR

AMAZON INSPECTOR FEATURES

Amazon Inspector is an automated security assessment service that helps improve the security and compliance of applications deployed on AWS.

Amazon Inspector automatically assesses applications for exposure, vulnerabilities, and deviations from best practices.

After performing an assessment, Amazon Inspector produces a detailed list of security findings prioritized by level of severity.

Amazon Inspector tests the network accessibility of your Amazon EC2 instances and the security state of your applications that run on those instances.

Amazon Inspector security assessments help you check for unintended network accessibility of your Amazon EC2 instances and for vulnerabilities on those EC2 instances.

After performing an assessment, Amazon Inspector produces a detailed list of security findings that is organized by level of severity.

These findings can be reviewed directly or as part of detailed assessment reports which are available via the Amazon Inspector console or API.

With Amazon Inspector, you can automate security vulnerability assessments throughout your development and deployment pipelines or for static production systems.

This allows you to make security testing a regular part of development and IT operations.

BENEFITS OF INSPECTOR

Configuration scanning and activity monitoring engine – Amazon Inspector provides an agent that analyzes system and resource configuration.

Built-in content library – Amazon Inspector includes a built-in library of rules and reports.

Automation through an API – Amazon Inspector can be fully automated through an API.

AMAZON INSPECTOR AGENT

Amazon Inspector also offers predefined software called an agent that you can optionally install in the operating system of the EC2 instances that you want to assess.

The agent monitors the behavior of the EC2 instances, including network, file system, and process activity. It also collects a wide set of behavior and configuration data (telemetry).

RULES AND PACKAGES

You can use Amazon Inspector to assess your assessment targets (collections of AWS resources) for potential security issues and vulnerabilities.

Amazon Inspector compares the behavior and the security configuration of the assessment targets to selected security rules packages.

In the context of Amazon Inspector, a rule is a security check that Amazon Inspector performs during the assessment run.

Amazon Inspector assessments are offered to you as pre-defined rules packages mapped to common security best practices and vulnerability definitions.

Examples of built-in rules include checking for access to your EC2 instances from the internet, remote root login being enabled, or vulnerable software versions installed.

These rules are regularly updated by AWS security researchers.

An Amazon Inspector assessment can use any combination of the following rules packages:

Network assessments

Network Reachability – The rules in the Network Reachability package analyze your network configurations to find security vulnerabilities of your EC2 instances. The findings that Amazon Inspector generates also provide guidance about restricting access that is not secure.

Host assessments

Common vulnerabilities and exposures – The rules in this package help verify whether the EC2 instances in your assessment targets are exposed to common vulnerabilities and exposures (CVEs).

Center for Internet Security (CIS) Benchmarks – The CIS Security Benchmarks program provides well-defined, unbiased, consensus-based industry best practices to help organizations assess and improve their security.

Security best practices for Amazon Inspector – Use Amazon Inspector rules to help determine whether your systems are configured securely.

AWS TRUSTED ADVISOR

AWS TRUSTED ADVISOR FEATURES

Trusted Advisor is an online resource that helps to reduce cost, increase performance, and improve security by optimizing your AWS environment.

Trusted Advisor provides real time guidance to help you provision your resources following best practices.

Advisor will advise you on Cost Optimization, Performance, Security, and Fault Tolerance.

Trusted Advisor scans your AWS infrastructure and compares is to AWS best practices in five categories:

- Cost Optimization.
- Performance.
- Security.
- Fault Tolerance.
- Service Limits.

Trusted Advisor comes in two versions.

Core Checks and Recommendations (free):

- Access to the 7 core checks to help increase security and performance.
- Checks include S3 bucket permissions, Security Groups, IAM use, MFA on root account, EBS public snapshots, RDS public snapshots.

Full Trusted Advisor Benefits (business and enterprise support plans).

Full set of checks to help optimize your entire AWS infrastructure.

Advises on security, performance, cost, fault tolerance and service limits.

Additional benefits include weekly update notifications, alerts, automated actions with CloudWatch and programmatic access using the AWS Support API.

AWS GUARDDUTY

AWS GUARDDUTY FEATURES

Intelligent threat detection service.

Continuously monitors for malicious activity and delivers detailed security findings for visibility and remediation.

Monitors AWS accounts, workloads, and data in Amazon S3.

Detects account compromise, instance compromise, malicious reconnaissance, and bucket compromise.

Amazon GuardDuty gives you access to built-in detection techniques developed and optimized for the cloud.

AWS Security continuously maintains and improves these detection algorithms.

The primary detection categories include:

- **Reconnaissance:** Activity suggesting reconnaissance by an attacker such as:
  - Unusual API activity.
  - Intra-VPC port scanning.
  - Unusual, failed login request patterns.
  - Unblocked port probing from a known bad IP.

- **Instance compromise:** Activity indicating an instance compromise, such as:
  - Cryptocurrency mining
  - Backdoor command and control (C&C) activity.
  - Malware using domain generation algorithms (DGA).
  - Outbound denial of service activity.
  - Unusually high network traffic volume.
  - Unusual network protocols.
  - Outbound instance communication with a known malicious IP.
  - Temporary Amazon EC2 credentials used by an external IP address.
  - Data exfiltration using DNS.

- **Account compromise:** Common patterns indicative of account compromise include:
  - API calls from an unusual geolocation or anonymizing proxy.
  - Attempts to disable AWS CloudTrail logging.
  - Changes that weaken the account password policy.
  - Unusual instance or infrastructure launches.
  - Infrastructure deployments in an unusual region.
  - API calls from known malicious IP addresses.

- **Bucket compromise:** Activity indicating a bucket compromise, such as:
  - Suspicious data access patterns indicating credential misuse.
  - Unusual Amazon S3 API activity from a remote host.
  - Unauthorized S3 access from known malicious IP addresses.
  - API calls to retrieve data in S3 buckets from a user with no prior history of accessing the bucket or invoked from an unusual location.

AWS CERTIFICATE MANAGER

AWS CERTIFICATE MANAGER FEATURES

Create, store, and renew SSL/TLS X.509 certificates

Single domains, multiple domain names and wildcards

Integrates with several AWS services including:

- Elastic Load Balancing.
- Amazon CloudFront.
- AWS Elastic Beanstalk.
- AWS Nitro Enclaves.
- AWS CloudFormation.

Public certificates are signed by the AWS public Certificate Authority.

You can also create a Private CA with ACM.

Can then issue private certificates.

You can also import certificates from third-party issuers.

AWS KMS

AWS KMS FEATURES

AWS Key Management Store (KMS) is a managed service that enables you to easily encrypt your data.

AWS KMS provides a highly available key storage, management, and auditing solution for you to encrypt data within your own applications and control the encryption of stored data across AWS services.

AWS KMS allows you to centrally manage and securely store your keys. These are known as AWS KMS keys (formerly known as customer master keys (CMKs).

AWS KMS KEYS

A KMS key consists of:

- Alias.
- Creation date.
- Description.
- Key state.
- Key material (either customer provided or AWS provided).

KMS keys are the primary resources in AWS KMS.

The KMS key includes metadata, such as the key ID, creation date, description, and key state.

The KMS key also contains the key material used to encrypt and decrypt data.

AWS KMS supports symmetric and asymmetric KMS keys.

KMS keys are created in AWS KMS. Symmetric KMS keys and the private keys of asymmetric KMS keys never leave AWS KMS unencrypted.

By default, AWS KMS creates the key material for a KMS key.

A KMS key can encrypt data up to 4KB in size.

A KMS key can generate, encrypt, and decrypt Data Encryption Keys (DEKs).

A KMS key can never be exported from KMS (CloudHSM allows this).

AWS Managed KMS keys:

- KMS keys managed by AWS are used by AWS services that interact with KMS to encrypt data.
- They can only be used by the service that created them within a particular region.
- They are created on the first time you implement encryption using that service.

Customer managed KMS keys:

- These provide the ability to implement greater flexibility.
- You can perform rotation, governing access, and key policy configuration.
- You are able to enable and disable the key when it is no longer required.

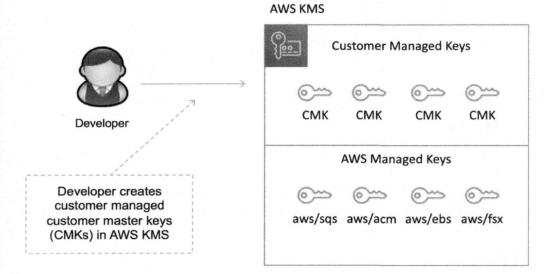

CUSTOMER MANAGED KMS KEYS

Customer managed KMS keys are KMS keys in your AWS account that you create, own, and manage.

You have full control over these KMS keys, including establishing and maintaining their key policies, IAM policies, and grants, enabling and disabling them, rotating their cryptographic material, adding tags, creating aliases that refer to the KMS key, and scheduling the KMS keys for deletion.

Customer managed KMS keys incur a monthly fee and a fee for use in excess of the free tier.

AWS MANAGED KMS KEYS

AWS managed KMS keys are KMS keys in your account that are created, managed, and used on your behalf by an AWS service that is integrated with AWS KMS.

You cannot manage these KMS keys, rotate them, or change their key policies.

You also cannot use AWS managed KMS keys in cryptographic operations directly; the service that creates them uses them on your behalf.

You do not pay a monthly fee for AWS managed KMS keys. They can be subject to fees for use in excess of the free tier, but some AWS services cover these costs for you.

AWS OWNED KMS KEYS

AWS owned KMS keys are a collection of KMS keys that an AWS service owns and manages for use in multiple AWS accounts.

Although AWS owned KMS keys are not in your AWS account, an AWS service can use its AWS owned KMS keys to protect the resources in your account.

You do not need to create or manage the AWS owned KMS keys.

However, you cannot view, use, track, or audit them.

You are not charged a monthly fee or usage fee for AWS owned KMS keys and they do not count against the AWS KMS quotas for your account.

DATA ENCRYPTION KEYS

Data keys are encryption keys that you can use to encrypt data, including large amounts of data and other data encryption keys.

You can use AWS KMS keys to generate, encrypt, and decrypt data keys.

AWS KMS does not store, manage, or track your data keys, or perform cryptographic operations with data keys.

You must use and manage data keys outside of AWS KMS.

The GenerateDataKey API can be used to create a data encryption key using a KMS key:

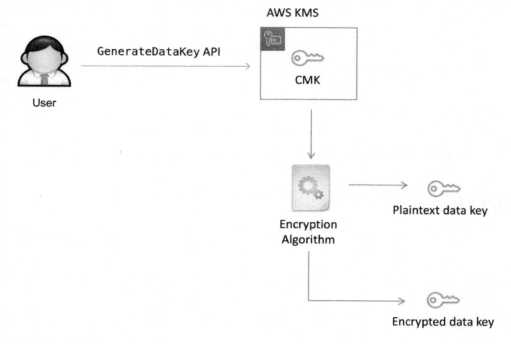

KMS DETAILS

You set usage policies on the keys that determine which users can use them to encrypt and decrypt data and under which conditions.

Key material options:

- KMS generated.
- Import your own.

You can generate KMS keys in KMS, in an AWS CloudHSM cluster, or import them from your own key management infrastructure.

These master keys are protected by hardware security modules (HSMs) and are only ever used within those modules.

You can submit data directly to KMS to be encrypted or decrypted using these master keys.

KMS now has the option for symmetric and asymmetric keys.

KMS is for encryption at rest only (not in transit, use SSL).

KMS is tightly integrated into many AWS services like Lambda, S3, EBS, EFS, DynamoDB, SQS etc.

Data keys are not retained or managed by KMS.

AWS services encrypt your data and store an encrypted copy of the data key along with the data it protects.

When a service needs to decrypt your data they request KMS to decrypt the data key using your master key.

If the user requesting data from the AWS service is authorized to decrypt under your master key policy, the service will receive the decrypted data key from KMS with which it can decrypt your data and return it in plaintext.

All requests to use your master keys are logged in AWS CloudTrail so you can understand who used which key under which context and when they used it.

You can control who manages and accesses keys via IAM users and roles.

You can audit the use of keys via CloudTrail.

KMS differs from Secrets Manager as its purpose-built for encryption key management.

KMS is validated by many compliance schemes (e.g. PCI DSS Level 1, FIPS 140-2 Level 2).

Exam tip: Encryption keys are regional.

KEY MANAGEMENT WITH KMS

You can perform the following key management functions in AWS KMS:

- Create keys with a unique alias and description.
- Import your own key material.
- Define which IAM users and roles can manage keys.
- Define which IAM users and roles can use keys to encrypt and decrypt data.
- Choose to have AWS KMS automatically rotate your keys on an annual basis.
- Temporarily disable keys so they cannot be used by anyone.
- Re-enable disabled keys.
- Delete keys that you no longer use.
- Audit use of keys by inspecting logs in AWS CloudTrail.

- Create custom key stores*.
- Connect and disconnect custom key stores*.
- Delete custom key stores*.

* The use of custom key stores requires CloudHSM resources to be available in your account.

DATA ENCRYPTION SCENARIOS

Typically, data is encrypted in one of the following three scenarios:

1. You can use KMS APIs directly to encrypt and decrypt data using your master keys stored in KMS.

2. You can choose to have AWS services encrypt your data using your master keys stored in KMS. In this case data is encrypted using data keys that are protected by your master keys in KMS.

3. You can use the AWS Encryption SDK that is integrated with AWS KMS to perform encryption within your own applications, whether they operate in AWS or not.

CUSTOM KEY STORE

The AWS KMS custom key store feature combines the controls provided by AWS CloudHSM with the integration and ease of use of AWS KMS.

You can configure your own CloudHSM cluster and authorize KMS to use it as a dedicated key store for your keys rather than the default KMS key store.

When you create keys in KMS you can chose to generate the key material in your CloudHSM cluster. Master keys that are generated in your custom key store never leave the HSMs in the CloudHSM cluster in plaintext and all KMS operations that use those keys are only performed in your HSMs.

In all other respects master keys stored in your custom key store are consistent with other KMS keys.

KEY DELETION

You can schedule a customer master key and associated metadata that you created in AWS KMS for deletion, with a configurable waiting period from 7 to 30 days.

This waiting period allows you to verify the impact of deleting a key on your applications and users that depend on it.

The default waiting period is 30 days.

You can cancel key deletion during the waiting period.

AWS KMS API'S

The following APIs are useful to know for the exam:

Encrypt (aws kms encrypt):

- Encrypts plaintext into ciphertext by using a customer master key (KMS key).
- You can encrypt small amounts of arbitrary data, such as a personal identifier or database password, or other sensitive information.
- You can use the Encrypt operation to move encrypted data from one AWS region to another.

Decrypt (aws kms decrypt):

- Decrypts ciphertext that was encrypted by an AWS KMS key using any of the following operations:
  - Encrypt
  - GenerateDataKey
  - GenerateDataKeyPair
  - GenerateDataKeyWithoutPlaintext
  - GenerateDataKeyPairWithoutPlaintext

Re-encrypt (aws kms re-encrypt):

- Decrypts ciphertext and then re-encrypts it entirely within AWS KMS.
- You can use this operation to change the customer master key (KMS key) under which data is encrypted, such as when you manually rotate a KMS key or change the KMS key that protects a ciphertext.
- You can also use it to re-encrypt ciphertext under the same KMS key, such as to change the encryption context of a ciphertext.

Enable-key-rotation:

- Enables automatic rotation of the key material for the specified symmetric customer master key (KMS key).
- You cannot perform this operation on a KMS key in a different AWS account.

GenerateDataKey (aws kms generate-data-key):

- Enables automatic rotation of the key material for the specified symmetric customer master key (KMS key).
- You cannot perform this operation on a KMS key in a different AWS account.

GenerateDataKeyWithoutPlaintext (generate-data-key-without-plaintext):

- Generates a unique symmetric data key.
- This operation returns a data key that is encrypted under a customer master key (KMS key) that you specify.
- To request an asymmetric data key pair, use the GenerateDataKeyPair or GenerateDataKeyPairWithoutPlaintext operations.

KMS ENVELOPE ENCRYPTION

AWS KMS is integrated with AWS services and client-side toolkits that use a method known as envelope encryption to encrypt your data.

Under this method, KMS generates data keys which are used to encrypt data and are themselves encrypted using your master keys in KMS:

- A KMS key is used to encrypt the data key (envelope key).
- The envelope key is used to decrypt the data.

LIMITS

You can create up to 1000 KMS keys per account per region.

As both enabled and disabled KMS keys count towards the limit, AWS recommend deleting disabled keys that you no longer use.

AWS managed master keys created on your behalf for use within supported AWS services do not count against this limit.

There is no limit to the number of data keys that can be derived using a master key and used in your application or by AWS services to encrypt data on your behalf.

AWS SECRETS MANAGER

AWS SECRETS MANAGER FEATURES

AWS Secrets Manager helps you protect secrets needed to access your applications, services, and IT resources.

The service enables you to easily rotate, manage, and retrieve database credentials, API keys, and other secrets throughout their lifecycle.

Users and applications retrieve secrets with a call to Secrets Manager APIs, eliminating the need to hardcode sensitive information in plain text.

Secrets Manager offers secret rotation with built-in integration for Amazon RDS, Amazon Redshift, and Amazon DocumentDB.

Also, the service is extensible to other types of secrets, including API keys and OAuth tokens. In addition, Secrets Manager enables you to control access to secrets using fine-grained permissions and audit secret rotation centrally for resources in the AWS Cloud, third-party services, and on-premises.

	Secrets Manager	SSM Parameter Store
Automatic Key Rotation	Yes, built-in for some services, use Lambda for others	No native key rotation; can use custom Lambda
Key/Value Type	String or Binary (encrypted)	String, StringList, SecureString (encrypted)
Hierarchical Keys	No	Yes
Price	Charges apply per secret	Free for standard, charges for advanced

AWS Secrets Manager encrypts secrets at rest using encryption keys that you own and store in AWS Key Management Service (KMS).

When you retrieve a secret, Secrets Manager decrypts the secret and transmits it securely over TLS to your local environment.

Secrets Manager does not write or cache the secret to persistent storage.

You can control access to the secret using fine-grained AWS Identity and Access Management (IAM) policies and resource-based policies.

You can also tag secrets individually and apply tag-based access controls.

With AWS Secrets Manager, you can rotate secrets on a schedule or on demand by using the Secrets Manager console, AWS SDK, or AWS CLI.

For example, to rotate a database password, you provide the database type, rotation frequency, and master database credentials when storing the password in Secrets Manager.

Secrets Manager natively supports rotating credentials for databases hosted on Amazon RDS and Amazon DocumentDB and clusters hosted on Amazon Redshift.

You can extend Secrets Manager to rotate other secrets by modifying sample Lambda functions.

You can store and retrieve secrets using the AWS Secrets Manager console, AWS SDK, AWS CLI, or AWS CloudFormation.

To retrieve secrets, you simply replace plaintext secrets in your applications with code to pull in those secrets programmatically using the Secrets Manager APIs. Secrets Manager provides code samples to call Secrets Manager APIs, also available on the Secrets Manager Resources page.

You can configure Amazon Virtual Private Cloud (VPC) endpoints to keep traffic between your VPC and Secrets Manager within the AWS network.

You can also use Secrets Manager client-side caching libraries to improve the availability and reduce the latency of using your secrets.

AWS Secrets Manager enables you to audit and monitor secrets through integration with AWS logging, monitoring, and notification services.

AWS WAF AND SHIELD

AWS WAF & SHIELD FEATURES

AWS WAF and AWS Shield help protect your AWS resources from web exploits and DDoS attacks.

AWS WAF is a web application firewall service that helps protect your web apps from common exploits that could affect app availability, compromise security, or consume excessive resources.

AWS Shield provides expanded DDoS attack protection for your AWS resources. Get 24/7 support from our DDoS response team and detailed visibility into DDoS events.

We'll now go into more detail on each service.

AWS WEB APPLICATION FIREWALL (WAF)

AWS WAF is a web application firewall that helps protect your web applications from common web exploits that could affect application availability, compromise security, or consume excessive resources.

AWS WAF helps protect web applications from attacks by allowing you to configure rules that allow, block, or monitor (count) web requests based on conditions that you define.

These conditions include IP addresses, HTTP headers, HTTP body, URI strings, SQL injection and cross-site scripting.

Can allow or block web requests based on strings that appear in the requests using string match conditions.

For example, AWS WAF can match values in the following request parts:

- Header – A specified request header, for example, the User-Agent or Referer header.
- HTTP method – The HTTP method, which indicates the type of operation that the request is asking the origin to perform. CloudFront supports the following methods: DELETE, GET, HEAD, OPTIONS, PATCH, POST, and PUT.
- Query string – The part of a URL that appears after a ? character, if any.
- URI – The URI path of the request, which identifies the resource, for example, /images/daily-ad.jpg.
- Body – The part of a request that contains any additional data that you want to send to your web server as the HTTP request body, such as data from a form.
- Single query parameter (value only) – Any parameter that you have defined as part of the query string.
- All query parameters (values only) – As above buy inspects all parameters within the query string.

New rules can be deployed within minutes, letting you respond quickly to changing traffic patterns.

When AWS services receive requests for web sites, the requests are forwarded to AWS WAF for inspection against defined rules.

Once a request meets a condition defined in the rules, AWS WAF instructs the underlying service to either block or allow the request based on the action you define.

With AWS WAF you pay only for what you use.

AWS WAF pricing is based on how many rules you deploy and how many web requests your web application receives.

There are no upfront commitments.

AWS WAF is tightly integrated with Amazon CloudFront and the Application Load Balancer (ALB), services.

When you use AWS WAF on Amazon CloudFront, rules run in all AWS Edge Locations, located around the world close to end users.

This means security doesn't come at the expense of performance.

Blocked requests are stopped before they reach your web servers.

When you use AWS WAF on an Application Load Balancer, your rules run in region and can be used to protect internet-facing as well as internal load balancers.

Web Traffic Filtering

AWS WAF lets you create rules to filter web traffic based on conditions that include IP addresses, HTTP headers and body, or custom URIs.

This gives you an additional layer of protection from web attacks that attempt to exploit vulnerabilities in custom or third-party web applications.

In addition, AWS WAF makes it easy to create rules that block common web exploits like SQL injection and cross site scripting.

AWS WAF allows you to create a centralized set of rules that you can deploy across multiple websites.

This means that in an environment with many websites and web applications you can create a single set of rules that you can reuse across applications rather than recreating that rule on every application you want to protect.

Full feature API

AWS WAF can be completely administered via APIs.

This provides organizations with the ability to create and maintain rules automatically and incorporate them into the development and design process.

For example, a developer who has detailed knowledge of the web application could create a security rule as part of the deployment process.

This capability to incorporate security into your development process avoids the need for complex handoffs between application and security teams to make sure rules are kept up to date.

AWS WAF can also be deployed and provisioned automatically with AWS CloudFormation sample templates that allow you to describe all security rules you would like to deploy for your web applications delivered by Amazon CloudFront.

AWS WAF is integrated with Amazon CloudFront, which supports custom origins outside of AWS – this means you can protect web sites not hosted in AWS.

Support for IPv6 allows the AWS WAF to inspect HTTP/S requests coming from both IPv6 and IPv4 addresses.

Real-time visibility

AWS WAF provides real-time metrics and captures raw requests that include details about IP addresses, geo locations, URIs, User-Agent and Referers.

AWS WAF is fully integrated with Amazon CloudWatch, making it easy to setup custom alarms when thresholds are exceeded, or attacks occur.

This information provides valuable intelligence that can be used to create new rules to better protect applications.

AWS SHIELD

AWS Shield is a managed Distributed Denial of Service (DDoS) protection service that safeguards applications running on AWS.

AWS Shield provides always-on detection and automatic inline mitigations that minimize application downtime and latency, so there is no need to engage AWS Support to benefit from DDoS protection.

There are two tiers of AWS Shield – Standard and Advanced.

AWS Shield Standard

All AWS customers benefit from the automatic protections of AWS Shield Standard, at no additional charge.

AWS Shield Standard defends against most common, frequently occurring network and transport layer DDoS attacks that target web sites or applications.

When using AWS Shield Standard with Amazon CloudFront and Amazon Route 53, you receive comprehensive availability protection against all known infrastructure (Layer 3 and 4) attacks.

AWS Shield Advanced

Provides higher levels of protection against attacks targeting applications running on Amazon Elastic Compute Cloud (EC2), Elastic Load Balancing (ELB), Amazon CloudFront, AWS Global Accelerator and Amazon Route 53 resources.

In addition to the network and transport layer protections that come with Standard, AWS Shield Advanced provides additional detection and mitigation against large and sophisticated DDoS attacks, near real-time visibility into attacks, and integration with AWS WAF, a web application firewall.

AWS Shield Advanced also gives you 24×7 access to the AWS DDoS Response Team (DRT) and protection against DDoS related spikes in your Amazon Elastic Compute Cloud (EC2), Elastic Load Balancing (ELB), Amazon CloudFront, AWS Global Accelerator and Amazon Route 53 charges.

AWS Shield Advanced is available globally on all Amazon CloudFront, AWS Global Accelerator, and Amazon Route 53 edge locations.

Origin servers can be Amazon S3, Amazon Elastic Compute Cloud (EC2), Elastic Load Balancing (ELB), or a custom server outside of AWS.

AWS Shield Advanced includes DDoS cost protection, a safeguard from scaling charges because of a

DDoS attack that causes usage spikes on protected Amazon EC2, Elastic Load Balancing (ELB), Amazon CloudFront, AWS Global Accelerator, or Amazon Route 53.

If any of the AWS Shield Advanced protected resources scale up in response to a DDoS attack, you can request credits via the regular AWS Support channel.

AWS RESOURCE ACCESS MANAGER

AWS RESOURCE ACCESS MANAGER FEATURES

AWS Resource Access Manager (RAM) is a service that enables you to share AWS resources easily and securely with any AWS account or within your AWS Organization.

You can share AWS Transit Gateways, Subnets, AWS License Manager configurations, and Amazon Route 53 Resolver rules resources with RAM.

RAM eliminates the need to create duplicate resources in multiple accounts, reducing the operational overhead of managing those resources in every single account you own.

You can create resources centrally in a multi-account environment, and use RAM to share those resources across accounts in three simple steps:

1. Create a Resource Share.
2. Specify resources.
3. Specify accounts.

RAM is available at no additional charge.

Key benefits:

- **Reduce Operational Overhead** – Procure AWS resources centrally and use RAM to share resources such as subnets or License Manager configurations with other accounts. This eliminates the need to provision duplicate resources in every account in a multi-account environment.
- **Improve Security and Visibility** – RAM leverages existing policies and permissions set in AWS Identity and Access Management (IAM) to govern the consumption of shared resources. RAM also provides comprehensive visibility into shared resources to set alarms and visualize logs through integration with Amazon CloudWatch and AWS CloudTrail.
- **Optimize Costs** – Sharing resources such as AWS License Manager configurations across accounts allows you to leverage licenses in multiple parts of your company to increase utilization and optimize costs.

EXAM SCENARIOS FOR AWS SYSOPS ADMINISTRATOR

AMAZON EC2 AND AWS LAMBDA

Exam Scenario	Solution
Administrator needs to check if any Amazon EC2 instances will be affected by scheduled hardware maintenance	Check the AWS Personal Health Dashboard
Scheduled hardware maintenance will affect a critical EC2 instance	Stop and start the instance to move it to different underlying hardware
When launching an EC2 instance the InsufficientInstanceCapacity error is experienced	This means AWS does not currently have enough capacity to service the request for that instance type. Try a different AZ or instance type
The error InstanceLimitExceeded is experienced when launching EC2 instances	EC2 instance limits have been reached, need to contact support to request an increased limit
System status checks are failing for an EC2 instance	Stop and start again to move to a new host

ELASTIC LOAD BALANCING AND AUTO SCALING

Exam Scenario	Solution
Design required for highly available and secure website on EC2 with ALB, and DB on EC2	Launch ALB in public subnets, web servers in private subnets and DB layer in private subnets – all layers across AZs
HealthyHostCount metrics for an ALB have dropped from 6 to 2. Need to determine the cause	The health checks on target EC2 instances are failing
An instance attached to an ALB exceeded the UnhealthyThresholdCount for consecutive health check failures. What will happen?	Health checks will continue and the ALB will take the instance out of service
Requirement to track the source IP of clients and the instance that processes the request	Check the ALB access logs for this information
503 and 504 errors experienced and instances have high CPU utilization	Use EC2 Auto Scaling to dynamically scale

AMAZON EBS, EFS, AND AWS STORAGE GATEWAY

Exam Scenario	Solution
User deleted some data in an Amazon EBS volume and there's a recent snapshot	Can create a new EBS volume from the snapshot and attach it to an instance and copy the delete file across
EBS volume runs out of space and need to prevent it happening again	Use CloudWatch agent on EC2 and monitor disk metrics with CloudWatch alarm
Low latency access required for image files in an office location with synchronized backup to offsite location. Local access required and disaster recovery	Use an AWS Storage Gateway volume gateway configured as a stored volume
EBS volume capacity is increased but cannot see the space	Need to extend the volume's file system to gain access to extra space
Need to replace user-shared drives. Must support POSIX permissions and NFS protocols and be accessible from on-premise servers and EC2	Use Amazon EFS

AWS SYSTEMS MANAGER

Exam Scenario	Solution
Application running on EC2 needs login credentials for a DB that are stored as secure strings in SSM Parameter Store	Create an IAM role for the instance and grant permission to read the parameters
Linux instances are patched with Systems Manager Patch Manager. Application slows down whilst updates are happening	Change maintenance window to patch 10% of instances in the patch group at a time
Custom Linux AMI used with AWS Systems Manager. Can't find instances in Session Manager console	Need to add permissions to instance profile and install the SSM agent on the instances
Multiple environments require authentication credentials for external service. Deployed using CloudFormation	Use an AWS Config rule to identify noncompliant keys. Create a custom AWS Systems Manager Automation document for remediation
IAM access keys used to manage EC2 instances using the CLI. Company policy mandates that access keys are automatically disabled after 60 days	Use an AWS Config rule to identify noncompliant keys. Create a custom AWS Systems Manager Automation document for remediation

AWS CLOUDFORMATION

Exam Scenario	Solution
Need to review updates to an AWS CloudFormation stack before deploying them in production	Use change sets
Stack deployed and manual changes were made. Need to capture changes and update template	Use drift detection and use output to update template and redeploy the stack
Need to update new version of app on EC2 and ALB. Must avoid DNS changes and be able to rollback	Update template with AutoScalingReplacingUpdate policy and perform an update
Need to write a single template that can be deployed across several environments / Region	Use parameters to enter custom values and use Ref intrinsic function to reference the parameter
Tried to launch instance in a different region from a working template and it fails	Probably due to incorrect AMI ID

AMAZON VIRTUAL PRIVATE CLOUD (VPC)

Exam Scenario	Solution
Need to identify the instances that are generating the most traffic using a NAT gateway	Use VPC flow logs on the NAT gateway ENI and use CloudWatch insights to filter based on source IP address
Latency on a NAT instance has increased, need a solution that scales with demand cost-efficiently	Swap with a NAT gateway
NAT gateway is NOT highly available across AZs, only within an AZ	Use multiple NAT gateways for HA across AZs
NAT instance deployed but not working	Make sure to disable source/destination checks
Need to enable access to S3 without the instances using public IP addresses	Use a NAT gateway or VPC endpoint

AMAZON ROUTE 53

Exam Scenario	Solution
Use Route 53 to direct based on health checks with (2xx) traffic to primary and other responses to secondary	Need to create an A record for each server and a HTTP (not TCP) health check
Route 53 health check uses string matching for	The search string must appear entirely within the

"/html". Alert shows health check fails	first 5,120 bytes of the response body
Need to make a website promotion visible to users from a specific country only	Use Route 53 geolocation routing policy
New website runs on EC2 behind ALB. Need to create record in Route 53 to point to the domain apex (e.g. example.com)	Use an alias record
Hosted zone in Account A and ALB in Account B. Need the most cost-effective and efficient solution for pointing to the ALB	Create an Alias record in Account A that points to ALB in Account B

AMAZON S3 AND CLOUDFRONT

Exam Scenario	Solution
Static website on Amazon S3 with custom domain name	Requires that the bucket name matches the DNS name / record set name in Route 53
503 errors experienced with new site and thousands of user	Request rate is too high
Discrepancy with number of objects in bucket console vs CloudWatch	Use Amazon S3 Inventory to properly determine the number of objects in a bucket
Need to enforce encryption on all objects uploaded to bucket	Use a bucket policy with a "Condition": { "Bool": { "aws:SecureTransport": "false" statement for PutObject and with the resource set to the bucket
Unauthorized users tried to connect to S3 buckets. Need to know which buckets are targeted and who is trying to get access	Use S3 server access logs and Athena to query for HTTP 403 errors and look for IAM user or role making requests

AMAZON RDS AND ELASTICACHE

Exam Scenario	Solution
Automated failover of a multi-AZ DB occurred	This may be due to storage failure on primary DB or the instance type could have been changed
Need to encrypt unencrypted RDS database	Take a snapshot, encrypt it, then restore a new encrypted instance from the snapshot
RDS DB query latency is high and CPU utilization is at 100%	Scale up with larger instance type
Need to share RDS DB snapshots across different	Use an AWS KMS key for encryption and update

accounts. Data must be encrypted	key policy to grant accounts with access then share snapshot
DB needs to be made HA to protect against failure and updates cannot impact users in business hours	Change to Multi-AZ outside of business hours

MANAGEMENT, GOVERNANCE AND BILLING

Exam Scenario	Solution
Audit requests to AWS Organizations for creating new accounts by federated users	use CloudTrail and look for the federated identity user name
Employees have created individual AWS accounts not under control. Security team need them in AWS Organizations	Send each account an invitation from the central organization
Need to restrict ability to launch specific instance types for a specific team/account	Use an organizations SCP to deny launches unless the instance type is T2, create an IAM group in the account granting access to T2 instances to the relevant users
Need to test notification settings for CloudWatch alarm with SNS	Use the set-alarm-state CLI command to test
Need to automatically disable access keys that are greater than 90 days old	Use an AWS Config rule to identify noncompliant keys and use Systems Manager Automation to remediate

SECURITY AND COMPLIANCE

Exam Scenario	Solution
Company wishes to force users to change their passwords regularly	Create an IAM password policy and enabled password expiration
Need to restrict access to a bucket based on source IP range	Use bucket policy with "Condition": "NotIpAddress": statement
Need to control access to group of EC2 instances with specific tags	Use an IAM policy with a condition element granting access based on the tag and attach an IAM policy to the user or groups that require access
IAM policy for SQS queue allows too much access. Who is responsible for correcting the issue?	According the AWS shared responsibility mode, this is a customer responsibility

Data is encrypted with AWS KMS customer-managed CMKs. Need to enable rotation ensuring the data remains readable	Just enable key rotation in AWS KMS for the CMK (backing key is rotated, data key is not changed)

CONCLUSION

We trust that these training notes have helped you to gain a complete understanding of the facts you need to know to pass the AWS Certified SysOps Administrator Associate exam the first time.

The exam covers a broad set of technologies. It's vital to ensure you are armed with the knowledge to answer whatever questions come up in your certification exam. We recommend reviewing these training notes until you're confident in all areas.

BEFORE TAKING THE AWS EXAM

AWS certification exams such as the SysOps test your hands-on knowledge and experience with the AWS platform. It's therefore super important to have some practical experience before you sit the exam.

Our AWS Certified SysOps Administrator Associate video course provides a practical approach to learning. Through over 15 hours of on demand video you'll learn how deploy, manage, and operate scalable, highly available, and fault tolerant systems on AWS. Our mixture of in-depth theory, logical diagrams and practical exercises, will fully prepare you for the AWS SysOps Certification exam.

By the end of the course, you will have developed a strong experience-based skillset. This will really help you when it comes time to answer exam questions.

Assess your exam readiness with practice exams from Digital Cloud Training

These popular practice questions are the closest to the actual exam and the only exam-difficulty questions on the market. If you can pass these mock exams, you're well set to ace the real thing. To learn more, visit https://digitalcloud.training/aws-certified-sysops-administrator-associate

Challenge Labs
Learn by doing and gain practical, real-world cloud skills with our scenario-based hands-on exercises that run in a secure sandbox environment. Simply the best way to gain hands-on skills. To learn more, visit https://digitalcloud.training/hands-on-challenge-labs/

REACH OUT AND CONNECT

We want you to have a 5-star learning experience. If anything is not 100% to your liking, please email us at support@digitalcloud.training. We promise to address all questions and concerns. We really want you to get great value from these training resources.

The AWS platform is evolving quickly, and the exam tracks these changes with a typical lag of around 6 months. We are therefore reliant on student feedback to keep track of what is appearing in the exam. If there are any topics in your exam that weren't covered in our training resources, please provide us with feedback using this form https://digitalcloud.training/student-feedback/. We appreciate your feedback that will help us further improve our AWS training resources.

Also, remember to join our private Facebook group to ask questions and share your knowledge with the AWS community: https://www.facebook.com/groups/awscertificationqa

BONUS OFFER

To assess your AWS exam readiness, we have included one full-length practice exam from Digital Cloud Training. These 65 exam-difficulty practice questions are timed and scored and simulate the real AWS exam experience. To gain access to your free practice exam with 65 exam-difficulty questions on the interactive online exam simulator, follow the steps below:

Step 1: Visit https://digitalcloud.training/product/aws-sample-practice-exam-certified-sysops-administrator-associate-bonus/ or simply scan this QR code.

Step 2: Click "Add to cart" and add coupon code "AMZBONUS" to reduce the price from $9.99 to $0.

Step 3: Upon registration, **log in** to http://digitalcloud.training/login and go to '**My Courses**' to access your practice exam.

For those who have already purchased the full set of practice questions, please note that these 65 questions are included in the pool of questions.

REQUEST YOUR FREE PDF VERSION

Based on the feedback we've received from our Amazon clients, we understand that studying complex diagrams in black and white or accessing reference links from a kindle device may NOT offer the best learning experience.

That's why we've decided to provide you with a PDF version at no additional charge. To access your free PDF version, simply attach a **screenshot of your review on Amazon** to SYSTNPDF@digitalcloud.training with **SYSTNPDF** in the subject line. You will then get FREE access to the PDF version within 48 hours. Should you encounter ANY problems with your review, please reach out. We're here to support you on your cloud journey.

LEAVE US A REVIEW

Your reviews help us improve our courses and help your fellow AWS students make the right choices. We celebrate every honest review and truly appreciate it. You can leave a review at any time by visiting amazon.com/ryp or your local amazon store (e.g. amazon.co.uk/ryp).

Best wishes for your AWS certification journey!

ON-DEMAND TRAINING, CHALLENGE LABS AND LIVE BOOTCAMPS

At Digital Cloud Training, we offer a wide range of training courses that help students successfully prepare for their AWS Certification exams and beyond. Check out the range of training options below.

ON-DEMAND / SELF-PACED AWS TRAINING

Prepare for your next AWS certification with video courses & practice exams / exam simulator. We also offer training notes and practice tests in PDF format for offline study.

All of our on-demand courses are available on digitalcloud.training/aws-training-courses

With our Membership Program, you gain unlimited access to ALL of our on-demand courses – current and future – with early access to new content and updates. To get a taste, start your Monthly Membership or sign up for 12 months of unlimited access to our entire library of AWS training courses. To learn more, visit https://digitalcloud.training/all-access/

CHALLENGE LABS

Keen to gain practical, real-world cloud skills? Then Challenge Labs are for you. Hone your skills across the most in-demand technologies, practice role-based cloud skills, and get the hands-on experience you need for certification exams.

Hands-on Challenge Labs are scenario-based exercises that run in a secure sandbox environment. These online scored labs offer extensive hands-on opportunities for all skill levels without the risk of cloud bills!

Ranging from fully guided to advanced hands-on exercises, Challenge Labs cater for all skill levels. At Digital Cloud Training we offer Challenge Labs for different levels of learners:

- **Guided** – Simply follow the step-by-step instructions in the guided labs with detailed hints to learn the fundamentals.
- **Advanced** – Create solutions according to requirements with supporting documentation – each step is checked / validated.
- **Expert** – Create solutions according to requirements with basic instructions and no supporting information – receive a final score.

Our Challenge Labs catalog includes over 1000 on-demand challenges across multiple cloud platforms and technologies including AWS, Azure, Docker, Linux, Microsoft, VMware and Cybersecurity. To learn more, visit https://digitalcloud.training/hands-on-challenge-labs/

LIVE BOOTCAMPS (VIRTUAL CLASSROOM)

Get ready for your next cloud job with real-world projects in a virtual classroom. AWS bootcamps are our most intensive training programs with live training sessions in a virtual classroom (via zoom).

The expert-led training sessions provide you with the opportunity to deep dive into AWS through real-world projects and hands-on exercises to help you develop practical experience. Delivered by experienced AWS instructors, our cloud bootcamps will fully prepare you for your next AWS certification and a successful cloud career.

ABOUT THE AUTHOR

Neal Davis is the founder of Digital Cloud Training, AWS Cloud Solutions Architect and successful IT instructor. With more than 20 years of experience in the tech industry, Neal is a true expert in virtualization and cloud computing. His passion is to help others achieve career success by offering in-depth AWS certification training resources.

Neal started **Digital Cloud Training** to provide a variety of training resources for Amazon Web Services (AWS) certifications that represent a higher standard of quality than is otherwise available in the market.

Digital Cloud Training provides AWS Certification exam preparation resources including instructor-led Video Courses, guided Hands-on Labs, in-depth Training Notes, Exam-Cram lessons for quick revision, Hands-on Challenge Labs and exam-difficulty Practice Exams to assess your exam readiness.

With Digital Cloud Training, you get access to highly experienced staff who support you on your AWS Certification journey and help you elevate your career through achieving highly valuable certifications. Join the AWS Community of over 750,000 happy students that are currently enrolled in Digital Cloud Training courses.

CONNECT WITH NEAL ON SOCIAL MEDIA

All Links available on https://digitalcloud.training/neal-davis

 digitalcloud.training/neal-davis

 youtube.com/c/digitalcloudtraining

 facebook.com/digitalcloudtraining

 Twitter @nealkdavis

 linkedin.com/in/nealkdavis

 Instagram @digitalcloudtraining